Advance Praise for *Lean Selling*

"*Lean Selling* is the most important sales management book of the last 25 years. Why? Most people who manage sales departments are winging it. Nearly all of them have learned by doing and they became sales managers because they were very good salespeople. Most have been trained by other sales managers who never had any formal training either. With this in mind, *Lean Selling* shows us why 90% of today's sales processes are broken. This book will change forever the way you sell and manage. Enjoy the 'aha' moments."

—Al Davidson
President, Strategic Sales & Marketing, Inc.

"Most sales leaders struggle to get their entire sales team to perform at the level of their 'A-Players.' Too many sales books focus on trying to change a salesperson's behavior to achieve this. Robert Pryor's book focuses on defining a sales *process* to yield consistent sales results for your company's product or solution. *Lean Selling* provides the tools you require to define then refine your sales process as market and competitive conditions change. The end result is achieving both predictable sales and customer satisfaction."

—Craig Jack
Former Managing Client Partner, Verizon Enterprise Solutions
Former Managing Director, KPMG Consulting

"Robert Pryor has written a book on a subject already covered by tons of books over the years but managed to give it a twist that makes it very engaging and relevant. The book is well written, insightful, and timely; the emergence of Internet commerce has had a profound impact on the sales profession as we know it."

—Ake Persson
Retired CEO, Ericsson Wireless Communications, Inc.

T0367222

"Tired of the dreaded *'slow no'* emerging after months of sales resources turn out to have been poured into a black hole? *Lean Selling*, by Robert Pryor, really woke me up to how complacent some of us are about our sales processes, and how that complacency connects directly to those sub-optimal results. Starting with the same lean thinking that produced the Toyota Production System, Robert has suggested some very practical and effective ways to get better bang for your sales investment dollar. It's a 'must read.' "

—J. Jeffrey Campbell
Brinker Executive in Residence and Director, Master of Science Program, San Diego State University School of Hospitality & Tourism
Former Chairman and CEO, Burger King Corporation

"*Lean Selling*? I love it. I've been using lean principles with my inside sales organization for a year now to improve customer fit and the buyer experience. The result has been astronomical growth in sales for my company. My biggest challenge now is getting salespeople on-boarded with our lean sales process fast enough to take advantage of the opportunities we have in front of us."

—Kevin Gaither,
Vice President of Inside Sales, ZipRecruiter, Inc.
President, Los Angeles Chapter of the American Association of Inside Sales Professionals

"For me, *Lean Selling* turns the traditional sales management process on its head—in a good way. Sales process improvements are usually internally-focused. This book looked at that part of the journey. However, it was the *external* focus of *Lean Selling* that really opened my eyes. This book helped me to see how an organization can manage the customer process more intelligently—and ultimately more effectively. I've had exposure to lean manufacturing and lean management process improvement in the past, but this is the first time I have seen these powerful ideas applied to the sales process. Great work!"

—Jim LaMarca
Director, Brand Strategy & Sales
IDEA Health & Fitness, Inc.

LEAN
SELLING

Slash Your Sales Cycle and Drive Profitable,
Predictable Revenue Growth by
Giving Buyers What They *Really* Want

ROBERT J. PRYOR

Foreword by J. Jeffrey Campbell,
Former Chairman and CEO, Burger King Corporation

authorHOUSE®

AuthorHouse™
1663 Liberty Drive
Bloomington, IN 47403
www.authorhouse.com
Phone: 1-800-839-8640

Published by AuthorHouse 01/28/2015

ISBN: 978-1-4969-5553-1 (sc)
ISBN: 978-1-4969-5554-8 (hc)
ISBN: 978-1-4969-5552-4 (e)

Library of Congress Control Number: 2014958414

Lean Selling is a trademark of CEO Cubed LLC

About This Book

Lean Thinking, pioneered by Toyota Motor Corporation, is the twenty-first-century way to produce goods and services. *Lean Selling* explains how these revolutionary principles can transform sales organizations and the value they provide for customers.

- Eliminate salespeople's wasted time on unnecessary activities and unqualified prospects
- Dramatically reduce sales cycle time
- Broaden and deepen your organization's competitive advantage and differentiation
- Significantly improve the accuracy of revenue forecasting
- Bind your customers more closely to your organization

Acknowledgements

When you write a book about an uncharted area like Lean Selling you require a lot of help from smart people around you. I didn't know I was forming a team, but somehow it turned into one. It's a good thing, because now I realize this book could not have gotten done the way it did without the "accidentally-recruited" team around me.

First I would like to acknowledge Ken Schmitt, the president of Turning Point Executive Search, Inc., and also the president of the Sales Leadership Alliance, for offering to introduce me to senior sales executives I could talk to about Lean Selling. Three of these introductions resulted in Case Examples in this book, which I believe will be valuable material for readers.

Along this line I would also like to thank the interview participants for their Case Examples: Kevin Gaither of ZipRecruiter, Doug Peterson of HD Supply, and Denise Rippinger and Thomas Schutz of Communicare. Two other sales executives I interviewed preferred that their names and companies remain anonymous for personal or professional reasons.

I would like to acknowledge and thank Ariela Wilcox, Literary Agent and President of The Wilcox Agency, who oversaw the writing of this book. Without her guidance I could not have gotten to the finish line as quickly as I did. I knew that Ariela was, among other things, an expert in helping first-time writers like me. I didn't expect she would have so much to contribute to the subject matter or that she would bring so many creative ideas. Ariela's touch is definitely throughout this book.

I couldn't be writing a book about Lean Selling—or Lean anything—without building on the work of the Lean pioneers who came before me. These include James Womack, Daniel Jones, and Daniel Roos, for their seminal work documenting the significance of the Toyota Production System, and later work by Womack and Jones to capture the principles of Toyota's system as Lean Thinking and show practical applications of it, not only in manufacturing but in service industries as well, which opened the door for Lean Selling. Kent Beck was a different kind of Lean pioneer who illustrated the versatility of Lean Thinking by showing how it could be applied to a different type of production, software development.

I am grateful to Roger Damphousse, my former boss when he was president of Lockheed Martin Commercial Electronics division, for first introducing me to Lean. I also appreciate that he gave me the opportunity to spread my general management wings early in my career. Roger demonstrated to me through his example what it means to be a life-long learner.

Finally, I am thankful to the Toyota Motor Corporation for inventing, refining, and sharing their Lean inventions. Most of all I am touched by the fact that Toyota offered to share all of its Lean knowledge and production techniques through a joint venture with General Motors (NUMMI) in 1984. Why would Toyota share its "secret sauce" with the then world leader in automobile manufacturing?

According to author Jeffrey Liker (*The Toyota Way*, Mc-Graw-Hill), one of Toyota's motivations was to help General Motors, which was struggling with its manufacturing at the time. Why would Toyota want to do that? Because the company wanted to give something back to the American people for the help provided to Japan to rebuild its industry after World War II. What a rare display of corporate character and repayment of appreciation! *(Disclosure: I have never had a business relationship with Toyota.)*

To my wife, Hiroko, and daughters, Crystal and Veronica
—the women in my life
whose support makes it possible for me to do what I do.

Foreword

If you've ever been through an extended and costly selling process with a big company only to receive the dreaded "slow no" after months of effort and thousands of dollars of investment, you might want to give this book your focused attention.

New ideas take time to percolate through the industrial landscape. I first read *The Machine That Changed the World*, about the Lean Revolution, back in 1990 when it first appeared on the bookshelves (the disappearance of those bookshelves represents another change percolating through the landscape). Since that time, the benefits of the Toyota Production System have become much more widely known and appreciated across multiple industries.

However, new ideas and new technologies also take time to create impact beyond their initial landing zones. This has certainly been true for the Lean concept.

Now Robert Pryor has applied the same Lean discipline and methodologies that transformed manufacturing to the selling process and the relationship between sellers and buyers. The result is something of a revelation . . . and you'll be hard pressed to find a better or more comprehensive guide to that tradition-shattering idea on the book market today.

The waste embedded in most sales efforts is significant. Perhaps this is a vestige of the happy days of yore when the pace of change was slower and firms could delude themselves into thinking that they were in possession of some form of "sustainable competitive advantage." Under circumstances like that—even if partially imaginary—perhaps some degree of waste and imprecision could be tolerated.

Well, those days are dead and gone. Today's only real competitive advantage, as Arie DeGeus has suggested, is the ability to learn faster than your competitors. And if your organization is used to depending heavily on a core process that remains unexamined, it just might turn out to be the fatal flaw that takes you down.

Hence, the relevance and urgency of this book.

As I read chapter after chapter, I realized that the thrust of the argument made complete sense and reinforced ideas I already considered to be powerful aids to leading in a complex and ever-changing environment. But new points and insights about "error-proofing customers" and "value stream mapping" were real grabbers, and I have become increasingly intrigued by the notion of multi-functional teams supporting the selling effort.

Like the best books do, this one has changed the way I think about the subject of selling. Even better, it has direct applicability to my current role as well.

As I proceeded through the book, it dawned on me that everything Robert Pryor talks about here applies directly to the recruiting effort I manage at San Diego State University for our new online Master's program. I had been thinking about that process as recruiting, but it really is selling . . . and the process by which we do that task is established enough now for a thorough review—and likely overhaul—according to the principles presented in this book. We'll be the better for it, I am sure.

If your organization counts on strong and effective selling capability, you'd be well advised to check out Robert Pryor's *Lean Selling*.

It's well worth your time.

J. Jeffrey Campbell
Brinker Executive in Residence and Director, Master of
Science Program, San Diego State University
School of Hospitality & Tourism
Former Chairman and CEO, Burger King Corporation

Table of Contents

Introduction

I'm Not Going to Waste Your Time

I assume you are a busy person. Why do I assume that? Because, since you are reading this book, you are likely involved in making sales, managing sales, or running an organization that has a salesforce. That means you are busy and time is money for you.

Because of this, I'm not going to waste your time. I am going to present you a business case right up front in this book for why you should learn about Lean Selling™, *now*. The primary reason for my sense of urgency is that I have learned that organizations are already applying Lean Selling techniques with breakthrough results, although most executives in organizations that depend on their salesforces for their existence have never even heard about Lean Selling.

Most business books save case studies until the end of a book, as a kind of proof of concept. However, I'm not going to do that. Since I am committed to saving you time I am going to present these cases at the end of Part I. By the time you finish the two chapters of Part I, I believe you will have enough information to decide if you want to invest any more of your valuable time into reading the rest of this book to further understand the potential for Lean Selling.

My argument for Lean Selling will take a senior executive point of view, focusing on the strategic implications of this new way of selling. There is ample evidence of remarkable successes in applying Lean Thinking to a broad range of business activities, ranging from manufacturing to service delivery, across a variety of industries. The evidence around Lean is so compelling, and the impacts so disruptive, that anyone involved in sales should think carefully before ignoring the impact that Lean Selling could have on the most important profession in the business world.

Five Premises for Predicting Lean Selling as the *Next Big Thing*

In the following section I construct my argument for why Lean Selling could become the **Next Big Thing** in the development and direction of global business. However, because you are a busy person I won't make you read any further before I give you the summary. These are the five premises that underlie my conclusion that Lean Selling can be the **Next Big Thing** in business:

1. **Lean as a methodology that revolutionizes the processes for producing products and for delivering services, and Lean Thinking that captures its principles, are the most disruptive and transformational management ideas since the Industrial Revolution that began over 100 years ago.**

2. **Sales is, or should be, a process, and therefore can benefit from Lean Thinking and can be continuously improved.**

3. **Sales is a service, which means its enduring value can be determined only by the recipient of the service, in this case a customer or Buyer.**

4. **Sales is a system, which implies that it functions within the context of a larger organization and not in isolation.**

5. **The adoption and deployment of Lean Selling is in its earliest stages but has already begun below the business "radar." Based on documented historical results yielded by adapting Lean to new application areas, the *early adopters* of Lean Selling are likely to enjoy significant competitive advantages for some time to come.**

If you categorically reject any one of these premises and your mind is made up about that, then this book is not for you. I will save you the time of reading it by suggesting you give this book to someone else, or return it for a refund if you still can. But if you are resonating with my five fundamental premises above or are open to the possibility that they all may indeed be true then I ask you to read at least the next section, Part I, ending with the Case Examples, as quickly as you can.

Then you can make up your mind whether you want to invest more time into reading the rest of this book and in learning more about Lean Selling.

What Can You Do If You Become a Believer?

Once you conclude that you cannot risk being on the sidelines of the emerging Lean Selling movement while vicariously watching your competitors rack up successes with it, you will want to move quickly to gain your own first-hand experiences using it in your own organization. This book will help you get started by illustrating how the proven principles of Lean Thinking can be applied to initiate a Lean Selling evolution—or revolution—in your organization. Even if you have no experience with Lean Thinking and terminology, this book will provide the basics you require to understand how Lean Thinking can be implemented in Lean Selling.

At the end of this book there are a couple of chapters devoted to providing ideas and specifics of how your organization can get a "taste" of Lean Selling, or a "full meal," including a *90-day plan for a Lean Selling transformation*. The ideas and plans presented in these chapters are designed to be "do-it-yourself," but there is also information in the Resources section in the back of the book that explains how you can get additional help, if you want it, for your Lean Selling journey.

Selling System Assessment

At this point you may be thinking, "This Lean Selling stuff sounds interesting, but how do I know if it's for me?" Good question. Lean Thinking advances the idea that *all* processes can be improved, continuously. However, your level of motivation to do something to improve the selling system your organization is currently using will, practically speaking, be influenced by how effective you believe your current selling system is. How can you know just where your own selling system stands?

I have included a 10-question assessment below to provide a perspective on how your current selling system stacks up against the typical company. If you take five minutes now to complete this assessment, you will immediately get an idea about where your organization stands. Alternatively, you can complete it on the Web at www.LeanSellingBook.com/assessment. When you take the assessment on the website, it will calculate the score for you automatically and provide a graphical representation of your ranking. Further, on the website you will be able to drill down into the individual components that make up your overall score as well as learn about specific actions you can take to improve each of these components in order to achieve a higher score.

Selling System Assessment

Instructions: In each *row*, circle **one** box that contains the word, phrase, or percentage that best describes the current state of the selling system in your organization. After completing all rows, count the number of circled boxes in *each column* and enter that count in the corresponding box in the *Number of Circled Boxes* row in that column. Then multiply the number in each box in this row by its multiplier below the box and enter that number in that column's box in the *Column Score* row. Add up the numbers in all the boxes in the *Column Score* row and enter it in the TOTAL SCORE box. Mark an "X" on the line below the table that represents where your score falls.

The Promise

I believe that the transition to Lean Selling can eventually show the same indisputable and game-changing results for sales as it has in every area of business and service delivery. I don't think it's a stretch to envision how Lean Selling can provide minimally the following five benefits to organizations that make the commitment:

1. **Eliminate the time wasted by both Buyers and Sellers on unnecessary activities and unqualified prospects, increasing sales productivity while reducing the cost of customer acquisition.**

2. **Dramatically reduce sales cycle time and–at the same time–reduce the likelihood a Buyer will go away or choose another provider.**

3. **Broaden and deepen your organization's competitive ad-**

Selling System Attributes	Circle *One Box in Each Row* That Best Describes Your Sales Situation				
Regularity of Achieving Your Revenue Plan	Rarely	Sometimes	Half the Time	Mostly	Almost Always
Frequency That Sales Forecast Is Met	< 15%	15–25%	26–35%	36–50%	> 50%
Percentage of Salespeople Meeting Quota	< 20%	20–40%	41–65%	66–85%	> 85%
Number of Prospects in Sales Pipeline	Almost None	Very Few	Not Enough	Almost Enough	Enough
Sales Cycle Time	Too Long	Long	Moderate	Acceptable	Short
Percentage of Total Sales from New Customers	< 15%	15–25%	26–40%	41–60%	> 60%
Number of Repeat Customers	< 5%	5–10%	11–15%	16–20%	> 20%
Year-over-Year Sales Growth	< 0%	0%	1–10%	11–20%	> 20%
Annual Loss of Existing Customers (Churn)	> 30%	21–30%	11–20%	5–10%	< 5%
Annual Salesperson Turnover	> 40%	31–40%	21–30%	10–20%	< 10%
# Circled Boxes in Column (This Row Total Must = 10)	⬜	⬜	⬜	⬜	⬜
Multiplier	x2	x4	x6	x8	x10
Column Score	= ⬜	= ⬜	= ⬜	≈ ⬜	= ⬜
TOTAL SCORE (Sum of Column Scores)	= ⬜				

Mark Your Total Score with an "X" on the line below

Below Average		Typical		Above Average		Excellent		World Class
20	30	40	50	60	70	80	90	100

vantage and differentiation *above and beyond* that which is already provided by the product or service you produce and deliver.

4. Significantly improve the accuracy of revenue forecasting and reveal new revenue streams available for your organization to pursue.

5. Greatly increase the value salespeople add for potential Buyers, binding your customers more closely to your organization.

Transformational results from adopting Lean Selling will not happen overnight, but your investment in a new direction for your sales organization could be the best investment your organization ever makes. Lean Selling is not a sales methodology *du jour* that has a shelf life or a season. The benefits of continued commitment to Lean Selling will accrue indefinitely to those who make it.

About the Structure of This Book

Part I of this book provides the business case for Lean Selling. It does so by presenting an introduction to Lean Thinking, including its history and successful applications, and also through explaining why disruptive changes in today's sales environment, largely driven by technology adoption, make this a ripe time for the application of Lean Thinking to Lean Selling. Part I also provides Case Examples of nascent applications of Lean Selling that represent a variety of sales environments and challenges across a wide range of industries.

Part II of this book is about clarifying why we are stuck where we are with today's selling process and how we get from where we are to where we inevitably must go: as CEOs, executives, managers, and sales professionals. It proposes a redefinition of the traditional relationship between buyers and sellers.

Part III addresses, from various perspectives, what a Lean Selling process can look like. It attempts to incorporate nearly all the pertinent objectives of Lean Thinking within a context that should be immediately familiar to anyone who has been exposed to sales. In addition, it suggests a way to integrate the Buyer's process with the Seller's process, and the Seller's process with the rest of his or her organization.

Part IV shifts the focus from the static implementation of a Lean Selling process to the dynamic management of a **Lean Selling System**. It also introduces proven Lean tools to capture the "Current State" of the sales process and to develop and communicate a collective vision of an improved state called the "Future State." The most important cultural mindsets during this stage of ongoing effort are *collaboration, teamwork, and continuous improvement.*

Some Lean purists may argue that Parts III and IV are actually elements of one thing, not two; that from the viewpoint of Lean, there is no difference between a process and a system. It is a fair argument (and one I would probably make if I weren't the book's author). I believe that one of the reasons Lean has not seen more adoption in the selling profession is that it is not presented in a way that is accessible to sales-people, sales managers, and business executives.

For that reason, I decided that the best way to make the connection between Lean principles and sales would be to start with a model well understood by sales professionals, that of the sales process commonly represented (and referred to) as a sales "funnel" or "pipeline." I first wanted to show how this concept might change after the application of Lean principles, from initial contact with a potential Buyer to closing of a sale. This is the most common view of the "scope" of the sales process and I wanted to dedicate Part III to it.

However, Lean also encompasses other important ideas that cannot be fully exploited using the classic sales process model. These can include inputs into and outputs from the sales process, as well as Lean concepts such as flow, teamwork, and continuous improvement. Indeed, to have a sustainable Lean process, you must create a complete system around it. Since many of these ideas from Lean don't have good predecessor concepts in the classic sales pipeline, I decided to present them separately in Part IV, as a continuation of Part III. Either way, at the end of Part IV, we will end up in the same place. I have merely for expediency separated the two sections to make it, hopefully, more digestible for readers.

In order to properly set reader expectations, there are a few points

I would like to make regarding what this book is *not* about. **It is not about a specific sales methodology, as that term is commonly understood in the industry.** The **Lean Selling System** is a larger container within which a company can, if it chooses to, implement its favorite selling methodology (as long as it doesn't conflict with the objectives or philosophy of a Lean implementation). The end product of a Lean transformation, even though it employs well-understood methods and established best practices, will always be unique to the company undergoing the transformation. Further, unlike a selling methodology, Lean Selling is a way of thinking, doing, testing, and evolving, rather than a specific unchanging set of behaviors. It is adaptable to fluctuating circumstances in the marketplace, technological innovation, regulatory change, and perturbations in the overall business environment.

   This book is also not a primer on Lean. The resource section in the back of this book provides many resources that are great for understanding the basics and history of Lean. You might conclude from this statement that a certain foundational understanding of Lean is necessary before being able to benefit from this book. I have tried hard to make sure that is not the case. I have aimed this book at people who have at least a rudimentary understanding of sales, but not of Lean. My research of the currently available information on Lean sales is that it is too technical to be of interest to most sales professionals and business executives. For that reason, I have attempted to familiarize the reader with Lean Selling without getting bogged down in the technical details.

   I believe the more important thing I can convey to readers is the compelling business case for considering Lean Selling, not its technical underpinnings. That being said, in order to remain respectful to the vaunted history of the Lean industry I have attempted to link every important new idea in this book to its foundational Lean principle, tool, or methodology. I have attempted, wherever possible, to provide examples that can help make the reader see the linkage. However, I have endeavored to write this book so its main purpose—making the case for a Lean Selling transformation—can be gleaned without reading these examples or fully understanding the Lean principle that underlies each idea.

   Finally, a style note: In this book I have capitalized the words Buying, Selling, Buyer(s), and Seller(s). This is to clarify that I am talking about a Buyer and Seller who are the main protagonists or actors in this book, and Buying and Selling as the two mutual journeys they are undertaking together. This is to distinguish these references from the more general statements made about sales, salespeople, selling and buying, and sellers and buyers, as we understand them in the common vernacular. I have also capitalized the phrase Lean Selling as I use it as a proper noun in this book.

To the Early Adopter Go the Spoils

The business world is at the very early stages of discovering and refining exactly how to best apply proven Lean principles to the important work of selling. In the years to come, there will doubtless emerge many compelling examples of successes with Lean Selling, along with agreed-upon best practices for implementing it. We just don't see them today. As Fujio Cho, President of Toyota Motor Company was quoted as saying in the book, *The Toyota Way*:

> Applying the Toyota Production System outside of the shop floor can be done, but this takes some creativity. . . . There are many more opportunities that we need to work on using our creativity.[1]

I can personally attest to the fact that applying Lean Thinking and methods to a new application area like sales does indeed require creativity. I have attempted in this book to apply my own creativity to putting forward a **Lean Selling System** model that organizations can experiment with and refine over time to best serve their own unique situations. I have done this within the context of what I have learned from three decades of business experience in sales, marketing, and general management, as well as exposure over that period of time to Lean implementations in different industries. I have also dissected how employing Lean Thinking and practices in new application areas—while remaining faithful to the foundational principles of Lean—has been achieved, in order to help inform how this might also be creatively accomplished for sales.

Today, Lean Selling is for early adopters: those who, in return for the promise of gaining considerable competitive advantage, are willing to invest in something yet unproven; to be one of the first, to be a trailblazer. It is my hope that this book can help awaken and identify the early adopters of Lean Selling. If achievement of one or more of the improvement benefits mentioned above is important to your organization's ongoing success and growth, you may be one of them.

When you or your sales organization *is* ready for Lean Selling, the benefits that await your company can be incomparable. The Case Examples in Part I illustrate the depth and breadth of the impacts that adopting Lean Selling principles can have on sales organizations. These Case Examples may provide the motivation you require to seriously consider undertaking a Lean Selling transformation, *now*. They will also, hopefully, motivate you to read this book from cover to cover.

Part I

Lean Secrets to Building Your Company's Competitive Edge

Chapter 1

What's Lean Got to Do with It?

In Chapter One
- → The Selling Crisis
- → Introduction to Lean Thinking
- → The Business Case for Lean Selling
- → My Personal Journey with Lean
- → Sales is a Different Kind of Process

The Selling Crisis

There is a crisis in selling. Let me be more specific. Today there is a crisis in selling anything that's *not* sold over the Internet. Internet sales are doing terrific, and are projected to continue their double-digit growth for at least the next four years.[1] It's the rest of selling—the traditional type of selling—where there is a crisis. And it's not just because Internet sales are gobbling up more of the retail sales pie to the detriment of brick-and-mortar stores at an increasing rate. The impact of the Internet on sales of all kinds goes deeper than that.

The Internet has completely changed the relationship between buyers and sellers, irrevocably and forever. Buyers are much more educated than they used to be about the things they are considering for purchase, and sellers are scrambling to keep up with them. Here are some statistics that illustrate the extent of the problem:

- **Today, as much as 70% of a buyer's purchasing decision process can be completed before he or she even talks to a salesperson.[2]**

- **Forty-one percent of salespeople feel that their inability to effectively communicate value to the customer is a main cause for them not meeting their sales quotas.[3]**

- **Forty percent of salespeople believe improvements are needed to help them better understand the customer's buying process.[4]**

- **In certain business-to-business (B2B) sales environments, only 30% of sales cycles end with the buyer actually making a decision to buy anything from anyone.**[5]

How did we get into this situation where salespeople are struggling to maintain their relevance? Is it simply collateral damage from the rapid development of the Internet and the Web? Or is there something else going on?

As you will learn more about later in this book, **Lean Thinking** is a set of principles derived by distilling more than 60 years of wildly successful applications of innovative Lean approaches used to revolutionize the automobile and other manufacturing industries and, more recently, services. One of the many lessons Lean Thinking teaches is to always search for the *root cause* of problems instead of stopping at the superficial level that is merely a *symptom* of the issues.

What, then, is the root cause of the issues we are facing today in sales? The Internet has definitely driven a change in the relationship of buyers and sellers, but that's only because the relationship between buyers and sellers *was already broken* and ripe for an alternative. **Traditional selling simply got too expensive. Not for the companies that salespeople work for—although that is an issue as well—but for *buyers*.** The cost for a customer to engage with a salesperson—as measured by the required investment of time and effort—primed the marketplace to be open to and ready for an alternative. There just hasn't been a good substitute to obtain much of the value that traditional salespeople provided—*until now.*

But even *that* is a symptom and not the root cause of the problem. Rather, the deeper cause lies within the belief system about what salespeople should do and how they should do it. These limiting beliefs have been solidly rooted in a state of mind that can best be classified as twentieth-century-industrial thinking. Twentieth-century-industrial selling puts the salesperson in the center of the selling universe and underemphasizes the process that salespeople follow.

There really hasn't been any significant shift in the *focus* of selling methodologies for more than 50 years. Billions of dollars are being spent annually on sales training worldwide, despite the fact that salespeople may retain as little as 13% of what they learn in a sales training session after just 30 days.[6] Much less investment has been made—and attention paid—to the *processes* that enable salespeople to do what they do.

This focus, on improving the skills and capabilities of individual salespeople as the means to greater sales, has all but run out of gas. It is based on very similar thinking as that which led to increased investment in industrial automation and other technologies in manufacturing over the past 30 years. However, those investments proved not to be the answer to increasing growth and profits. The U.S. and European auto manufacturing industries demonstrated that beyond a shadow of a doubt.

What can be done to turn the tide for professional salespeople and the organizations that depend on their success? Should companies simply give up their traditional salesforces and sell everything over the Internet?

That is not a realistic option for the vast majority of companies that currently have traditional salesforces. First of all, many companies provide products and services that are simply too complex, expensive, risky, or strategic for the customer to buy them over the Internet. Second, we have to remember that less than five percent of U.S. GDP, for example, comes from e-commerce sales.

So, for the foreseeable future, the vast majority of goods and services out there will still be bought and sold in more traditional ways that involve professional salespeople. Still, unless those salespeople, and particularly the organizations they work for, change the way they view the role of selling and correspondingly modify their behaviors with buyers, salespeople will become increasingly ineffective and unproductive—and therefore more expensive—leading to a forced obsolescence.

Fortunately, Lean Thinking can provide the light to lead executives, sales managers, and salespeople out of the current sales darkness. This book will make the case that **the right focus for sales organizations concerned about these issues today should be on improving the *process* of selling, not just the skills of sellers.** The changing landscape of buyers is not something we should expect sellers to deal with completely on their own. It's unrealistic to expect that additional training of individual salespeople will allow each of them to singlehandedly address the macro changes that the Internet has wrought upon the sales environment. There is ample evidence that excellent, motivated people working within a substandard process, or one that is out of step with the times, can *at best* provide less-than-excellent products and services.

The Internet has affected every consumer and the way every company does business more than any other technological innovation in our lifetimes. A systemic response is the only viable and appropriate one to address such a global and pervasive change in the environment. This means that ***the entire system and all the processes that support and guide salespeople must adapt to respond appropriately to this new reality.***

If you are going to improve a process from a system perspective, there is no better set of proven practices and methodologies than those that have been encapsulated under the term Lean Thinking and applied successfully to a variety of industries in forms known as Lean Manufacturing, Lean Health Care Delivery, and many others. I believe Lean Thinking is the best tool that organizations have available to them today to pull out the roots of the twentieth-century-industrial selling mentality, which *is* the root cause of our current dilemma in sales.

What is Lean?

Soon after WWII, a then largely unknown Japanese company, the Toyota Motor Corporation, was busy defining and refining what would become the second major revolution in manufacturing in the twentieth century, nearly 50 years after the introduction of mass production by Henry Ford at the century's beginning. The new methodologies, principles, and underlying philosophies, collectively called the Toyota Production System (TPS), were popularized in the ground-breaking book, *The Machine that Changed the World.*[7] TPS is now commonly referred to as Lean Manufacturing or Lean Production. Toyota's invention and its commitment and leadership in Lean Thinking and implementation, applied to manufacturing and other areas such as product development and customer service, are widely credited for the company's ascendance from obscurity to leadership in global automotive production in 2007, surpassing General Motors for the top spot.[8]

Toyota's success with Lean resulted from methodically repeating the following five steps in every one of its production processes:

1. **Eliminate activities that are unnecessary and don't add value for the customer**

2. **Minimize activities that are necessary but don't add value for the customer**

3. **Complete activities from beginning to end as quickly as possible**

4. **When things don't go as planned or expected, find out why, make a change and see if it fixes the problem**

5. **Empower the people who are carrying out activities to continuously improve the process**

What is Lean Selling?

Lean Selling™ borrows principles and practices that were developed and refined in hardware and software manufacturing and service industries for more than 60 years, and applies them to the sales process. *Lean* is about focusing on the value you deliver to customers, while eliminating the waste that exists in the process of delivering that value. In Lean Selling, waste is defined as any activity that is unnecessary or does not add value *from the customer's perspective.*

Buyers can extract value by engaging with Lean sellers. The methods and tools to accomplish this will necessarily be different for Lean Selling than for manufacturing and service industries, given the special nature of the sales process, but the objectives will be the same:

• **Create more value (as defined by the customer)**

• **Eliminate the waste that accompanies the creation and delivery of that value**

• **Empower those involved in providing the value to continuously improve the process of doing so**

The Business Case

When you review the improvement numbers attributed to Toyota's new Lean system so carefully documented in *The Machine*, it is easy to see why you can't afford to ignore Lean Thinking and how it might benefit your organization. Here are some examples of the *typical* improvement in performance metrics that would warm the heart of any plant manager, CFO, or CEO of a manufacturing company:[9]

- **Productivity increases of 82%**
- **Quality improvements of 49%**
- **Required assembly space reductions of 27%**
- **Days of inventory reductions of 92%**
- **Absenteeism reductions of 58%**
- **Suggestions per employee increases of 15,200%**

"Impressive numbers," you may be thinking, "but what does this have to do with sales?" Good question. That's what the rest of this book is about. Before we get there, though, let's first look at how Lean has evolved.

Toyota realized that its Lean innovations could be applied to other *customer-facing processes* outside of the factory. The first non-production area the company tackled was the provisioning of replacement and repair parts to dealers in the U.S.[10] This can be seen as Lean Thinking *crossing over* from being applied to a tangible product (assembly of automobiles or the manufacturing of parts) to an intangible service (availability of the right replacement parts when you need them and where you need them).

Although the specific procedures and ideas to support a Lean supply chain required different thinking and a different implementation than Lean in the factory, the underlying goals and philosophy employed in approaching the challenge were the same. The results Toyota achieved by moving toward a Lean supply chain of replacement and repair parts were no less impressive than those listed above for production processes.[11]

Once Lean was successfully applied to service processes and the provision of intangibles, the floodgates of potential applications were opened. There are now initiatives, success stories, and Lean best practices across a broad spectrum of business, government, and education,[12] including:

- **Supermarket and convenience store stocking**
- **Hospitals and health care provisioning**
- **Software development**[13]
- **Entrepreneurialism**[14]
- **Accounting**
- **Government**
- **Education**
- **Office and administrative processes**
- **New product development**
- **Pharmaceutical regulatory approval**[15]

While the robustness of the application of Lean and the maturity of best practices varies widely in these industries, *case studies routinely report startling, measurable improvements in line with those presented above for the automobile manufacturing industry.* (The metrics of success will naturally be adapted somewhat to be relevant to each industry and process that undergoes Lean transformation.)

I have spent more than 15 years of my career consulting with or advising CEOs of companies in the technology, manufacturing, and service industries on a broad set of operational and strategic challenges. Additionally, I have had multiple opportunities to run businesses myself.

Moreover, I have personally experienced the business impact of Lean transformations and implementations. In one particular consulting assignment with a company that produced customized aftermarket automobile parts, after working with their team for one month we got the delivery lead time *from 13 weeks to 3 weeks, a reduction of 77%, with zero dollars spent on capital improvements.* In another case I implemented a Lean Software Development methodology that reduced the time between new software releases to production, from my usual experience of *six months, to one week. That's a reduction of 96% in cycle time between releases.* As a bonus, the company attained 100% first-time production quality of releases. If you have any experience with software development as a provider or consumer, I challenge you to recall the last time you remember software being released without errors, let alone weekly.

It's difficult to fully capture the totality of economic benefits and strategic advantages that accrue from dramatically shortening production cycle times, getting products and services delivered to customers much more quickly and reliably providing first-time quality. Yet this is what Lean transformations have delivered time and time again for a variety of industries, products, services, and companies of all sizes.

How I Got to Lean

In the mid-1980s, at age 34, I became a director-level executive in a company that designed and manufactured complex electronic systems for both commercial and defense industry customers. This company, which eventually became a subsidiary of Lockheed-Martin, was a U.S. early adopter of so-called "Japanese methods" for improving production quality and on-time delivery, while *simultaneously* reducing fixed and variable costs. This is where I was first exposed to what is now widely known as Lean Manufacturing.

I wasn't much interested in manufacturing at the time, with my primary responsibilities lying outside the manufacturing realm in product management, marketing, sales, and eventually product development. To me, manufacturing was that place "downstairs" where stuff was built. However, as a senior member of the management team, I couldn't avoid constant exposure to foreign (literally) terminology and concepts such as *kaizen* (continuous improvement), *kanban* (pull-demand system), and JIT (Just-in-Time supply chain management).

My Lean learning at the time was by osmosis, and my lack of serious interest in the topic dissuaded me from delving deeper into understanding the Lean system and how it worked. Still, there was no doubting its effectiveness. Our organization was the sole supplier of a critical high-end product line to one of the world's largest computer companies at the time, which also happened to have a serious fixation with product quality and process consistency. Our organization designed the product, built it, tested it, private-labeled it, and shipped it directly to our customer's customers. That was showing trust in a supplier.

Later, when I became general manager of a business unit within this same organization, I took on the additional responsibility of hardware and software product development for a different product line sold directly under our own brand. It was then that I gained first-hand knowledge of the importance of Lean "feeders" to the manufacturing process, such as Design-for-Manufacturability (DFM). I also had the opportunity to successfully manage the implementation of certain emerging new Lean-related productivity improvement concepts in the engineering and product development areas such as concurrent (parallel) product development. These new approaches allowed us to bring complex new electronic systems products from concept to product delivery in record time. In some cases, we achieved this in a third of the time of the previous product development cycles, with first-time manufacturability straight out of engineering.

After five years, I left this organization, but not before I had the opportunity to lead, manage, and integrate the activities of the product management, product development, marketing, sales, and finance functions as director of this business unit. After leaving, my new career focus was on the general management of software companies, which later evolved into Internet and Web-based software. I had little reason at that time to revisit my "manufacturing" experience. That is what I thought at the time.

Fast forward to 2004 when, for the fourth time, I took on the role of software company CEO. This particular startup company was developing and providing one of the first large-scale interactive Web applications. It was through my association with an offshore software development organization that I first learned about a new way of developing software called Extreme Programming[16] (later referred to as Lean Software Development[17]).

This novel process for developing software turned on its head everything I had learned about the way software was supposed to be developed, and the way software development organizations were supposed to be managed. Despite my previous successes in implementing leading-edge processes and seeing transformational performance improvements, some of the premises of Lean Software Development were too "out there" for me to swallow.[18] Becoming an adherent would require me to jump off a figurative executive cliff, tossing out a belief system that I knew worked for one that was unfamiliar, felt risky, and required me to reset my thinking process from scratch.

Nevertheless, I took the leap, and a few years later I deeply understood, comparing current and past experiences, just what the business (not just technical) implications were of implementing Lean Software Development. For me, there was simply no going back to traditional software development methods, ever. The traditional cycle time for software releases was six to twelve months or more, after completing an exhausting process where the only predictability was the pain that you would inevitably experience going through it. If you have ever managed an organization that develops or depends on software, you know what I am talking about.

Instead of six-plus-month development cycles, for several years our company made **weekly production (not "Beta") releases to the Web, without one major production failure due to quality problems** (a.k.a. software "bugs"). Our company also became one of the first in the world to successfully use this Lean development process with an offshore team. I eventually founded the Lean-Agile Software Business Interest Group within the San Diego Software Industry Council as a venue for sharing my discoveries and experiences with others in the business community.

I subsequently became a student of Lean and wanted to understand more about its origins. I was about to complete the Lean circle that started in the mid-1980s.

However, the most important management and leadership question you may be pondering at the moment is what enabled me to take the leap to Lean Software Development despite my gut discomfort. Well, as noted above, the old software development process worked; it just didn't work very well. The most common and chronic problems in software development across organizations include:

- **Inaccurate forecasts (product release dates and development cost)**
- **Consistently missing commitments** (near-zero on-time delivery across the industry)
- **Failure to provide the functionality that users actually want**
- **Wasted time** (developing features that users don't want and will never use)
- **A completely opaque process** (that doesn't lend itself to quality control or continuous improvement)

I would like to point out that the first four problems listed above are what Lean Thinking refers to as symptoms, and the last one is closer to what Lean Thinking refers to as a root cause. Lean Software Development promised to fix all of these problems. I took the leap, and it delivered as promised.

Back to the Future

In 2011, I started a firm to provide consulting services to CEOs on a variety of business challenges they faced. This provided me the opportunity over the last few years to work with CEOs in wide-ranging industries, sometimes on strategy and finance issues, but frequently on operations. One pattern I observed is how rare it was to find a CEO who was happy with his or her sales organization and sales results. I consistently found that nearly every company I got to know had significant challenges in its marketing and sales area, even if that was not the primary issue that triggered them to seek our help. The most common complaints were:

- **Inaccurate forecasts (revenues and deal-closing times)**
- **Consistently missing commitments** (only a fraction of salespeople consistently met their quotas and closed deals as forecasted)
- **Failure to provide the services and experience that users actually wanted**
- **Wasted time** (providing information and engaging in activities that customers didn't want and didn't benefit from)

- **A completely opaque process** (that didn't lend itself to quality control or continuous improvement)

Does this list look familiar? It's almost a cut-and-paste of the list of symptoms for the broken traditional software development process, with a few words changed for context. Because I have a fair amount of experience in managing sales and marketing functions as well as the software development process, I believe I am in the unusual position to assess the "state-of-the-art" as to how progressive the culture and practices of these professional functions are today. I find that sales and software development processes, from a CEO's perspective, exhibit very similar dysfunctions that they regularly present to their companies and to their customers. I have summarized these findings in Table 1 below.

Table 1 – Comparing Issues in Software Development to Sales

Symptom	Software Development	Sales
Inaccurate Forecasts	Release dates not met	Sales forecasts not met
Consistently missed commitments	Near-zero on-time delivery	Two in five salespeople do not make their quota[19]
Failure to provide what the customer wants	Failure to provide the desired product functionality or user experience	Failure to provide the desired services and experience Buyers want
Creating waste	Creating features and "just-in-case" architectures that users don't want and that will never be used	Providing information and engaging in meetings and other activities that customers don't want and don't benefit from
Opaque process	Lacking a consistent, repeatable, measurable process	Lacking a consistent, repeatable, measurable process
Typical level of CEO understanding about how the process works	Little to none	Little to none

It occurred to me that the same Lean Thinking and methodologies that solved these chronic problems in areas such as manufacturing, product development, customer service, and health care delivery might be used to revolutionize the way sales processes and organizations are designed and managed with similar breakthrough results. For those reasons, I began thinking: if Lean can create seeming miracles in every area it's been tried in **AND** I know how impactful it's been in software development **AND** looking from the outside in–sales seems to have cultural and performance challenges in common with software development–then **WHY CAN'T** Lean be a solution for sales as well?

What then would Lean Selling look like? Although core Lean principles are maintained across various application domains, the implementations in new arenas have had to be adapted to a new context to achieve the desired result. Someone had to create the proper methods and tools for each new application context; in effect, inventing a new Lean system methodology and tools to support the traditional Lean objectives. Then I started scouring the Web for case studies of Lean transformations in companies' selling processes. To my shock and amazement, I couldn't find any. **Today there are no universally agreed-upon best practices for applying Lean to sales** (and to tightly linked organizations such as marketing).

In addition, I couldn't find a single comprehensive place where one could go to get a model or even to start thinking about applying Lean to the selling process. Now I know there will be some who are in the sales training and coaching industry who will disagree with this statement. Also, I acknowledge that there are numerous blogs, whitepapers, articles, and websites that have some excellent thinking about areas where Lean can hypothetically be applied to sales, and even ways it might be implemented.

Still, I'll stand by my assertion because the operative word for me is "comprehensive." As a Lean practitioner myself, I know Lean doesn't have its full impact except as a complete end-to-end implementation, not as a piecemeal, isolated island of improvement opportunity. If you think I am mistaken and can point me to something, please let me know or post the information at the LinkedIn® group or Facebook® page, "Lean

Selling"; you can also direct message me on Twitter® @LeanSelling.

At first I couldn't believe it. I thought there must be something wrong with the way I was searching for the information. I tried different ways to find what I was looking for. I was still unsuccessful, although I gained more insight into the state-of-the-art of applying Lean to sales. It also became clearer to me that there was a hole in the market that was not being filled. That is when I decided to write this book.

At first I had to resolve in my own mind how it could be possible that the methodologies for applying Lean to sales weren't fully established many years ago. It just seemed like such an obvious application, particularly in an area that is so close to every company's heart, and which is often near or at the top of an organization's departmental expenditures.

I asked myself how that could be the case. It can't be that the benefits of Lean practices are in question. There is probably more agreement on the benefits of Lean approaches than there is on the topic of global warming. It couldn't be for lack of motivation. Companies are always looking to improve their sales productivity and lower their cost of new customer acquisition. There must be another reason. Was it just too hard to figure out how to do it?

I knew from my experience with Lean Software Development that the implementation details, methodologies and tools were quite different than those used in Lean Manufacturing. I was very impressed by the system developed for Lean Software Development and how the elements to implement it were "invented" to accomplish the goals of Lean, but in the context of software development.

An example is the "extreme" idea of "pair programming" where two developers work together to create a line of code. I don't mean each of them working at their own desks. I mean both of them sharing a keyboard and screen; *creating the same code together*. It seems like that would double the cost of development, but it doesn't. It actually *reduces* it. How is that possible? It is because one of the biggest costs in software development is the cost of poor quality code, manifesting as "bugs." It turns out that bugs are very time-consuming (and therefore costly) to find and fix. And the longer they are in the code, the more expensive it is to fix them. It is also one of the greatest contributors to software releases missing their scheduled dates for delivery.

The Lean principle at work here is to build quality in, also known as *error-proofing*. Having two pairs of eyes (and the collaborative discussion and reflection that ensues from having two programmers program together) reduces software quality defects (bugs) from getting into the code to such an extent that it more than pays for the doubling of staff.

Most Lean service applications I looked at appeared very similar in terms of their Lean implementation methodologies, across a wide range of industries. Still, I struggled with how to map a "comprehensive" Lean approach to sales. Was the sales function so different that it would require new "inventions" to make it Lean?

My instincts told me that the fact that I was having such conceptual challenges building on previous novel Lean adaptations to create a selling adaptation meant that something was indeed very different about selling when it came to pursuing a Lean implementation. What was it? **I knew selling was a process (or should be) just like any other. Was it not like any other?** I knew that unless I resolved this conundrum in my own mind, I could never embark on clarifying what a comprehensive Lean Selling approach might look like. As Lean had taught me, if you don't really understand the problem, you can't solve it. Maybe others had my same difficulty, which is why there is a paucity of information on the topic of my pursuit.

How Sales is Different

As I struggled with this dilemma, it occurred to me that there were some truly unique aspects of selling that must be considered in thinking about how Lean applies to it:

1. **With all other products and services where Lean has been implemented, the ultimate consumer is not interested in how the product or service is produced, only in his or her experience with the output, the ease of accessing it, and the number of "touch points" required.** In other words, the "production" of a product or service in these cases is a "black box" process to the consumer, and the less they have to know about how a company does what it does, the happier they are. A simple example is that

a buyer of a car is interested in the car, the features, quality, availability, and price. He or she doesn't much care how the manufacturer transports the car, how the car is assembled in the factory, how much manufacturing is outsourced, and so forth. Another example is in the provision of health services. A patient wants to receive a required medical service with the fewest touch points in the shortest amount of time, even when their insurance company is paying for it. He or she doesn't care about the medical facility's doctor or nurse scheduling system, their billing software (unless there are errors), and so on. *This is not the case with sales. In sales, the buyer must be involved in the process of producing the value that is created from engaging in the process.* This becomes immediately obvious when you consider that without the involvement of a buyer, there is no sale. Later in this book I will refer to the actions that buyers take as the *Buying Process*.

2. **Most salespeople (and their managers) think that a salesperson's value derives from, and is largely defined by, the product or service he or she is selling**. However, they fail to realize that the selling process in itself can create (or destroy) value in the buyer's mind *independent of the product or service being provided.* Still, very little time is invested in helping salespeople understand the aspect of what a buyer's expectation is for the *emotional* experience the buyer is seeking in making a decision to buy. The reality is that a salesperson's value to a buyer is partly related to the product or service the company provides (almost exclusively the common view) and partly to what he or she personally brings to the experience of buying.

3. **This leads to the next point, which is that companies rarely think of sales as a "service" that its salespeople provide to a potential buyer.** It is much more common for sales to be thought of as a service to the company (in order to increase revenues). Maybe that is why it's hard to map it to other Lean service implementations unless you understand selling is a service for buyers. This is the focus of Part II of this book.

4. **The selling process must be synchronized to the buying process or it will not be effective or have value for the buyer.** Therefore, the seller must understand and track—even manage—the buyer's process if his or her interactions with a buyer are going to be meaningful and impactful. Very few sellers consider, let alone attempt to engage in, a buyer's process except at the most superficial level.

Let's recap and summarize what appear to be meaningful differences for a Lean implementation in the sales arena as compared to the provision of other types of services:

1. **It is a process that the buyer wants to be–and must be–involved in executing.**

2. **Salespeople have to orchestrate the delivery of three interconnected types of value:**
   - **Value that the product or service represents for the buyer (the foundational reason the buyer first engaged with a seller)**
   - **Value that the buying process provides for the buyer**[20]
   - **Value that the selling process provides for the buyer**

3. **Sales must be considered a service that synchronizes and integrates the processes and these three types of value "streams"[21] that produce ultimate value for the buyer.**

I now believe that the difficulty in applying Lean to the selling process derives from two fundamental gaps in thinking:

1. **Lack of recognition that the buying process is integral to the selling process and that you cannot create a Lean Selling process without fully integrating the buying process into one overall buying *and* selling process *that must be synchronized at every point of the process from beginning to end.***

2. **Lack of recognition that sales is indeed a service from the viewpoint of the buyer. It is a service the company delivers,**

**not one that the company receives. Realizing this is the first
step toward Lean Thinking in the area of sales.**

Acknowledging these two gaps, this book will attempt to be the
first to comprehensively describe a Lean Selling process end-to-end,
collectively referred to as the ***Lean Selling System***. This book is not
intended as a cookbook or a "how-to" for comprehensive Lean implementations. There are many excellent ideas and instructions that are
available in books or across the Web on how to transform into a Lean
organization in general, as well as many implementation examples in
particular. Additionally, today there are many Lean coaches and trainers
with years of real-world experience in effecting Lean transformations
in organizations.

Use This Book as an Excuse

The primary purpose of this book is to expose senior executive
team members and sales managers to the possibilities Lean can
provide for their company's selling process.

If you are not yet a sales manager or a member of the senior
executive team, but are intrigued by the ideas presented in this book
and think they might be helpful to your company, pass this book on
to the most innovative person you know at the executive level of your
organization when you are finished reading it. At a minimum, it will
make for a great excuse to talk business with that senior executive in
your company, and that can't be bad!

As a side note, I would *not* recommend that an organization
undertake a full Lean transformation without qualified outside guidance. This is the case even where there is significant, broad experience
with Lean inside the organization (a rarity). The importance of engaging a Lean ***Sensei*** (teacher or coach) to lead Lean transformations is a
well-established custom in the Lean world. While the outcomes Lean
provides are dramatic and desirable, getting there is not easy, or without
its share of setbacks. In my experience, a big part of the difficulty is that,

although Lean ideas are common-sense, they are often counter-intuitive (as most good, innovative ideas are). Organizational transformation to Lean Thinking requires a shift in mindset and in firmly held (but often erroneous) beliefs about the way things are and the way things can be. It is exceedingly rare that an insider can drive the cultural change necessary to institutionalize new beliefs to a point where the organization will not slip back (even unconsciously) into old ways of thinking and old patterns of behavior. Some examples of these ways of thinking and behaviors will be covered in Part II of this book.

I do not mean to imply that bringing in an outside person or team to coach a Lean transformation is all that is necessary for success. It may be necessary, but it is not sufficient. The most important element is the commitment of senior management (including the CEO) to the Lean transformation *and to stay the course*. This is especially true when, as is inevitable, things don't always go as desired and the beneficial results are hard to see, especially in the early stages of transition.

Selling Is Not for the Faint of Heart

Selling is not an easy profession. Most people are just not cut out for it. We have all heard about how the requirement to deal with continual rejection is one factor that supports that assessment. Still, in the same vein we don't often mention tenacity, self-motivation, a competitive spirit, and a true desire to help, which are also common characteristics of successful salespeople. Most salespeople are true entrepreneurs: usually paid for performance, not activity, left pretty much to their own devices to figure out the best way to close sales, constantly having to discover new ways to find additional prospects, and frequently navigating uncharted waters.

Unfortunately, the world of sales is not getting easier or kinder to salespeople. I will go into more detail about the reasons for this in Part II of this book. I will also explain why every CEO and senior executive should be concerned about the effects that current marketplace trends are having on salespeople, as much or more than the salespeople themselves are concerned.

Fortunately, I believe Lean Selling™ offers a way to address all the current and future challenges salespeople may experience. My goal is to present an argument for Lean Selling as a remedy for what ails sales today, in the hope that it will initiate some new thinking, discussion, and action toward a way out of the current sales dilemma salespeople everywhere face.

Key Takeaways from Chapter 1

1. *There is a crisis in sales driven largely by Internet adoption.*

2. *Salespeople are struggling to maintain or recapture the relevance they once had.*

3. *There is hope for the sales profession offered by Lean Selling, a new application of the proven principles of Lean Thinking.*

4. *The sales process has similarities with many other processes but also significant differences that must be recognized.*

5. *Early adopters of Lean Selling can see substantial productivity improvements in their sales organizations while building competitive advantage.*

Chapter 2

Lean Selling Case Examples

In Chapter Two

Case Examples
→ Cloud-Based Software—*Inside Sales*
→ Business Services—*Field Sales*
→ Industrial Distribution—*Hybrid Sales*
→ Healthcare—*Independent Sales Representatives*
→ Pharmaceuticals—*Field Marketing*

Focus on Quality

Sales Function: Inside Sales Management
Industry: Cloud-Based Business Service

Kevin Gaither, Vice President of Inside Sales at ZipRecruiter, Inc., and also the President of the Los Angeles Chapter of the American Association of Inside Sales Professionals, spoke to me about his own sales situation. It's a very different set of circumstances than the other case examples of field sales that follow in several ways, but there are also similarities from a Lean Thinking perspective. ZipRecruiter is not a recruiting firm, but provides a cloud-based service that helps companies get more results from their recruiting efforts.

His company is growing very rapidly, due in large part to the contributions made by the inside sales function. When Kevin joined the company a little more than a year ago there were only two inside salespeople. Now there are 50, and that number will double in the next four months. What is the key to this company's growth?

Unlike the typical situation, this company is generating thousands of leads for the inside sales team every month. The inside salespeople spend *zero* time on prospecting. With inside sales, the "connect rate" in business-to-business (B2B) sales (how often you get someone to pick up the phone when you call) is typically 10% or less, depending on the size of the company and the organizational level you are calling at. This company's rate is twice that, due largely to brand recognition. However, these are *outcomes* of what Kevin feels is a deeper cause of their success.

Rather, Kevin believes the foundation of their achievements can be traced to the company's focus on ***quality*** and its willingness to take a ***long-range view*** in its sales process. Both of these guiding principles are consistent with Lean Selling™.

What type of quality does the company focus on? Primarily the quality of the customer fit with the company *and* the quality of the Buyer experience during the Buying process along with the customer experience post-sale. While the inside salespeople don't spend time prospecting since there are an abundance of leads, they do spend a lot of time ***qualifying the Buyer,*** employing their proprietary seven-step qualifying process. They do so to ensure customer fit, but also to help **avoid *buyer remorse*.** Kevin told me **they intentionally "slow down" the sales process** by not pushing for a sale to close prematurely, in order to ensure these two higher-level goals are not compromised.

Kevin also told me that his inside salespeople are providing a ***service*** for the Buyer, to help Buyers make sure his company's offerings are right for them. They have reduced the pressure to buy, and as part of their process they insist that a Buyer first engage in a free, no-obligation trial of their Web-based service before becoming a customer. He says this approach has yielded a larger initial customer commitment and greater use of the company's service by customers over time.

The ironic thing about this Case Example is that ***by thinking long-term instead of short-term, and by focusing on quality rather than a transaction, the company has achieved sales growth in the short-term that is astronomical***, but also manageable. Better yet, that's not the end of the story.

To my surprise I learned that Kevin is already a believer in Lean Thinking and that he has been applying it to everything the company does in sales. He was inspired to do so by the book *The Lean Startup*, and he has embraced the concept this book presents of an MVP (Minimally Viable Product) and a scientific approach to sales experimentation.

In fact, Kevin has a small group he fondly calls the "sales hackers" (similar in concept to groups previously chronicled as "skunk works"), which is a petri dish of sorts where "experiments" in the form of pilot implementations of new ideas can be tested. The pilot programs his group undertakes are based on the scientific method of capturing and evaluating metrics to determine whether the new idea works in the real world. Based on what the company learns, tweaks are made to the new idea until it either yields the results the company is looking for (a success) or the company moves on to a different idea (another type of success). This process corresponds to an additional concept from *The Lean Startup* of "Validated Learning." As a result, in essence, Kevin views each of his pilot programs as a mini-startup exercise.

Lean Selling Principles Employed

There are several Lean Selling concepts that are being employed to achieve the results of this Case Example. Here is a list and brief explanation.

Error-Proofing – Much of the salespeople's time is devoted to ensuring that the Buyer is a fit with the type of customer the company wants to have. Further, much time is also invested in making sure the service the company offers is a good fit for the Buyer. This prevents "bad quality" Buyers (misfits) from taking space and time away from the sales pipeline or from becoming customers who do not realize the benefit of the company's service. *(See Chapter 16.)*

Reduce Waste – The approach of investing in better qualification saves time that otherwise would be wasted on prospects that are not going to close or don't support the company's long-term objectives. *(See Chapter 20.)*

Reducing Inventory – By improving the quality of the leads coming into the pipeline, Kevin is reducing inventory in the pipeline, the Buyers in progress who otherwise would have had expensive time and energy put into them only to leave the funnel before making a decision. *(See Chapter 14.)*

Leveling – Because of the steady stream of leads available and the removal of pressure to close a transaction, the company is able to balance or level its sales pipeline. This allows realistic, consistent, and achievable monthly goals for the company's salespeople. It also allows for revenue forecasts that are highly reliable. *(See Chapter 21.)*

Opportunity for Lean Selling Improvement

This is a company that is already very successful based on the Lean Thinking it has already applied to its sales process. However, Lean Thinking also informs us that organizations should always pursue Continuous Improvement *(see Chapter 23)* regardless of how successful they become. Now, what is there that could be improved?

Continuous Improvement thinking looks at metrics or Key Performance Indicators (KPIs) to determine where improvement efforts should be prioritized. While this company's "connect rate" is currently twice as good as the industry average, it is still only 20%. Could it be better? Is there something else that could be done to improve it? Since this sales organization already has experience with the benefits of doing pilot projects, it would be interesting to see if there is some experimentation that could be done in this area.

For example, is there a way other than phone calling—perhaps with email or social media outreach—to entice a potential Buyer to schedule a call with an inside salesperson using a tool like TimeTrade® (www.TimeTrade.com)? Who knows what the connect rate could go up to if the company experimented, measured, tweaked and ultimately found a model along these lines that worked?

Leaning the Sales Pipeline

Sales Function: Field Sales
Industry: Business Services

Sue (not her real name) is among the top salespeople in her company, a large national provider of business outsourcing services with over $2 billion in annual transactions. Sue talked to me about her sales pipeline. Some of her leads are provided by a corporate telemarketing function, but Sue is responsible for finding the vast majority of her leads by herself. She estimates that she spends about 60% of her time prospecting and qualifying prospects.

Sue is managing complex sales that are technical, consultative, and require trust to be established with the Buyer. The average close ratio for her industry is 25% (which means 75% of leads that come into the sales pipeline don't close at the end, implying they end up in *No Decision,* or the default state, *Status Quo*). Remarkably, Sue's closing ratio is more than two times the industry average. I wanted to know how she is able to do this consistently.

Sue told me that she only brings leads into her pipeline that she believes have a high probability of closing. She said she doesn't want to waste time with leads that have a lower chance of closing because that is time that she can't be spending with her better prospects, and time is money.

Sue added that the key to her success is this philosophy of qualifying the leads that come into her sales pipeline and making sure she avoids the pressure to compromise her lead quality standards. She believes that she is able to Lean her sales pipeline because she has a specific minimum for the number of prospects she wants to have in her pipeline at any one time. This is so Sue can be comfortable that she will make her sales closing goals. Further—and this was the most fascinating part for me—Sue knows *instinctively* that if her pipeline falls below her minimum number, she will unconsciously tend to be less selective about the leads that come into her sales pipeline. She keeps track of when she is getting close to her minimum number as a warning signal or indicator to step up prospecting.

I also found it interesting that Sue is further aware that if she gets too many prospects into her pipeline, things can get out of control. Therefore, Sue also has a maximum number for prospects as well. As she approaches this number, she begins to "weed out" or "schedule out" prospects that are less likely to close in the near term, in order to bring her number of active prospects back to a controllable number. This is similar to the Lean Manufacturing principle of leveling production in a factory so people and machines don't get overworked and break down.

Finally, her company is organized around a cross-functional team to support the customer post-sale, including service delivery. The field salesperson is the *de facto* leader of that client team.

Lean Selling Principles Employed

There are several Lean Selling concepts that are being employed to achieve the results of this Case Example. Here is a list with brief explanations.

Error-Proofing – Leads are compared to a list of criteria to determine if they are likely to close. The ones that don't meet the criteria don't go into the pipeline. This prevents "bad quality" from entering the process and allows the process to yield a higher close rate and less waste of time and energy spent on leads that are unlikely to close. *(See Chapter 16.)*

Visual Signal – By setting minimum and maximum numbers of prospects for the pipeline, it is easy to determine when the process is in control simply by looking at the count of prospects in the pipeline. Approaching these minimum or maximum numbers serves as a type of signal to "request" more leads or to stop prospecting. *(See Chapter 24.)*

Reduce Waste – The approach of investing in better qualification saves time that otherwise would be wasted on prospects that are not going to close. *(See Chapter 20.)*

Reducing Inventory – Improving the quality of the leads coming into the pipeline reduces inventory in the pipeline, particularly the Buyers in progress, who otherwise would have had expensive time and energy invested into them only to leave (or get stuck in) the pipeline before closing. *(See Chapter 14.)*

Leveling – Determining in advance the minimum and maximum numbers of prospects to have in the pipeline allows salespeople to level their workload so they can be confident about making their goals, without having so much to do that they become inefficient in dealing with too many prospects at the same time. *(See Chapter 21.)*

Pull – The idea that when a prospect leaves the pipeline it needs to be replaced supports the idea of "pulling" sales from the pipeline, with the awareness that when the number of prospects gets to a certain minimum level the process must "pull" in more leads. *(See Chapter 22.)*

Teamwork – Organizing teams around customers and formalizing the people on the team goes a long way toward breaking down functional silo thinking and provides a focus on adding value for the customer. *(See Chapter 18.)*

Opportunity for Lean Selling Improvement

Sue is currently spending 60% of her time prospecting and qualifying, not because she wants to, but because she has to in order to make her sales numbers. As a pilot project, it would be interesting to provide her a *dedicated* lead generation resource that she would manage and personally train in her techniques of prospecting and qualifying.

The goal of this experiment would be to see if this additional resource could bring in *at least* the same quantity and quality of leads as Sue does. If this pilot project is successful, it would free up significant time that Sue could spend with customers closing deals. Of course, like any process, this endeavor would have to be approached with the mindset of Continuous Improvement *(see Chapter 23)*, as it might take some time and a lot of collaboration to get another person to deliver the same results that Sue currently does.

Continually Innovating Customer Value

Sales Function: Managing a Hybrid Sales Organization
Industry: Industrial Distribution

Doug Peterson is the Market Vice President of Hospitality Sales for HD Supply Facilities Maintenance, which is a $2.3 billion division of HD Supply, Inc., an $8.5 billion publicly-traded industrial distributor. Facilities Maintenance focuses on the multifamily apartment, hospitality, healthcare, and institutional markets. The revenues of Doug's hospitality sales division have been growing at double-digit rates for the last five years.

The responsibilities of Doug's team of nearly 200 salespeople encompass inside and outside sales, as well as national account sales. Unlike most companies, Doug's sales organization does not have significant challenges in the areas of client prospecting and qualifying. This is because his division's penetration into their markets is very high. For example, in one of Doug's target markets, 78% of their potential customers have bought something from them within the previous six months. Instead, Doug's selling challenge is how to get a greater share of the purchases made by the customers they already have a relationship with.

Doug is certain that the key to this will be to continually offer customers new products and services that address new requirements and add new forms of customer value. The responsibility for driving this type of innovation has fallen traditionally on Doug's organization. He believes that, while his group is making good progress, there is an opportunity to pursue innovation with customers in a more systematic way.

Doug also is a believer in the power of Lean Thinking based on his past experiences with a very large client company that was steeped in Lean Manufacturing. He sees a lot of potential opportunity in applying Lean principles to the challenge and opportunity for innovation in his own customer base, but wonders how to balance the required investment (mainly time) with the short-term financial requirements of a publicly-traded company.

Opportunity for Lean Selling Improvement

There are two areas where Doug's objectives and Lean Thinking perfectly align. The first is the premise that value is defined solely by the customer. The second is that continuous improvement, a bedrock foundation of Lean Thinking, is a broader term for the continuous innovation of value-added services Doug seeks with his customers.

Additionally, as I discuss in Chapter 11, Toyota constantly finds itself with excess employees as a result of its relentless pursuit of productivity improvements. The company therefore regularly has to find new products and services to offer its customers—and new businesses to enter—in order to gainfully engage these excessed resources. Toyota is able to continually innovate in this area because it applies the same rigor to this process as it does to the continuous improvement of a manufacturing process: understand what can be improved *based on customer value*, thoroughly discuss various ways you might make the improvement, create or deliver the improvement or new service, and see what customers think about what you have done. Then do this all over again.

From a practical perspective, Lean Selling prescribes that customer value and unmet needs should be collected in a systematic, data-driven way. Doug's sales organization is ideally suited to gather such information, assuming his salesforce is brought into a formal process of identifying opportunities for new services that can be offered to the current customer base. Of course, there could be the tension that Doug alludes to between salespeople meeting their near-term sales objectives and building a platform for continued growth. There is also potentially an issue of focus when salespeople are asked to close business and do customer research at the same time.

I believe that this tension arises partly from the definition we have of a salesperson's role. I cover this at length in Part II of this book when discussing the mindset change necessary to think about sales as a service and salespeople as coaches. It appears the same principle might apply here.

It seems quite logical, since Doug's salespeople are primarily engaged in account management rather than prospecting for new customers, that the salespeople would want to open an ongoing dialog with their customers about their unmet needs, brainstorm with them on potential solutions, and even occasionally come back to their customers with a "mock-up" or hypothetical example of how a new service they suggested might work for them.

What is that you say? This is not a traditional selling role? Maybe not, but it is a Lean Selling role and, as with all the other innovations in selling roles proposed in this book, if nothing else it would lead to highly differentiating this Lean Selling team of salespeople from their competitors in the eyes of their customers.

Once the difficult part, changing the mindset about the salesperson's role, is resolved, then many creative ways this new activity can be seamlessly integrated into the ongoing relationship with the customer can be discovered. It might be as simple as creating a standard procedure that salespeople follow, such as questions to ask when they are with customers. Or it could be built around a fun activity, like a "Question of the Month" to test new ideas with customers.

Finally, Lean Thinking and Lean Selling prescribe the use of experimentation as part of continuous improvement, sometimes in the form of a pilot project. The same approach can work here. Doug could identify a subset of his sales team that appear ideally suited for a pilot of this new role for salespeople. These would be the ones least likely to be distracted from their sales goals as a result of this new activity. In this way, data could be gathered and incremental improvements made to the program before expanding it to the entire salesforce. That would reduce any potential risk to near-term revenue as well as potential opposition to adoption of the new program from the salesforce.

Evaluating the Partnership

Sales Function: Managing Independent Sales Representatives
Industry: Non-Medical Products for Healthcare Facilities

Denise Rippinger is the President and CEO of three affiliated companies, two of which provide art products and art consulting services to corporate and healthcare environments. The third company provides a unique type of marker board called the Communicare-Board®, which meets the stringent requirements of healthcare facilities, including hospitals, surgery clinics, and assisted living.

Thomas Schutz is the Executive Vice President of Sales for Communicare Products. He was hired less than a year ago to set up an Independent Sales Representative (ISR) organization to bring a field sales presence to Communicare. ISR organizations are independent contractors that represent more than one company and typically sell multiple products and services from a variety of companies to their customers. Incidentally, Thomas shared with me that he was previously an executive with a major Cloud Consulting company that used something very similar to the Buying Plan *(see Chapter 21)* as a fundamental part of their sales process with outstanding results.

Thomas succeeded in recruiting 13 ISR organizations across the U.S. that collectively have 25 field salespeople selling Communicare's products. Thomas has personally trained these salespeople and provided them the tools he believes they require to sell Communicare's products successfully. As part of the training, Thomas created and provided each salesperson an Independent Sales Representative Manual that includes sales tools and case studies.

The company assigned internal people to each have responsibility for a territory containing several ISRs. Despite Thomas's efforts in recruiting and training the ISR organizations, sales results to date have been disappointing for both Thomas and Denise.

Based on in-depth discussions and data-gathering from ISRs, Thomas is clear about the fundamental issues that are keeping this new distribution channel from meeting expectations:

1. The ISRs require leads to get them started in this new area for them and they are not currently receiving any leads from the company. In certain territories, Territory Managers are providing the ISRs with suspect company names from industry data sources that provide contact and construction project data, but no actual "leads" of prospects who have expressed interest or are otherwise likely to buy.

2. The ISRs require the support of company subject-matter experts when they get engaged with a potential customer, and they are not currently getting that support.

Denise believes that the ISRs should be able to find opportunities without getting warm leads from the company or additional support in the sales process. She feels that the ISRs represented during the interview and hiring process that they would be able to function independently, and successfully sell the CommunicareBoard product along with the other product lines they represent to current clients.

It appears that the lack of success with the ISR channel is a symptom of a deeper issue. This deeper issue is the differing expectations among Communicare's CEO and the Territory Managers who manage the ISRs, and the ISRs themselves. As noted above, the ISRs expect support from Communicare in the areas of lead generation and pre-sales support, but the company's CEO and Territory Managers want the ISR organizations to prove they can sell their product before the company shares leads or commits its staff to help the ISRs during their sales process.

Based on these differing expectations among the players that are the key to the success of this new program, Communicare appears to be stuck in a "Catch-22" situation. There is widespread disappointment within the company and in the ISR channel with the lack of results. This could grow into a serious motivational problem if not addressed quickly. Denise and Thomas wanted to know whether there were any Lean Selling principles that could provide guidance as to what they should do next. I believe there are, and I have summarized them below for Denise's and Thomas' consideration.

Opportunity for Lean Selling Improvement

As I describe in Chapter 11, Toyota developed a very special way of working with their suppliers that is quite different from the relationship that U.S. automobile manufacturers have with their vendors. Consistent with Lean Thinking, Toyota treats its suppliers as true partners, makes a long-term commitment to them, invests in their success and continuous improvement, and shares the economic benefit of improvements with them. Toyota knows that the quality and value of their products is highly dependent on the quality of their suppliers, and after going through a rigorous selection process, their suppliers are considered a part of the Toyota family. This "win-win" mentality is in stark contrast to the "win-lose" thinking of Toyota's U.S. competitors that underlies many of their vendor relationships.

The first recommendation Lean Selling has for Communicare is to treat their channel partnerships based on "win-win" thinking, which means believing that their partners' successes translates to Communicare's success. Conversely, partners' failures mean a failure for Communicare, at least regarding this major sales channel initiative, in which the company has invested significant time, effort, and money. This implies that once you have selected a partner you must do everything reasonable to ensure they are successful. It further counsels that a plan must be put in place to prevent or resolve potential channel conflicts (competition) between Territory Managers and ISRs.

There must have been a compelling motivation for Communicare to proceed down the path of expanding their field sales presence. The issue or goal underlying that motivation has not disappeared, despite the disappointing sales results to date. The company now has to decide what to do next. Broadly speaking, I see that there are two main options the company can pursue:

1. Abandon the ISR strategy and develop another plan to create a field sales presence.

2. Understand the reasons why the current process is not working, decide what to do to address them, try something to fix the underlying problems, and see if it works.

If Communicare chooses option number two, then the second recommendation based on Lean Selling is to treat the ISR initiative as an experiment. The company rolled out the ISR initiative nationwide without first testing some of the assumptions it was based on. The failure to meet expectations is now affecting all the key staff.

Communicare should now make a "strategic retreat" and restart with a *pilot* ISR program to determine whether a focused effort that includes the support requested by ISRs will prove that the channel can meet the company's goals. Communicare should select the Territory Manager and ISRs that are the most enthusiastic about the ISR program—and that are most likely to succeed with it—for this pilot project.

Communicare should form a process improvement team that includes top management—in this case, Denise and Thomas—to work closely with the selected Territory Manager *and the selected ISRs* (collectively, the *Improvement Team*) to get to the root causes of the problems with the ISR channel process. The Lean Thinking technique of the Five Whys *(see Chapter 24)* can be of great help in getting to the root causes.

Communicare may find, for example, that it has to generate a certain number of leads per month for each ISR salesperson in order to make sales plan goals. If so, a plan has to be created to achieve that numeric objective for leads, and this metric should also be monitored as the improvement plan is executed, making adjustments as necessary to the assumptions underlying the plan.

Next, the Improvement Team should agree on additional specific metrics that they will use to determine whether the experiment is making sufficient progress. There should be a sales plan in place reflecting what the ISR channel is forecast to accomplish, and it should include these important process metrics—or Key Performance Indicators (KPIs)—that the company believes lead to sales. All of these metrics should be closely monitored after an improvement plan for the ISR channel is put in place.

Further, to help address the motivation issue, the entire company should be made aware of the pilot program. Metrics on progress should be displayed in a public area and updated as regularly as possible. This will send a message to company employees about transparency and about the commitment from the top of the organization to make this channel initiative work. It will also communicate that experimentation is a good thing and that failure is another name for continuous learning.

Approaching Buyers Strategically

Sales Function: Field Manager, Sales and Marketing Initiatives
Industry: Pharmaceuticals

Karen (not her real name) is a Field Manager of Sales and Marketing Initiatives for a product line of a major pharmaceutical and medical products firm. Karen's responsibilities are to create, implement, and monitor the success of field sales plans for her product area, which will be carried out by several hundred field salespeople.

Karen's company has been applying Lean Thinking for a number of years. Its adoption started in manufacturing processes. Based on its success there it migrated to other non-manufacturing business processes throughout the organization, with great accomplishments there as well. Based on these achievements, the company decided to pursue the application of Lean Thinking to field sales processes. This is a relatively new initiative for her company.

Karen told me that she uses Lean Thinking techniques in everything she does to make a sales rollout plan successful. These include such methodologies as Continuous Improvement *(see Chapter 23)*, the Five Whys *(see Chapter 24)*, and collecting and monitoring metrics *(see Chapter 10)* for Key Performance Indicators (KPIs—*see Chapter 24)*. I was pleasantly surprised to learn how many Lean Thinking and Lean Selling techniques Karen was already employing.

Karen said that in her previous experiences in the pharmaceutical industry with field sales before she adopted Lean Thinking, the biggest impediment to the sales process was a lack of understanding of where the client, or Buyer, was in their own Buying process. As a result, the Sellers would take actions that were not aligned with the Buyer's priorities. She described this approach as "shooting in the dark"; not understanding what was going on in the Buying process but taking action anyway. This led, according to Karen, to a lot of wasted selling time and effort and a low sales success rate.

Now, however, a key focus of the new sales process driven by Lean Thinking is—at the very beginning of a new client engagement with a new product—to understand where the Buyer is in their Buying

Process, and then to build the sales plan to achieve alignment with the Buyer. This has made all the difference in the world, according to Karen. Now the salespeople are much more focused with their clients regarding what has to be done to move the Buying process forward. This outcome has the same intent as the "Buying Plan" concept introduced in this book *(see Chapter 21)*.

According to Karen, by integrating with the Buyer's decision-making process, salespeople are "ten times more successful" than when the Buyer and the Seller each had their own separate process. Karen's entire sales team is now versed in this technique of aligning these two processes into one Buying process.

Now, Karen says her field salespeople can "jump in with a customer at a much deeper level than before," and they know exactly what to do in each selling situation. The relationship of the Buyer and Seller has been transformed into one of collaboration *(see Chapter 16)*. Karen believes that everything that they are doing to improve their sales "service" is benefiting their clients, such as being more effective and efficient in helping them to move forward from wherever they are in their Buying process, and not wasting their time. She also believes that this new approach differentiates her salespeople from those of the competitors, at the level of the relationship, not just the product they are selling.

Since customer value is the basis for measuring the success of Lean processes, it is important to constantly check assumptions about the value customers are seeking from your sales process and whether you are providing it. This becomes the basis for Continuous Improvement initiatives. Karen's organization has a formal process to measure twice a year the customer value they are adding. They are tackling head-on the challenge of getting a large sales group involved in process improvement so that it is from the bottom up, not from the top down. *(See Chapters 19 and 23.)*

Karen's organization also makes regular use of a form of Value Stream Mapping (VSM), a very powerful tool for the initial and continual improvement of processes. VSM events ideally should be held at least a couple of times a year to brainstorm on how the sales process can be improved (based on recent customer data about value) and also to consider any changes in the client environment that could justify a change to the sales process. *(See Chapter 20.)*

Karen believes that the greatest gain from applying Lean Think-ing to the sales process is that it causes salespeople to think more stra-tegically about their behaviors with clients, so they are not just taking actions for the sake of creating activity, but they are taking actions with a specific purpose. Additionally, however, Karen is convinced that there has been a real, quantifiable impact on sales productivity. She estimates that with their Lean Selling approach:

- *Selling waste* (time and effort) has been reduced by 25%
- *Sales productivity* has increased by 40%
- *Sales cycle time* has been reduced by 35%

Opportunity for Lean Selling Improvement

Karen's company has made great strides in applying Lean Think-ing to their sales organization. They are pioneers in this area and they have already seen significant tangible results. The implementation has been a home-grown one, and it appears to me that they have done a great job in figuring out how to apply Lean Thinking in their environ-ment, as well as executing the plan to do so. The decision to apply Lean Thinking to sales was a very purposeful one for this company based on their previous successes with Lean Thinking in other functional areas of the organization and in their industry.

So what else might Lean Selling have to offer? Here are some of the more advanced techniques presented in this book that Karen's company might want to consider.

Integrated Buying Process – While Karen's organization has made great progress in understanding the Buying process and plan-ning around it, it isn't clear whether the Buyer has joined the Seller in executing together one Buying Plan. This may be as simple as sharing the Seller's plan with the Buyer and, after getting suggestions from the Buyer, making it "their" plan. *(See Chapters 16 and 21.)*

Flow – Flow is a fundamental aspect of a true Lean system. Karen and her team should determine whether their current sales process has Flow. If not, then the team must determine what Flow means in their sales environment and propose and test ways to achieve it. *(See Chapter 21.)*

Pull – Another fundamental goal of Lean processes is that they are initiated by pull rather than push. As with Flow, if they don't have a Pull system now, the team will have to determine how Pull could work in their sales process, and experiment with ways to implement it. *(See Chapter 22.)*

Key Takeaways from Chapter 2

1. There is clear evidence that employing Lean Selling principles can significantly improve sales performance.

2. The value of Lean Selling applies to service industries as well as product industries.

3. We can see how Lean Selling techniques can be applied at the level of an individual salesperson or of a sales team.

4. Taking a long-term view of selling leads to consistent, predictable sales, and better short-term results as well.

Part II

Sales as a Service

Chapter 3

Are Salespeople Becoming Obsolete?

In Chapter Three
→ The Changing Customer
→ Where Sales Value Has Gone
→ Where Sales Value Is Now

Why Aren't Customers Calling You as Much Anymore?

The Internet began a broad commercial emergence in 1995, fueled by the introduction of the Netscape Navigator Web browser late the year before, which is considered by many as the first "killer app" for the Internet and is widely credited for popularizing the World Wide Web.[1] I first became involved with companies that were spawned based on this new Web technology in the mid-1990s, and I followed the development of the industry from its development of "plumbing" (infrastructure), to the introduction of new types of applications based on the Web (late 1990's, leading up to the Internet "bubble" in 2001), and today's pervasive social media services based on Web technology.

Twenty years after the Navigator Web browser was introduced, we are still seeing new applications and broader adoption of the Web that has disrupted many industries, creating new types of companies we couldn't have imagined previously. Because these new companies often introduced new business models (such as "free") to accompany their breakthrough services, they were very disruptive to existing companies whose business models were not based on the Web. Further, things that people never imagined could be done over the Internet are now commonplace as major Web applications. A couple of examples that come to mind are booking on-line travel and dating.

Advancement in technologies around the Internet, such as transmission speeds, has increased by hundreds of times since the Web browser was introduced. These advancements have created new ways to deliver all kinds of information, such as streaming videos, which are making elements of both the traditional movie business and even video rental (which itself was a disruptive business just a few years ago) obsolete.

Consumer behavior continues to follow the adoption curve with an increasing number of people choosing to shop online rather than going to a physical store. Companies such as Amazon and Zappos are innovating new consumer value propositions that can make buying over the Web an overall more pleasurable experience than going shopping in the brick-and-mortar world. In fact, no new enclosed mall has been built in the U.S. since 2006, and one prediction is that half of all enclosed malls will close in the next 10 years.[2]

As this book is being written, Internet shopping is about 8% of total retail sales in the U.S., and growing at three times the rate of retail brick-and-mortar sales.[3, 4] Maybe that's why warehousing space (for online product distribution centers) is currently the hottest segment of the commercial real estate market, growing twice as fast—while retail space is growing half as fast—as five years ago.[5]

Those who still bother to make the trip to a physical retail store are often armed with all the competitive information they acquired online before they arrive at the store, to make sure they are getting a good deal. Also, if they happen to consider an impulse buy when they are in a store, their Internet-connected smartphone will let them find the least expensive price available for the product they have an interest in. Increasingly, retail stores feel compelled to match that price rather than have a customer leave the store empty-handed.

We are fast approaching a tipping point of no return where the challenge of traditional retail businesses will be to convince Buyers why they *shouldn't* just buy the products they offer over the Web. Even Walmart, the Goliath of the retail brick-and-mortar world, has moved very aggressively to build out its Web sales strategy. While its online sales are still a fraction of Amazon's, Walmart's sales may be growing faster.[6]

What does this mean for salespeople? It means that if you are in sales, and you are lucky enough to have a potential Buyer actually talk to you, you'd better be prepared because that Buyer may know more about the product he or she is interested in than you do. The Buyer may also know more about the product's competition, and **your** competition, than you do. In a nutshell, it means that on initial contact with a potential Buyer, you'd better be ready immediately to add value to that person's Buying process. If you aren't, the Buyer won't waste his or her time talking to you. Forty percent of salespeople in a recent survey listed "Clearly understanding a customer's buying process" as one of the top three areas for improvement in their sales process.[7]

The balance of power between Buyers and Sellers has shifted, irrevocably. Sellers are at a strategic disadvantage at the time of "first contact" with a new potential Buyer, due to knowledge asymmetry. The Buyer knows what he or she knows—but the Seller knows nothing about what the Buyer knows. In other words, the old paradigm of Sellers driving a sales process is fast becoming ancient history. The Buyer is now taking charge of his or her buying process to make a pragmatic decision as to when and *whether* to engage a Seller.

Therefore, if you are a salesperson, and it seems that not as many people are interested in talking to you these days, don't take it personally. They just don't think they need your help, at least not yet. One survey found that nearly 70% of a buying process can be completed before the Buyer ever engages with a Seller.[8] I'm not sure what that percentage was five or ten years ago, but I'll bet it was much lower. **If the average salesperson is involved during less than a third or less of the Buying process, it is easy to understand why Sellers today may have a lot of extra time on their hands.** Does this mean that salespeople are now or soon-to-be obsolete? I would say it is not inevitable—unless they fail to change the understanding and definition of their role and their relationships with Buyers.

Where Did the Value Go?

The shift in Buyers' behavior to the Web being their first source to gather information (about anything) is actually a symptom of a deeper issue. At the core of the shift salespeople are experiencing is that there has been a displacement of value. Buyers seek value in many forms, and they gravitate to those sources that will provide that value. Because of the unprecedented technological upheaval the Web has caused across every industry and human endeavor, models of value acquisition are changing dramatically.

For example, when (it seems like decades ago) we wanted to know what flights were available for a trip we were planning, we would call our favorite travel agent. However, unless your trip is to an exotic location or has some other very unusual characteristics, today's trip planner will simply type a few words into a Web search engine to see what's available. It's often quicker and easier than making a phone call (and probably leaving a voice message for your favorite travel agent).

If a travel agent's primary value continues to be "finding flights," then they will see a gradual then increasing decline in the number of engagements they have with trip Buyers. They will eventually become obsolete. The issue is not with the travel agents. The problem is that the value they traditionally added is no longer wanted or needed from them. That means it no longer qualifies to be called a value–at least not from the Buyer's perspective. In order to remain relevant, travel agents have had to find new ways to add value, above and beyond what the trip planner can do by himself or herself online. Case in point: while the number of traditional travel agents has declined by half in the last 20 years, the majority of the agents remaining saw their business increase two years in a row. Another strategy employed by still–successful travel agents is to "up-scale" the services they offer; in other words, to provide a more personalized and consultative, even customized service.[9] For the other striving—not simply surviving—agents, two approaches have been the key to competing with online travel sites:

1. Changing the value they add for a traveler so they are generally superior to what can be provided by online services

2. Exploiting and resolving the *new* problems travelers now face using online travel services[10]

I hope this example of what's happened to travel agents will stimulate thinking about what is happening in your own business regarding the way that Buyers today perceive the value your salespeople have traditionally provided. Self-service is not free for the Buyer. It isn't that the traditional value that salespeople provided has gone away. It is still required by the Buyer. It's just that it is now being delivered and received in a different way; one that Buyers increasingly think doesn't require salespeople.

Where Is the Value Now?

For the purposes of this book, we are concerned with the value that salespeople can still provide. As stated earlier, there is still a shrinking fraction of the Buyer's process where salespeople are supposedly adding value. Few salespeople or their managers are comfortable with the current trend once they understand what is going on at a macro level. Unless salespeople plan to find a new career, they have no choice but to find new ways to add value. Still, what is that value, and why is it so difficult to determine what it is? Before we answer both of those questions, let's establish what we already know about the value Sellers add to Buyers:

1. **Much of the traditional value added is no longer considered valuable**

2. **That kind of value will never be considered valuable again**

The question of what kind of value Sellers can add today is not a simple one, and the answer will be unique to each type of organization and the selling it does. It's much easier to see what the value *won't* be than what it *will* be. Fortunately, this book will provide proven methods to uncover new, currently unrecognized opportunities for organizations to provide new types of value to their customers. The reason it is so difficult to determine what this value will look like is symptomatic of the traditional sales process, where selling is telling.

Those salespeople who are going to be survivors of their professions amidst the turmoil the Web has wrought on their world will have to learn to listen better, and probe for unmet Buyers' needs in ways that they haven't been trained to do in the past. Later in this book, I will argue that all the selling challenges we have been discussing have created new needs for the Buyer that weren't there before. In order to discover these, salespeople have to completely change their mindset regarding their relationship with the Buyer and the value of Selling in today's world.

Still, salespeople–even if ready, able, and willing–cannot make this transition alone. The organizations they work for will have to not only accommodate but also lead the transition to a new selling reality. At the most basic level, the type of training provided to salespeople will have to change. However, that is only the start. Sellers will have to have a new support system that is designed to maximize the value they provide to Buyers in their interactions with them. The elements of this new support system will likely include redefinition of job roles throughout the organization, culture change, and—only then—possibly some new applications of information technology.

The good news is that there is a bright future for Sellers who can make the transition, especially if their organizations make the transition with them. Some good salespeople will find it necessary to migrate to companies that provide the infrastructure to support them being value-added Sellers. For the rest who won't or can't change, they hopefully will be able to find new careers that fit their skill sets and interests.

Key Takeaways from Chapter 3

1. *The Internet has changed the relationship between salespeople and Buyers–forever.*

2. *Much of the value that salespeople used to add is not considered valuable by Buyers anymore*

3. *Salespeople will have to re-envision their relationship with Buyers and find new ways to add value.*

4. *Salespeople who make the transition to adding new types of value can be very successful in this new environment.*

5. *Salespeople who do not make the transition risk becoming obsolete.*

Chapter 4

Why CEOs and Senior Executives Should Care About Trends in the Sales Profession

In Chapter Four

→ Are Salespeople Still Relevant?
→ Is Selling Too Expensive?
→ Salespeople as a Solution

Do You Still Need Salespeople?

If you are the CEO or senior executive in your organization, I am assuming that you are reading this book because you have or manage some type of salesforce. It might be a retail salesforce, an outside salesforce, an inside salesforce, or a hybrid. Still, it is a salesforce. If that's the case, then I'm also going to make an assumption that you have a salesforce for a reason. It's only rational that the products or services you provide can't sell themselves or you wouldn't be spending all the money you currently are on a salesforce.

It may be that your offerings are complex or Buyers require help to understand how to use them in their environment. It may be that there are technical or regulatory issues that Buyers need to have addressed. It may be that you offer either customized or custom-configured products. Lastly, it may just be that the nature of your industry compels customers to choose interaction with experts (your salespeople) to discuss their goals.

Unless one of your competitors has already figured out how to sell what you provide without using salespeople, then it's a safe bet that the Buyer requires something that salespeople are providing in order for them to buy. Despite all the trends previously noted about the impact the Web is having on salespeople and their perceived value, the reality may be that nothing has really changed about your offering and the Buyer's ultimate needs. It may be that it is primarily the way the Buyer makes a decision that has changed. As a result, it would seem rash to conclude that salespeople are no longer needed in your organization unless you have a strategy to replace what they currently do, which is fundamentally close a gap (or multiple gaps) in the Buying process to enable a sale to happen.

I think **the sales function is at the heart of most organizations.** Even if you make a terrific, revolutionary product or provide a wonderful, ground-breaking service, if the heart stops beating (sales stop being made) then the organization, and all the great work it does, will die. Arthur Motley, former publisher of Parade Magazine, is credited with creating the famous sales axiom, "Nothing happens until somebody sells something."[1]

In my experience, the financial metric that CEOs worry about most is the "top line," which roughly translates into revenues or sales. CEOs and CFOs know that all other financial performance derives from this number, including profitability. Without sufficient top line revenue (sales) there can be no profitability, no matter how efficient a company may become or what kind of technological advances it may make.

"Hiccups" in the sales plan do not escape the scrutiny of the top executives of an organization for very long. That's how important it is to the life of the company. Companies routinely live with delays in product releases, and executives are not happy, but they do not generally view such delays as existential threats. This is not so with sales. Business executives know instinctively how quickly things can unravel when sales are declining.

It would appear that the choices facing business executives who have to decide how their company should respond to the Web-driven shift in Buyer behavior are along the lines of the following:

1. **Plan to reduce the number of salespeople you employ as demand for them decreases.**

2. **Invest in accelerating the Web-driven buying trend and help Buyers to buy without the need to engage with your salespeople.**

3. **Find new ways for your salespeople to add value.**

Theoretically, any of these approaches can be a possible way to deal with the changing landscape in sales. On its face, #1 appears to be a reactive and defensive approach, sort of like a plan to reduce staff broadly (a.k.a. rightsizing) as sales decline, rather than looking at new sources of revenues and profits. This should, in my opinion, be pursued only after other options have been eliminated as realistic alternatives.

The approach in #2 is akin to following the axiom, "If you can't beat them, join them." Hopefully none of you are stuck hoping beyond hope that the current Web-driven sales trends we are seeing will reverse themselves anytime soon. The question is whether it is realistic for any given company that currently has a salesforce to move to a Web-only sales model, one without live salespeople injected into the Buying process. Even if it is theoretically possible, is it practical? What would it take to pull it off? The answer to this question will be exclusive to each individual organization, not only because of its unique combination of industry and market position but also because the capacity of the organization's senior staff to think far out of the box will be a major determinant of whether their organization can envision a novel solution to implement and execute on it.

For practical and cultural reasons, I suspect that the vast majority of organizations will choose alternative #3. I believe this will be the case because few companies are willing to do nothing in the face of a clearly declining business (although some major companies, particularly in the U.S. auto industry, appeared to do just that over many decades). I also think that any organization that has a salesforce now and can figure out a way to do completely without it will be a very unique and rare one. It will be interesting to see if some case studies along these lines develop in the future.

I believe that the fastest and most promising route for the vast majority of organizations who want to address the shifting role of sales will be to focus on option #3. Although it won't be an easy one and it will require some very creative out-of-the-box thinking as well, it is likely a realistic goal for most organizations that commit to this path, especially considering the alternatives, including maintaining the *status quo*. Also, pursuing this plan does not require radically new infrastructure, but rather a redefinition of sales and other roles, along with an investment in training and support systems for the newly transformed salesperson and the supporting organization.

Is Our Sales Service Too Expensive?

Your first reaction to the subhead title of this section may be to think about it from the perspective of how much your salesforce costs your organization to deploy and maintain. What if it weren't referring to that at all, but to the price a potential Buyer pays for this service. Now, you are probably thinking instead that the subtitle of this section is silly. The following may be going through your head at this moment: "We don't charge our customers for the time we spend selling. It's free to them. Besides, who says sales is a service?" We will address the latter objection in Chapter 6, but for the moment, whatever sales is if it's not a service, let's consider whether it's too expensive *from the viewpoint of the Buyer.*

Surely you would agree that something is free only if the recipient is not expected to offer anything valuable in return for the value he or she receives. Therefore, that would necessarily mean that Buyers do not have to offer anything they value in order to be recipients of our Selling services (defined here as engaging and interacting with a Seller).

Really? What about the Buyer's time? Must he or she invest time in order to engage with a Seller? Of course that's the case. Is time valuable to Buyers? Of course it is. In fact today, at least in the rich-world countries, time is the most precious commodity many people cherish. It is also one of the few commodities that cannot be replaced, regardless of how much you are willing to spend for it.

Most organizations today are trying to do more with fewer people, which has increased the pressure on their staff to produce more. In this environment, time becomes even more compressed and valuable. Both business and consumer Buyers have time pressures with family and other obligations, not to mention a desire for some uninterrupted leisure time, in addition to the demands on their time from their work.

Make no mistake; Buyers pay for the privilege of engaging with salespeople with their time, a most precious commodity to them indeed. However, does your organization realize this and respect Buyers' time, or do you consider it "free" from your organization's perspective, because Buyers' time doesn't cost your company anything (or so you think)?

If Buyers sense you are wasting, don't value, or don't respect their time, or that you are focused on your own objectives rather than theirs, they will, as a matter of self-preservation, disconnect from the Seller's process and try to find a less expensive way to get what they think they require. I believe that is, together with the availability of so much content and information, one of the main factors driving Buyers away from Sellers and to the Web. Now that we understand that, we can begin to think about ways to change the Buyers' desire to connect with Sellers.

Don't Blame the People, Blame the Process

Far too often, when things don't go as planned, the first place we as managers look to find the problem is with the people responsible for delivering the goods. This occurs even though these same people seemed to be performing just fine in the past. *And why is it that so many of them have gone bad all at the same time?* This management tendency is particularly prevalent when it comes to sales.

In my experience, more often than not the problem is not primarily with the people, but with the process (or lack of one). Most business outputs, including sales, are the result of a process. **A defective or poorly designed process will yield less-than-satisfactory results,** *even if you have great people.*

Replacing people is harder and much more costly than fixing or improving a process. So, the next time things are not going the way they are supposed to, use some of the tools and tips in this book to take a critical look at your processes *first,* before looking anywhere else. You may just find the underlying source of the problem there.

Salespeople are Part of the Solution, Not the Problem

I hope by now I have presented a persuasive argument that when the environment changes in a such a radical way (such as the "Webification" of much of the sales process across so many industries and markets), it is fruitless to look for the problem in the current people (who were doing just fine previously or you would have let them go a long time ago). Now, I will admit that sometimes the changes required for personnel to adapt to a new reality is beyond their capability, but that is the minority case in my experience.

Rather, what I often see in the case of sales is that CEOs and senior executives conclude that salespeople just need to work harder. Some of that is true; many of us are working harder than we were in years past, seemingly to achieve the same level of results, largely due to increasing competition from all fronts. Although it may sound trite, how often do we, as leaders of our organizations, *first* think about how we can work *smarter* and ask ourselves, "What's changed?" Asking this type of question and looking deeply for the cause of a problem or change in results[2] is one of the fundamental problem-solving techniques in Lean Thinking.

I have stated my belief that salespeople are not the fundamental cause of the challenges facing companies with salesforces today. What about their being part of the solution? Actually, that's easy. Even though we may not know exactly how we will get Buyers to feel that the value they get from the Selling process is worth their time, we do know that whatever new ideas we devise will have to be delivered by our newly re-fitted Sellers. Therefore, the sooner we start thinking about how we can leverage the existing Selling resource in our organizations to bring more value to Buyers, the closer we will be to finding an answer to how to deepen the relationship and mutual collaboration of Buyers and Sellers.

Now, where do we begin to achieve that? I believe that the key to opening up new possibilities to redefine the relationship between Buyers and Sellers lies in a recasting of sales as a service and Sellers as service providers. The next two chapters go into further detail about what this means for organizations that choose to begin this journey.

Key Takeaways from Chapter 4

1. *While the role of salespeople is changing, their value to certain organizations is increasing.*

2. *When calculating the total cost of sales, the investment the Buyer has to make should be included as well.*

3. *Redirected salespeople can become a strategic asset in addressing the new challenges organizations face.*

Chapter 5

Buying, Selling, and Coaching

In Chapter Five
→ The Uniqueness of Sales
→ Salespeople as Coaches
→ Buyers as Coaches

The Uniqueness of Sales, Revisited

In Chapter 1 of this book, I discussed possible reasons that Lean had not yet found its way into the realm of sales to any significant extent. I hypothesized that one of the primary reasons may be that sales requires Buyer involvement in creating the deliverable (product or service), whereas, in all other major areas where Lean has been applied, the Buyer is not really involved–or interested–in the process of creating a deliverable. Rather, the Buyer's objective is in achieving his or her ideal outcome while minimizing his or her investment to achieve it.

A topic I didn't pursue is whether there are any good *non*-Lean models for processes that currently require Buyer involvement, which could provide clues as to what a Lean implementation of a Buyer-involved process might look like. I think one potentially powerful candidate to serve this purpose is the process of coaching.

Coaching comes in many forms and flavors. For the purposes of this discussion, I am going to focus on individual, not team, coaching. This is because, in the latter case, it is generally the coach who sets the objectives for the outcome of the coaching, not the individual being coached. This happens to be an important distinction for our purposes here.

- **Personal or life coaching (motivation, life purpose, career, relationships)**

- **Organizational and business coaching** (leadership, strategic, communications, teamwork, sales)

- **Skills coaching** (technical, professional, and "soft")
- **Sports performance coaching** (football, baseball, golf, tennis, swimming)

It's difficult to envision a coaching process that could deliver anything of value without the involvement of the person being coached. The value of a coaching relationship is measured against achievement of the trainee's objectives in being coached. Success or failure of a coaching process will be determined by whether the coach is able to help the individual to get closer to the ideal state the trainee desires.

In Chapter 3, I discussed the importance of today's Sellers rediscovering and redefining the value they bring to Buyers. As in coaching, the Buyer has an ideal outcome he or she would like to achieve. The Buyer will engage with a Seller if he or she believes it will help achieve his or her objective more directly or predictably. This is the "value" that the Buyer wants to extract from the relationship.

The Buyer defines the value and also decides whether it has been delivered. Value being defined by the recipient (user) of a process output (which is the deliverable) is a very foundational concept in Lean implementations. Similarly, in Lean Selling™, the Buyer is the one who is defining the value that he or she wants to realize from the Selling process. Using coaching as a model might provide a way that a Seller can identify this value and deliver it to the Buyer. Possibly, a Seller can employ the mindset and persona of a coach in his or her interactions with a Buyer. Still, is the Seller the only one in the relationship acting as a coach?

Who Is Leading and Who Is Following?

People voluntarily engage with coaches because they presume a coach has knowledge, experience, or a proven process that they don't have, which can help them achieve their goals more quickly and directly. However, since only the person being coached can determine the ideal outcome for the coaching process (the "value"), the trainee also has knowledge and information that the coach doesn't have, but requires to fulfill his or her role. Therefore, there is a symbiotic and interdependent relationship between a coach and a trainee that requires good, honest communication and a shared vision for both of them to become more successful in working with each other.

Let's consider for a moment what relevance, if any, this has for sales. In a sales process, the Seller has specialized knowledge, experience, or a proven process, just as a coach does. However, the Seller cannot be successful unless he or she understands what the Buyer wants to get out of the relationship (the "value"). Accordingly, without good, honest communication and a shared vision with the Buyer on an ideal outcome, he or she is unlikely to be successful. In that sense, the Seller is dependent on the Buyer to fulfill his or her role successfully, because the Buyer has information and knowledge (and often a Buying process) that the Seller must understand. There appears to be an opportunity for this Buyer-Seller relationship to be symbiotic and interdependent.

Is it possible the Buyer can sometimes play the role of coach as well? It is not unusual at all for a successful salesperson to ask potential Buyers questions along the lines of, "What does my company have to do in order to become a trusted supplier to yours?" or, "Who is it that I should be speaking with besides you?" or, "What other suppliers are you considering in addition to us?" All of these questions and the endless variations of them that salespeople use every day expose an honest vulnerability that a Seller has for information only the Buyer can provide, without which the Seller's job is going to be much more difficult.

When we think about it, the ideal Buying and Selling process requires a very collaborative relationship between a Buyer and Seller, who only together can maximize their mutual benefits through a relationship that depends on sharing and cooperation. Further, when a Seller exposes his or her vulnerability and asks for information from a Buyer (probably multiple times in different ways during a single sales process), he or she is asking the Buyer, in essence, to "coach" him or her on what direction he or she might take next. As a result, we can see that, **without necessarily being consciously aware of it, both Buyers and Sellers can, and often do, function as coaches to each other at different points in the Buying and Selling process.** What if we were to make the reality of this relationship explicit, rather than implicit, and bring it to a level of shared conscious awareness between Buyer and Seller where it could be viewed, evaluated, and discussed? How might this "dance" between Buyer and Seller unfold?

Doing the Coaching Pivot

Once we realize that Buyers and Sellers are frequently passing off the baton of coach to each other, back and forth during a sales process, the question is what steps they take to synchronize their performance. The key lies in the concept of a "pivot." Once both a Buyer and Seller agree that they are both part of providing a service that has value for both the Buyer and Seller and agree to work together to maximize the mutual benefit of their engagement, they must clarify the roles each will play during various stages of the process. They must also accept the fact that they will have to pivot, or change their roles, multiple times from coaching to being coached and back again.

Not all Buyers and Sellers will be comfortable acknowledging and committing to these roles. It requires an admission of vulnerability for both parties, one that involves some emotional and professional risk. Still, if they are going to successfully perform together, they will have to agree on who is leading and who is following at each point in the process.

The somewhat radical idea (in relation to today's sales mindset) is that both parties will have to reveal, at the outset, their objectives for the relationship. This is completely counter-intuitive to the behaviors that Buyers and Sellers have been taught to exhibit, which is based on the idea that knowledge is power, and shared knowledge weakens one's position. But such sharing will lead to another, very important outcome: the Buyer and Seller will be able to determine up-front if their objectives are aligned and compatible.

A Buyer may be unable or unwilling to commit to the outcome that the Seller seeks, for example, to become a provider within a certain period of time with the promise of earning a long-term relationship and additional business based on performance. And the Seller also may not be able to agree to the Buyer's objectives, for example, to get educated on the industry and competition merely for research purposes or in preparation for a Request for Proposal (RFP), without a commitment that the Seller will be included in the RFP process.

Think about how many times Sellers and Buyers engage with each other in a costly and time-consuming sales process, only to find out after a significant investment of time, money, and emotional energy that they don't have the same goals in mind. Such a waste and so demoralizing in the end, for both parties! By having honest and open "alignment" discussions up front, many of the more unpleasant aspects that accompany being a Seller or Buyer can be avoided.

We shouldn't expect Buyers to initiate this dialogue. Sellers have to take the lead and courageously put their cards on the table and let the Buyer decide if he or she wants to play. Regardless of how agreeable a Buyer may appear, a Seller must be brave enough to ask for evidence. This can come in many forms but *actions* are the truest indicator of Buyer intent.

It can be something as simple as the Buyer sharing information or committing to do something and then doing it. By explaining the Coaching Pivot process at the beginning of the relationship, the Seller is making a commitment to the Buyer to act as a coach in his or her Buying process and asking the Buyer if he or she is willing to be coached. Further, the Seller is asking the Buyer if he or she is willing to act as his or her coach through the sales process.

Next, the Seller can share his or her objectives for the relationship in terms of ideal outcomes and ask the Buyer directly what his or her objectives are. The Seller (acting now as the process coach) can clarify any ambiguity through questions and can also highlight any areas of potential disconnect. This will be the first test of whether the Buyer is willing to engage in a collaborative relationship with the Seller to mutually develop a valuable outcome, in this case, a clear, unambiguous statement of mutual goals and points of synchronicity.

The Seller can then explain how the process works and give examples of when the Buyer and Seller may have to participate in a Coaching Pivot and what that might look and feel like. They can agree on "homework" assignments they each commit to complete in order to move one step further together on their shared path toward their mutual goals. They can also settle on a timeframe to achieve these assignments (gathering information required, clarifying requirements, and so forth), at which time they will share what they have learned and establish another mutual set of commitments.

With this type of relationship, there should never be big surprises, although there will likely be adjustments to goals, timeframes, and

ways of achieving objectives, as more learning is achieved. Because of
the power of collaboration, it is very likely that the vision for the outcome of the relationship could be very different than either party had
initially envisioned. At that point, this vision will be unique and owned
cooperatively by the Buyer and Seller. The Seller will now become, in
the Buyer's eyes, a sole-source provider for the value that they have envisioned together—and that the Buyer has now internalized.

Key Takeaways from Chapter 5

1. *The sales process has unique characteristics that other
   production processes do not; the customer must be involved in creating the value of the process.*

2. *Buyers and Sellers naturally swap leading roles at different
   points in a sales process, even if they are not consciously
   aware of it.*

3. *Buyers and Sellers must act as coaches to each other to
   maximize their mutual benefit from a sales process.*

Chapter 6

What's Service Got to Do with It?

What Is Customer Service Called Before a Buyer Becomes a Customer?

In the Introduction, I made the case that thinking about Sales as a Service (SaaS) would open creative new ways of thinking about the relationships between Buyers and Sellers. Some who have been around the sales world for a while might initially have difficulty processing such an idea because it seems so foreign to the way they think about the role of salespeople.

This cognitive difficulty is puzzling since forward-looking companies have invested so much time and money in improving customer service. Any executive who scratched his or her head when told that customer service is a service would probably be taken to task, ridiculed, or worse. **Why then is it that we provide a service to customers but not Buyers?** It must be because they haven't bought anything from us yet, so they haven't earned our service. That seems counterproductive to me. Aren't the significant investments made in fielding a sales organization based on the objective of turning Buyers into customers—as frequently and quickly as possible? Shouldn't we be looking at how to accelerate that process and make it flow better, faster, and more predictably?

I submit that the shift in mindset from sales as something a Seller does primarily for his or her company to something a Seller does primarily for a Buyer will make all the difference in the outcome, not to mention the relationship. Let's take a look at how this new type of selling compares to today's customer service department.

Table 2 – Customer Service vs. Sales Service

Category	Customer Service	Sales Service
User	Customer	Buyer
Cost	Free (generally)	Free (almost always)
Reason to use	Solve a problem	Solve a problem
Success metrics	Problem solved first time Advocacy Loyalty	Problem solved first time Advocacy Loyalty
User's Value	Speed Minimal time investment Painlessness Avoiding buyer's remorse	Speed Minimal time investment Painlessness Avoiding buyer's remorse

Based on the contents of the right two columns being nearly identical in this chart, it seems the question we should be asking is not, "How is sales a service?" but "How is it not?" It occurred to me that, while countless investment continues to be made in customer service, little has been made in recasting Sales as a Service. In one survey, 25% of companies indicated that customer service would be their number-one priority for increased expenditures.[1] Why is that? One reason could be that two-thirds of people surveyed were willing to spend more for a given product or service if they believed they could get excellent customer service.[2] How much more might they be willing to spend if they could get excellent sales service? How much is being invested in that?

What Buyers Want

Once we view the role of a salesperson through the lens of a coaching model, it becomes clear that the Seller is a Buyer's Coach.

Additionally, this perspective clarifies that the Buyer is the only one who determines what he or she wants to get out of the coaching relationship. Of course, there are as many different requirements Buyers have as there are Buyers. This will be driven by the product or service they are interested in, the industry they are in, the culture of their company, the urgency of the problem or opportunity they are attempting to address, and many other factors.

However, I believe we can safely conclude that, **despite the uniqueness of each sales opportunity, there are some things that Buyers value universally.** Here are a few:

- **Making an informed decision about selecting a product, service, or vendor which the Buyer can comfortably justify**
- **Avoiding the experience of "buyer's remorse"**
- **Limiting risk to their career or personal life because of the Buying choice they make**
- **Keeping the length of the buying cycle to a minimum**
- **Reducing their personal investment of time to realize the above values**

For a Buyer, an ideal outcome (always an important thing to clarify and document so that a Buyer can concur) can be stated in a way similar to the following, from the Buyer's perspective: "I want to be able to make an informed decision on <u>the best vendor</u> to select for <u>Planetary Retro Gearing parts</u> as quickly as possible, invest the minimum amount of time in doing so, and be confident I will never regret the decision." Isn't that simple? You can replace the underlined text with your own product, service, and specific object of a sales situation, and see how it sounds. If you like, try it on a prospect, starting with, "I'm guessing what you want is . . ." and see how they respond. You will immediately differentiate yourself as a Seller from your competition.

I would like to point out a few subtleties included in this statement of universal Buyer value. For starters, nowhere does it mention the *details* of the product or service. However, that is what salespeople are usually taught to lead with. Of course, your product or service is important, and the Buyer is interested in what you have to offer. He or she wouldn't be talking to you otherwise. It's a given.

The second subtlety I want to highlight is how much of the value as perceived by the Buyer is contained within the *making of a decision*. We sometimes fail to realize how emotionally stressful it can be to make a buying decision about any kind of important purchase or relationship. Still, if we remember the last time we had to make a decision about selecting a vendor, hiring a person, buying a house, or choosing a financial advisor, we might be able to transport ourselves psychologically to the place of the Buyer.

While salespeople are trained to tell Buyers how much better (or less expensive) their products or services are, these are "left-brained" (logical and rational) arguments. How often are salespeople coached to deal with the emotional side of the sales process, where the Buyer has to deal with the risk of not making an optimal decision, or worse, one that is flat-out bad? The answer is, unfortunately, not very often.

This brings me to the third subtlety. Do you find it surprising that the Buyer wants to minimize the buying cycle? **Given how lengthy—or worse, open-ended—sales cycles often are might make you think that Buyers actually *enjoy* the sales process and don't want to see it end!** I sincerely doubt that is the case. I'm sure that most Buyers have other projects queued up, which they would like to have some extra time to work on, and which may be more enjoyable than engaging in a sales process. Here's a clear-cut case where a Seller's and Buyer's values completely align: make the sales process as quick (and painless) as possible. Nevertheless, extended, unpredictable sales cycles are the bane of the selling world. What's going on here?

Is it possible that Sellers are not helping Buyers get what they require to make a decision? How often do Sellers even explicitly know what Buyers require to make a decision? Increasingly, Buying decisions require group consensus from multiple types of stakeholders. Is your Buyer the one who can bring the group to consensus if he or she wants to buy from you? If your Buyer is not, then find and start working with that person or persons.

Unpleasant surprises happen too often for a Seller toward the (forecasted) end of the sales process. Sellers should ask themselves why there was a surprise and what they can do to avoid one in the future.

(This is Lean Thinking applied to problem solving, and also an example of a continuous improvement mindset.)

There are many other ways that Sellers can add value for a Buyer in addition to what was discussed above. Here are some examples:

- **Work with the Buyer to understand how your product or service can plug into their existing organization or plan.**

- **If you don't sell customized products, look for ways that your offerings can be configured to better meet the requirements of the Buyer.**

- **Help the Buyer to see what ongoing benefits, beyond the initial ones, might accrue from selecting your company as a partner for their business, and how you as a Seller can help the Buyer realize those benefits.**

These are highly leveraged activities because the Seller has unique insight into his or her own company's products and services and how they can be applied, and the Buyer has almost none. It helps to bring balance to the knowledge asymmetry we discussed earlier. The key to making this impactful to the Buyer is to resist bringing an "off-the-shelf" mindset to your interactions (even if you are providing a standard offering), but rather to think in terms of positioning what you have as a tailor-made solution. I think that many of the most successful Sellers are using these techniques already. Still, if you forget about the importance of supporting the Buying decision, then you are missing the big picture because it will all be for naught if the Buyer can't—or won't—make a decision to buy.

What Sellers Want

We have already identified at least a few areas where Buyers and Sellers share common objectives during a sales process. One is that they both would like to shorten, rather than lengthen, the sales process or cycle. Another is that they both would like a firm decision to be made at a given point in time. Lastly, they would both like to minimize the investment of their time in achieving an outcome.

Salespeople are practical. It's not that they don't enjoy the time they spend with Buyers; it's just that they want to limit it, in order to leverage their own time. The most successful salespeople are always thinking about how to maximize their performance (normally measured in number of sales or revenue volume), while minimizing their personal time investment. As with Buyers, the Seller's most irreplaceable investment is time, and time is money.

Sellers have other goals as well. The vast majority would genuinely like to have happy customers and to feel that they have helped someone through their efforts. This is the "psychic" satisfaction outside of the monetary compensation. Most would like to have a long-term relationship with a client, rather than a one-time transaction.

Again, for practical reasons, Sellers hope they can get their Buyers to refer other Buyers to them. This makes for a healthy influx of new opportunities with a minimum prospecting effort. Referred Buyers are much more likely to buy something from you. Life is good as a salesperson when the beneficial things you do for customers result in a steady stream of referrals.

Sellers also want to be treated by Buyers as professionals and as collaborators. No salesperson enjoys working with a Buyer who treats him or her as a commodity. Also, it is not much fun when a Buyer is demanding but fails to reciprocate by sharing information or helping the Seller in other ways. **Probably the thing that Sellers want the most is to have Buyers *not* waste their time. Interestingly, this is exactly what an honest Buyer wants as well.** It seems that there is a good basis for cooperation around not wasting each other's time. Getting the things that Sellers want may be more within their control then they might have initially thought, after all. Using Lean techniques, Sellers can create the type of Selling and Buying process that meets all their objectives as well as those of the Buyer. More on this topic will be coming in Part III.

What Organizations Want

Let's not forget the entities that are paying the bills for all the fine work Sellers and Buyers are doing. Without these organizations, there would be no Sellers and no Buyers because there would be nothing to sell and nothing to buy. What are the objectives of these organizations?

Table 3 – Organizational Objectives

Objectives	Seller Organization	Buyer Organization
Goals	Predictable revenues, growth	Efficiencies, competitive advantage
Preferences	Loyal, repeat customers	Loyal, competent vendors
Expectations	Meets commitments	Meets commitments
Success metrics	Long-term relationship	Long-term relationship
	Repeat business	Continued innovation, improvement
	Testimonials	Quality
Value	Fair price	Fair price
	Return on sales	Return on investment
	Honesty and integrity	Honesty and integrity
	Trusting, mutually beneficial relationship	Trusting, mutually beneficial relationship

Since there is so much overlap in what Buyers' and Sellers' organizations want from each other, there appears to be a solid foundation for Buyers and Sellers to work together to help achieve it. The key to creating this type of collaborative relationship between Buyers and Sellers is to begin to view Sales as a Service.

Key Takeaways from Chapter 6

1. *There should be a shift in thinking about what the selling process represents; from the Buyer's perspective, it is a service.*

2. *Companies that have been very committed to the post-sales customer experience have not put nearly as much investment into the pre-sales customer experience.*

3. *Buyers, Sellers, and their organizations have common ground on which to base collaboration.*

Chapter 7

What's a Salesperson to Do?

In Chapter Seven
→ A Seller's Stakeholders
→ Transitioning to Lean Beliefs
→ Buyer Fit
→ A Lean Transformation

What Kind of Selling Service Do You Want to Deliver?

Whether you are an individual salesperson, run a sales organization, or run a company, you have to decide what you want the sales service you deliver to feel like to a customer. In the customer service examples we discussed in the previous section, the most successful organizations have clear goals that they want to achieve through their investments to provide better customer service.

There are goals that customer service should pursue, such as speed of response, solving problems completely on the first call, and so on. There are also goals that are strategic to the organization that should come as a result of providing consistently excellent customer service. These include the likelihood that the customer will communicate positively about the experience to his or her network of friends and associates (online and otherwise), as well as respond positively to a professional survey where the research results might end up in a public ranking of companies' customer service.

However, both types of goals have an implicit "litmus test" of how the interaction "feels" to the customer, in addition to any objectively measurable outcomes (such as actually resolving the problem the customer initially called about). The company may feel they hit the mark in all areas that they are measuring, and still get a low ranking from their customers on their experience. This can happen, for example, when an otherwise very competent customer service employee, with an excellent record of solving problems, somehow causes a customer to feel uncomfortable, or that he or she was treated disrespectfully. Even though the engagement was successful from a rational perspective because the problem was solved without undue effort on the customer's part, the customer still *didn't feel good* about the "experience."

This is akin to a patient getting treatment from the doctor that cures his or her ailment, but the patient does not feel comfortable about the experience of interacting with the doctor, and does not look forward to repeating it. Another example is the experience of buying a new or used car. You may ultimately come away from the engagement with a car you love, and even a price you think was fair, but it is unlikely you will want to repeat the experience (including the painful investment of the time at the dealer) if you don't have to. For those reasons, we can see that **the customer ultimately determines whether the interaction was beneficial, emotionally as well as rationally.**

This perspective is very much aligned with Lean Thinking in that Lean stipulates that "value" can only be defined by the recipient or user of a product or service, not by the provider of the product or service. Let's take a look at how the objectives of a Lean Selling™ transformation might vary when we compare the individual, departmental, and organizational objectives.

Table 4 – Individual, Departmental, and Organizational Objectives for Lean Selling

Objectives	Salesperson	Sales Manager	Senior Executive
Near-term	Accelerate closing sales	Exceeding quota	Predictability of sales revenue
Long-term	Repeat sales	Reduced variability in monthly sales results	Revenue scalability, growth
Outcome	Differentiation from competition	Customer expectations are met	Positive referrals and reviews, social media
Value	More sales, quicker	Control and visibility	Lower cost of customer acquisition, higher rate of customer retention

While these three different types of stakeholders in the Lean Selling process are seeking value at different points along a spectrum of varying tactical and strategic importance, their ideal outcomes all derive from the same source, a positive experience (rationally and emotionally) on the part of the Buyer. The good news is that the salesperson who commits to being a Lean Seller will be supporting the goals of his or her department along with those of the company. Similarly, an organization that decides to commit to Lean Selling will be supporting the goals of its managers and salespeople. There is much common ground for organizational alignment here.

How then can you become a Lean Seller? It starts with a shift in mindset based on a shift in beliefs. The table below summarizes some current beliefs that have to be challenged in order to make a Lean transition.

Table 5 – Transitioning to a Lean Belief System

Category	Non-Lean Belief	Lean Belief
Activity	More is better	Less is better
Information	Everything available	Only what's required
Time	Sales just take time	Sales can go faster
Qualifying	Tread lightly	Go deeply
Approach	Win-Lose	Win-Win
Interaction	Transactional	On-going
Relationship	Confrontational or submissive	Collaborative and coaching
Driver	Quota attainment	Value provided to Buyer at every step

Some of these differences may seem provocative at first glance, so let's take a closer look at each in turn.

Activity

Many salespeople believe that the more time they spend in front of their prospects, the better chance they have of closing a sale. This may be true, but only if all the time they spend with Buyers creates value. **Confusing activity with value is a mistake.** Activities (such as presentations about how great your company is) that do not have value (as judged exclusively by the Buyer, not by you or your company) are referred to as "waste" in the **Lean Selling System** and should be eliminated. Remember: Buyers value their time (just like you do), so if they feel like you are wasting it, you are engaging in "anti-selling" activity.

Information

This is a close cousin of the previous one and comes from the same fundamental thinking. However, the bad outcome from providing too much information is even more insidious than wasting Buyers' time on unnecessary and valueless meetings and other activities. That is because too much information creates confusion on the part of the Buyer and complicates his or her Buying decision process.

Complication slows down decisions. Too much information actually increases the risk perception of a Buyer because there are new aspects to consider that they had not thought of (and are probably not helpful to them or you). A knee-jerk reaction of many salespeople on initial engagement with a new Buyer is to bury them with all available information their marketing or sales department has provided.

I'm not sure why salespeople think this is a good thing. Maybe they believe that if they overwhelm the Buyer with information, the Buyer will get confused and not ask challenging questions. Maybe they think that the Buyer will be pounded into submission and just decide to buy right away. Has anyone ever seen either of these outcomes from indiscriminate information sharing? From the perspective of the **Lean Selling System**, any information that a Buyer does not request (directly or indirectly) or require to make a decision is waste.

Time

At this point in this book we have discussed from several aspects how important the preservation of time is as we look at interactions between Buyers and Sellers. It is important to note that *time* is a foundational metric for evaluating and improving Lean systems, as we will discover in Part III of this book. *If you buy into the notion that sales have to take as long as they do but you have never delved deeply enough into your sales process to determine where time is wasted, then I would submit you are subscribing to a limiting belief, one without evidence.*

The application of Lean principles dramatically improves the speed of *every* process cycle they are applied to. A sale is not a "special exception." Remember that waste does not identify itself; it's buried in the current way of doing things. You have to actively seek it out and eliminate it.

Qualifying

Many salespeople are loath to push too hard in their initial engagement with a prospect for fear of losing the opportunity. However, *how do you know there's an opportunity?* Wouldn't you want to find out as early as possible in the engagement with a Buyer if there is or there isn't? I understand the emotional reluctance to asking hard questions of a Buyer early on because of the fear that he or she will reveal that he or she is really not a prospect. Still, wouldn't that be a good thing? In addition to the time that you will save the prospect by not working with him or her, think about the time you will save yourself that can be spent productively with qualified Buyers. In Part III we will describe some Lean Selling approaches that you can use to qualify quickly and professionally, while providing value for the Buyer in the process.

Approach

This one risks being disregarded as trite. It is very popular to speak about always acting to create a win-win outcome in all our interactions. However, at crunch time are you still committed to that goal? How about at the end of the month when you are behind on quota? Lean is not about appearance; it is about behaviors and results. There is no faking your commitment in a Lean system. In the best-selling book, *The Seven Habits of Highly Effective People*, Steven R. Covey entitled Habit 4, "Think Win-Win."[1] While this phrase may be overused or sometimes inappropriately used today, the **Lean Selling System** will enforce such a mindset and alert us when we are unconsciously deviating from it.

Interaction

This category refers primarily to bringing a mindset to consummate an immediate sale into the relationship with the Buyer when you should be thinking of building a profitable relationship that can continue to pay dividends for the long term. Even if you are in a business where you engage primarily in single transactions with many customers, rather than ongoing relationships with a few customers, vendors, or partners, it doesn't mean you have to bring a transactional mindset into the relationship with a Buyer. I would argue that **a transactional sale can have many of the same elements as one that is considered to be more "consultative" or "relationship" based. It simply has a highly compressed sales cycle.**

Let's take the purchase of a mobile phone, for example. Many would consider this to be a transactional sale. However, before today's "transactional" Buyer goes to a retail outlet to purchase a new smartphone or new mobile service, chances are he or she has done significant Web research to decide what features are most wanted or valued.

The chances are also good that he or she is still not ready to make a decision because there are a few important things that couldn't be figured out from online sources. A Seller who takes a Lean approach similar to the one described in this book, including acting as a Coach to the Buyer, is much more likely to help the Buyer to make a decision that he or she is confident about, rather than leaving the store without making a purchase. **All Buyers want to avoid buyer's remorse, and all Sellers can help them do that, using Lean Selling techniques.**

Relationship

By confrontational, I don't mean to imply that Sellers are arguing with Buyers, but rather that they believe their goals are not aligned and the process of getting to a sale (or not) is a test of wills, where the more dominant person will get his or her way. On the opposite end of the scale, a submissive relationship can exist where a salesperson is not sufficiently assertive, thinking that he or she exists to serve the Buyer and provide whatever that Buyer asks for without asking anything in return.

In other words, rather than acting as a service provider, the Seller acts as a servant. In Lean Selling, the relationship is not confrontational (because the Buyer and Seller have the same goals), and it is not subservient (because the Buyer and Seller are both contributors). Rather, it is collaborative, which not only implies an equality of peers, but also that the relationship will yield more real value than either participant could create by himself or herself.

Driver

This will probably be the toughest one for the manager and the organization to commit to. Sales quotas are seen as the single most efficient way to "manage" (control) the behavior of salespeople. But is it the most effective, or even the most productive? It is this kind of thinking that makes it so difficult for sales managers and their organizations to troubleshoot the sales process and to know where efforts and resources should be applied when things don't go according to plan.

Lean Selling asserts that while a quota is both a goal and a metric (good things), its achievement is the result of activities and a process based on a particular philosophy about how to do things, rather than something that can be controlled directly. Lean Thinking always points first toward looking at the causes of results and putting efforts there in order to change the result itself.

Changing Beliefs

Now that you have an overview of which firmly-held sales beliefs will require changing in order to make a Lean transformation, you can decide if you are ready to continue learning what these changes in mindset might ultimately mean for your organization. Feeling uncomfortable about changing certain beliefs is not a reason to reject a Lean transition out of hand. In Chapter 1, I shared how uncomfortable I was when first introduced to Lean concepts in software development before I became a believer and advocate of it.

Ultimately, your willingness to continue to learn about Lean Selling will primarily be based on two things:

- **How satisfied you are with your current situation and results**
- **What you think the potential cost is of continuing to do things the way you are doing them today**

We will expand on these and on the psychic investment required for a Lean transformation following the next section.

Is Your Buyer a Fit for You?

After you have clarified in your own mind the type of selling you want to do and the kind of relationships you want to have with your Buyers, it is time to think about what your ideal Buyer looks like. Simply because the transition in beliefs we discussed in the last section is difficult for Sellers does not imply that it is easy for Buyers to make, either. Buyers have similar beliefs that mirror those of Sellers. After all, Buyers and Sellers have been working from complementary, reinforcing, negative belief systems for a long time.

Nevertheless, you have to find those Buyers who are willing to try something new. You don't have to tell them that it is something new or even mention Lean or Lean Selling. You just have to explain to them what your selling process is and what you should both expect from it. If they like what they hear and agree to play along, then you might have the beginnings of a great relationship. However, if they are resistant to the idea of a collaborative relationship based on mutual commitments, then you have a few options from which to choose:

1. **Walk away and find another Buyer**

2. **Revert to your old selling style and don't use Lean approaches with this customer**

3. **Ask this customer if he or she would be willing to take a "test drive" with you to experience how such a relationship might work for the organization**

I suggest you try #3 before punting (#1) or reverting (#2), if for no other reason than if the Buyer refuses #3, you still have #1 and #2 as options. Also, we are asking the Buyer to do something new and we know how resistant people are to trying something new. Maybe you can share your own reaction when first exposed to the concepts of Lean Selling. You can also create the opportunity for a limited set of Lean Selling interactions that would deliver something of value to the Buyer, and repeat that process until the Buyer is comfortable with committing to your new way of working with a Seller.

I have listed these options assuming you are in complete control over which of these options you can choose. The reality is that your organization may dictate which one you must pursue based on its overall commitment to a Lean Selling transformation—or not. Also, it is always easier to walk away from prospects or to hold fast to your position when you have enough prospect flow in your sales pipeline to keep you busy enough to meet your sales goals. This reinforces the notion that an environment supportive of Lean Thinking, for example, in the area of ample lead generation, is important to an individual salesperson's success and decision-making when making the transition to Lean Selling.

Nevertheless, your chances of finding the ideal Lean Buyer will be greater if you are very clear with yourself about the characteristics you are looking for. Make a list of the values and beliefs that a Lean Buyer should possess. Find a way to determine early in the process if your new prospect is a good fit, and if not, how you will deal with that situation.

Drafting Customers

The biggest single thing you can do to improve sales productivity is to improve the match between your ideal customer and the leads that get into the sales pipeline. Improving the quality (defined as "fit with your ideal customer") of the Buyers in the sales pipeline would immediately have the following impacts:

1. **Your salespeople will waste less time with prospects they shouldn't be spending time with.**
2. **Sales productivity will soar because your salespeople will be spending more time with prospects that are more likely to close.**
3. **You will have less attrition of prospects from the sales pipeline and a higher close rate, which will cause your sales return on investment to soar.**

What's that you say? You don't know what your ideal customer looks like? Better get on it right away if you want to see the results listed above. Some of the ideas in this and other chapters can help you get started.

Are You Ready to Make the Investment in a Lean Transformation?

There is an important misalignment that I am aware of but haven't yet shared in this book. Possibly you have already connected the dots and figured it out. Either way, it can't be ignored any longer, so I want to make it explicit here. Lean is for long-term thinkers, as it requires current investment (emotional as much or more than financial) for future returns and a commitment to continuous, steady improvement.

Sales is typically thought of as being focused on the short-term (quarters or months), extracting value immediately (in terms of a sale) from investments that have already been made (in developing and creating products and services), and has a bias toward a single point in time—*now* (closing a deal). Might this be the underlying reason that Lean has barely scratched the surface in terms of adoption in sales? Could this be the proverbial "elephant in the room"? Is it possible that Lean Thinking is simply incompatible with the prevailing sales culture?

Today, we would have to admit that it *is* largely incompatible with popular sales culture. Isn't that the entire point? There are important improvements in all areas of business and society that have come about despite the fact that they went counter to the common thinking and culture of the time.

The customer service example in the last section is one example. The change in thinking was from customer service as an expense to a source of revenues (in the form of larger and additional follow-on sales), profits (in the ability to charge more than competitors without the same level of customer service), and goodwill (as demonstrated by positive comments on social media).

Was it simply at one point in time that companies became enlightened to the fact that improving customer service was a good investment? Not really. Over time, evidence gradually mounted, particularly as products and services became more complex, that there was a payoff for increasing focus on customer service. Still, there had to be a tipping point to start a trend.

That tipping point was social media, and a change in the way that consumers spoke about and evaluated the companies they considered doing business with. A bad customer experience coupled with a willing news reporter was no longer a local phenomenon; it could become, in a CEO's worst nightmare, a global viral sensation. The cost of *not* investing in improving a customer's experience simply became too high.

The important points to draw from the customer service example that apply to our consideration of Lean Selling are that first there was evidence of inefficiencies and quality problems in the process, building over a long period of time, to justify a change. The second one is that there was a tipping point, largely caused by the evolution of the Internet, particularly social media.

There is general agreement that the state-of-the-art (term used generously—it's practically an oxymoron) in sales organizations is ripe for improvement in efficiencies, productivity, and quality. I previously listed some of the symptoms of sales dysfunction in Table 1. I also believe there is broad concurrence that there is significant room for improvement with the current sales processes in most organizations.

Still, how does one go about improving the sales process and organization? **The answer is that it requires more of a macro or system view than simply looking at the sales organization as an isolated entity,** as has been the case for far too long. Lean Selling provides such a perspective. However, before anything will happen, there will have to be a tipping point.

Once again, as I discussed in the introduction, social media and the Web in general may be setting up such a tipping point. The Web has been a significant contributor to permanently changing the relationship between Buyers and Sellers. The symptoms of this are getting more and more difficult to ignore, as salespeople struggle to stay relevant. Competition is increasing, and the commoditization of products and services is a broad financial threat to companies everywhere.

This issue, as I previously noted, is striking at the heart, not the periphery, of organizations everywhere. **The tipping point will be when CEOs *en masse* realize that the risk of doing nothing exceeds the cost of doing something about their current sales approach and philosophy, particularly as it relates to the roles of Buyers and Sellers.**

Fortunately, Lean provides tools, methodologies, and ways of thinking that can lead the way toward a transformation in sales and directly counteract the troubling signs we are seeing in the marketplace. Nevertheless, not every organization will embrace a Lean Selling transformation, at least not right away. We are at the very early stages of the Lean Selling adoption cycle without a lot of proven case studies in hand.

If you disagree with this statement, please contact me or post at the LinkedIn® group or Facebook® page, "Lean Selling"; you can also direct message me on Twitter® @LeanSelling. By definition then, Lean Selling will resonate with, and be embraced by, *early adopters.*

An early adopter is a person or company who tends to lead the pack when it comes to trying something new, something yet unproven. That much is well understood. More pertinent for our discussion on Lean Selling is what causes a person or entity to become an early adopter and take on the attendant risks that accompany embracing something new and not broadly proven. Early adopters often have one of the following characteristics:

- **Culturally based desire to be the first established player to change the game in order to gain competitive advantage (first-mover advantage)**

- **Weak market position coupled with lack of resources to compete with established players** (guerrilla approach)

- **Desperation based on business trends and failed attempts to counteract them with traditional approaches** (nothing-to-lose mindset)

While you might personally find Lean Selling intriguing, you or your organization is unlikely to commit to it without having one of the above characteristics. Also, while a lone salesperson may find that exposure to Lean Selling ideas helps him or her become more successful, the full benefits of a Lean Selling approach can only be realized in an organization that supports and embraces Lean Thinking.

A Lean transformation will ultimately require a change in culture and buy-in from all the people affected by it. As you might imagine, this organizational transformation is a complex topic and the subject of many excellent books and case studies on the topic (except, apparently, in sales). There are practical ways to mitigate the risk and ease the transition, such as by commissioning pilot Lean projects. The key point is that leaders of a Lean transformation will have to be committed to getting everyone moving together along the same path. This, in my view, is the biggest investment and commitment required for Lean Selling. Is your organization ready for it?

Key Takeaways from Chapter 7

1. The benefits of Lean Selling satisfy the objectives of salespeople, management, and senior executives.

2. Lean Thinking requires a change in beliefs about the way things are and the way they can be.

3. A Lean transformation requires commitment, and not every organization is ready for it.

Part III

Sales as a Process

Chapter 8

What Different Types of Processes Are There?

In Chapter Eight
→ Defining a Process
→ Process Characteristics
→ Lean Processes

What Is a Process?

A process is simply a series of steps or activities that someone or something (like a machine or software application) follows in order to create something. In the case of manufacturing, there is generally a raw material or component part or subsystem that is acted upon or assembled at each process step to reach a final product. In non-manufacturing environments, there are generally a series of steps that a product, person, or intangible is acted upon in each process step, leading to some output benefit for a user that didn't exist before.

In every case we say that value is added at every process step (or the step would be unnecessary), so the thing being acted upon becomes more valuable (and more complete) as it passes through each process step. Classic manufacturing refers to the product moving through the assembly process as Work-in-Process, or WIP. In financial accounting for manufacturing, WIP becomes more valuable as it moves further along in the assembly process.

On the face of it, this sounds like a good thing. However, it also increases the value of WIP inventory, and increasing the value of inventory is never desirable, but may not be unavoidable. This makes sense because labor, time, and other materials are continually added during the process, and these must be properly accounted for somewhere in the financial system.

Why is this important for our discussion of sales? As we will soon discuss, it may be helpful to think about all the time and effort that is continually being added by your salesforce to a Buyer as WIP inventory (or, to coin a new acronym, BIP, or *Buyer-in-Process*). In other words, the longer a Buyer is in your Selling process—and the longer he or she remains there—the higher your "sales BIP inventory" becomes. This is commonly referred to as a "sunk cost" because you can't get it back until you sell something.

If you are a sales executive, CFO, or CEO, and you consider the Buyers in your organization's sales process as "assets" (because you have invested in or added value to them), you might be shocked at the total cost of the inventory that is sitting there. Still, it is not customary financial accounting procedure (in the U.S. under rules called GAAP) to carry sales investment as an asset on the balance sheet. Universally, sales and marketing costs are expensed in the Profit and Loss statement, so most executives have no idea how much has been invested in each Buyer that is sitting (stagnating) in the sales process.

What happens to all that investment, the value-added of your sales process, when a sale doesn't close because the Buyer goes away or buys from your competitor? The time (and money spent on travel, meals, entertainment, literature, etc.) should now be accounted for as "waste" and written off. Of course, in the real world, that's not what happens. I have never seen a company account for its cost of sales in this way. Rather, sales cost is a blanket expense in the financial statement that reduces profits, whether the "investment" in any particular Buyer results in a sale or not.

The main benefit of thinking about the cost of the sales process from this new perspective of inventory is to help company management realize that they have no idea how much of their actual "value-added" leads become sales, and how many of these leads are wasted. Since companies don't have that information, it is nearly impossible to take actions or to create a plan to reduce the waste.

With a Lean Selling™ process, a company will know exactly how much of the process is wasted with non-value-added time and activity. The company will also be in a position to accumulate data on its cost of customer acquisition. The cost of customer acquisition, in my experience, is *one of the most strategically important statistics for any business*.

Let's first discuss a high-level classification of processes. As we are doing this, think of a process or two your company uses, ideally including one in sales, and see which side of the following categories you think it falls into.

Repeatable v. Non-Repeatable

A repeatable process is one that, as the name suggests, can be repeated over and over again, following the same steps to get the same results. This implies that the inputs and outputs of each process step are designed to be identical. Most large-scale manufacturing and service industries (such as automobile repair or delivery of health services) have repeatable processes. In fact, they likely have multiple repeatable processes for different classes of products or services.

A repeatable process is called for when your aim is to produce the same or a very similar outcome from a process, so that the deliverable (a product or service) is the same each time (a widget gets built and shipped, a car is fixed, a patient is treated). In order to improve the efficiency and consistency of a process, and make it predictable (how long it will take to get done with a certain level of quality), it must be designed with repeatability in mind. Repeatable processes will generally be documented in detail, spelling out what people do and how they do it.

A non-repeatable process is one where there is no expectation of following the same steps or having the same outcome each time. Crafting completely custom-designed pieces of furniture might be a reasonable example of this. Although the carpenter will almost always shape something from raw materials and put it together to create a finished piece of furniture, that's about all we can say about the steps of the process that we know for sure. We don't even know whether the craftsman will be working with wood or a synthetic (such as fiberglass). We don't know if he or she is making a table or a cabinet or a chair. In such a case, it is difficult to predict the time it will take or what the final product will look like (although the craftsman may have done something similar before and may have some idea).

The efficiencies of non-repeatable processes don't improve very much over time, because what is being produced and how it is being produced varies each time it goes through the process. There are no "economies of scale" to be realized with process knowledge gained through repeating the process (although individual skills may improve). On the contrary, costs will likely increase over time, assuming it is a labor-intensive process, as wages rise.

Scalable v. Non-Scalable

Simply put, a scalable process is one that "scales," or is able to be sized up or down to produce more—or less—with the same process. Organizations rarely want to scale down sales, but occasionally they want to scale down production if market demand for their product or service declines for an extended period. Processes that depend on large, expensive capital equipment, such as those often used in high volume manufacturing, are sometimes scalable up (to the limits of the equipment's utilization rate) but not easily scaled down, at least not economically. This may lead, as has been shown,[1] to management and process design decisions that optimize the use of expensive equipment, but generally do not optimize the delivery performance or profitability of the company.

On the services side, processes that are highly dependent on specific individuals or specialized skills are not easily scalable. Think of a rock band. The musicians can only play one venue at a time, and they have a limit of how many gigs they can do in a year before the members of the band burn out. Further, losing a star band member can sometimes mean the end of the band.

There are actually many instances of this phenomenon in business. **Whenever a single individual or sub-group is responsible for results, rather than the process they are following, there likely exists a non-scalable process.** That is because a star does things in his or her unique way. That's what makes him or her a star. There is no one else who can do exactly what he or she does in exactly the way that he or she does it.

Early-stage and developing companies often fall into this trap. Their business can often be built initially around the special talent (sometimes genius) of one or two individuals. These individuals might be the creators of the products or the first sellers of them. They are often founders of the company. The company first grows rapidly, then plateaus. It becomes increasingly difficult to increase growth because sales, product design, or some other competitive uniqueness the company possesses is highly dependent on people who can't easily be duplicated (nor, of course, be easily replaced). Unless a company at this stage begins to make investments in creating repeatable processes, it will likely be stuck at its current level of business. Making such a transition, however, is very difficult, and often doesn't happen without injecting new leadership at the very top of the organization, and even then, it is still painful.

The Lean Startup

Did you know that Jeffrey Immelt, the CEO of General Electric, is a Lean adopter, in the form of *The Lean Startup* methodology, and that he makes the book of the same name* *required reading* for all GE managers? I assume he did so because he likes the ideas the book presents, but I also think it might be because the book introduces a language for its key concepts that GE employees can adopt to facilitate discussing startup ideas, including such terms as "pivot" and "validated learning." Who would have thought that a set of principles that originated in the factory could be turned into a system that helps to make starting a new company a repeatable, efficient process? This is yet another example of how Lean Thinking can be adopted and adapted creatively into completely new arenas, with outstanding results.

If Lean can improve the way to run a startup, then why can't it improve the way to run sales as well? Will Lean Selling be the next success story in the creative application of Lean Thinking? I certainly hope so. If you are a CEO or executive, and you like the Lean Selling ideas presented in my book, *you also might want to consider making it required reading for your team or employees.* If nothing else, it will give your team a common language for discussing the novel concepts presented in this book, as they work toward improving sales productivity and performance.

The Lean Startup: How Today's Entrepreneurs Use Continuous Innovation to Create Radically Successful Businesses

Mature companies are also vulnerable to this syndrome. There continues to be much speculation in the popular and business press about whether Apple, following the untimely death of its charismatic and brilliant leader, Steve Jobs, still has the mojo for product innovation. There are reports that it took Jeffrey Immelt, the CEO of General Electric (GE), 13 years in the job to come out from under the shadow of the legacy of his world-famous rock-star-CEO predecessor, Jack Welch.[2]

Optimized v. Non-Optimized

As implied in the previous sections, non-repeatable and non-scalable processes cannot generally be optimized. In fact, optimization is not an objective or important value for these processes. For processes that *are* repeatable or scalable, or both, the question is whether they are optimized. A fully optimized process is one that is operating at a speed, cost, and level of quality that cannot be improved further.

Such a goal is generally a target but not a set or even reachable objective. In order to optimize a process, you must do a deep analysis of every step in the process and determine whether there is a better way of doing things that will improve one or all of the output metrics (such as speed, cost, and quality). Very few processes are ever completely optimized, or intended to be, simply because once the process is running smoothly, there is little organizational fortitude to mess with it. We've all heard the expression, "If it's not broken, don't fix it."

There is another reason, however, why most processes are not optimized. It is because processes are typically designed with an explicit priority to maximize (or *optimize*) the use of a particularly expensive piece of equipment, especially common in high-volume manufacturing or the airline industry.

As a result, while the usage rate of a particular piece of equipment (such as a commercial aircraft) is optimized, it is often at the cost of sub-optimizing other processes, leading to a higher (often unrecognized or hidden) overall cost, longer cycle times, or reduced quality of the entire collection of processes, or the system. This is the classic problem with mass manufacturing.[3] **The culprit in all these cases is a lack of systems thinking, resulting in optimization of a component (e.g., a single process step), rather than the entire process.**

In non-manufacturing environments, there are analogs to expensive capital equipment in the form of bloated functional departments and expensive staff (such as doctors and lawyers). Processes will often be designed to optimize the use of these expensive resources because it seems to be common financial sense to do so. However, this approach rarely optimizes the overall system, which is what the organization should be focusing on (and where the total costs are).

Characteristics of Lean Processes

Now that we have completed our overview of the three main characteristics of processes, it is time to itemize the characteristics of Lean processes. Lean processes must have the following capabilities in order to be considered Lean:

- **Repeatable**
- **Scalable (up or down)**
- **Optimized (at a system level)**

It is important to note that optimization in a Lean system is an ongoing, continuous effort referred to as continuous improvement. This is based on the belief that all processes can be continuously improved, without end.

Key Takeaways from Chapter 8

1. A process is a series of steps that can be repeated to yield a predictable result with acceptable quality of the output.

2. There are several different characteristics that processes should ideally have, including repeatability, scalability, and optimization.

3. Lean processes, by definition, exhibit these ideal qualities.

Chapter 9

Do You Have a Sales Process?

In Chapter Nine
→ Defining a Sales Process
→ Qualifying a Sales Process
→ Assessing Your Sales Process

Minimum Requirements for a Sales Process

When we use the term "sales process" in this section, we are assuming that it refers to a repeatable, scalable process, as defined in the previous chapter. There is really little value to a sales process that is not repeatable and scalable, except for use by a single, independent salesperson. For brevity, we will use the term "sales process" herein to imply that it is repeatable and scalable.

Why are these two attributes required to qualify as a sales process? It is because **repeatability and scalability are the primary objectives of instituting a sales process in your organization in the first place.**

You want the sales process to be repeatable to provide a reliable level of revenue predictability. You also want to know that there is a standard selling system that your salespeople are following. You would not get very far with an engineering organization that did not have processes around developing products. Likewise, finance and accounting departments where every employee had a different way of doing things would be unacceptable. Customer service organizations generally have well-spelled-out steps for how support personnel engage with customers. Why would sales, the heart of your organization, be allowed to function to any lower standard?

You want the sales process to be scalable because you likely want to be in a position to grow revenues. In most organizations, there is a correlation between the number of salespeople you have and the revenues you can expect. This relationship assumes you are able to bring new talent on to your sales team and, after allowing a certain amount of time for training and an inevitable learning curve, expect them to be as productive as your existing salespeople. If this is not the case, then the sales process is not scalable, and it will be challenging to figure out what levers you can pull in order to grow the top line.

Now, assuming you agree with the definition proposed above, the question becomes how you can determine whether you do have a sales process in place. The remainder of this chapter is devoted to helping you answer that question.

Is It Documented?

Unless your organization is unusual in that it uses a Zen form of communicating information, rules, and culture, it is a safe bet that any process that is not documented is not being followed by everyone, or maybe anyone. A well-documented sales process requires identifying explicitly all the steps in the sales process that salespeople are expected to follow, from the time a prospective Buyer is turned over to them until a product or service is successfully delivered. (In some sales processes, "successfully" also includes "paid for.")

The sales process should identify and document which individuals or teams (roles) have the primary responsibility for executing each step in the process. It will also list the inputs into, and the outputs out of, each process step. (Remember, all process steps have an input and an output; something must change about the item being processed, even if it is a Buyer that is being "processed.")

While you may have a sales process that is documented to meet the minimum requirements discussed above, the process is useless if it is not communicated. In this case, the standard for communication is not just that the information about the process is available if someone chooses to go find it, but rather that it is required reading in order to be a member of the sales team.

Incidentally, **simply having a list of customers and prospects buried deep in a Customer Relationship Management (CRM) system does not by itself qualify as having a sales process.** If you don't have a sales process, CRM software is not going to magically create one for you unless you make your sales process faithfully follow the default process that comes prebuilt into the CRM. Otherwise, the best a CRM can do is to give you the means to adapt it to *model* the process *your* organization *is* following within the CRM. According to Gartner, Inc., a research firm, Salesforce.com® and Microsoft Dynamics® are the two fastest growing[1] of the popular CRM software systems, used by companies of all sizes.

Here's what Dave Meagher, President of RedTeal, a Salesforce.com consulting firm specializing in solution architecture, custom development, integrations, and business automation, had to say about this topic:

> No matter how clean your data or how simple your configuration, the Salesforce platform is not a substitute for a well-managed sales process. We witness it over and over again. Organizations think that they can improve their sales numbers by simply getting a better tool in place. Nothing could be further from the truth. A better tool can only help at the margins.
>
> A better tool can enable your organization to institutionalize and report on the sales process. It can allow you to scale. It can increase transparency and efficiencies. But it is not a substitute for effective sales management. Salesforce only gives you the tools to drive the process, it's up to management to provide the one-on-one mentoring that creates great sales results.

Is Everyone's Role in the Process Clearly Spelled Out?

Salespeople rarely execute a sales process without working with others in their organization, unless what they are selling is very simple (conceptually as well as technically). Even in that case, as noted earlier, salespeople can't complete a sale without a Buyer, and for that reason alone, a salesperson has to work with *someone* on every sales opportunity.

A well-designed and well-considered sales process does not leave anything to anyone's imagination or interpretation as to what every participant's role (including the Buyer) is at every process step. It is equally clear at identifying who is responsible for orchestrating the overall process. (The salesperson is the conductor by default.)

Who is responsible to qualify a potential Buyer? Is it the marketing department, the lead generation department, the salesperson, or all of the above? Does it vary from time to time and by specific salesperson? Without consistency and an impersonal definition of roles and responsibilities, there cannot be a true sales process.

Is Every Participant Required to Follow It?

Let's assume that you have managed to document your sales process and clearly define the roles and responsibilities within that process. That's a great foundation. Now the question is whether everyone in your sales organization is required to conform to it. The operative words here are "everyone" and "required."

Is your sales process optional? Does it only apply to salespeople who are newly on-boarded or below quota? Are salespeople "supposed" to follow it, but rarely do? Do they follow it sometimes but not at other times? How do you require them to follow it? What are the benefits of conformance and the penalties for non-conformance to the sales process? Are there any?

Do They?

Unless you are a sales manager or otherwise deeply involved in the *process* of sales in your organization (as opposed to being involved in the output: closing sales), you may be struggling to answer some of the questions I posed above. Even if there is an established sales process in place, do you know if your salespeople are following it? (To repeat: having your customers and prospects in a CRM does not ensure that your salespeople are following the same process, or any process for that matter.)

Do your most productive salespeople get a "free pass" when it comes to following a process? Are you hesitant to enforce the process and procedures (including reporting) on them when they are "on a roll," not wanting to "disturb their flow" when they are closing sales? This is akin to the earlier example where a big, expensive piece of capital equipment dictates the processes on the manufacturing floor to the detriment of the productivity and quality of the entire system. Are you, too, loath to mess with something that appears to be working?

Are Your Salespeople Artisans?

Prior to the Industrial Revolution in the early 1900s, production was done by craftsmen, some of whom considered themselves artisans, producers of unique and exquisite things.

Many times salespeople (*particularly* if they are somewhat successful) consider themselves artisans. That is to say they believe that:

1. **What they do is unique (and magical)**
2. **It can't really be replicated by anyone else**
3. **It can't fit into a formalized process or the creative artistry would be destroyed**

Is that what you hear from *your* salespeople? Are you buying it?

"What's wrong with having an artisan in sales, especially if she's hitting her numbers?" you might ask. Well, the problem is the same problem Henry Ford faced when he started the Industrial Revolution. Craftsmanship cannot be scaled up, easily trained, or quality controlled. Neither can a salesforce of artisans.

If you are designing your sales strategy around artisans rather than a process, then you are optimizing it for individual producers, rather than the entire sales system.

History has shown that such an approach leads to long-term suboptimal performance in a company, although it may produce impressive "point" sales results in the short term.

How Do You Know?

Here's an important question you might be asking yourself at this point: "How can I know whether our salespeople are all following a standard process?" You could begin by asking your sales leader. If he or she doesn't know the answer, then the answer is almost certainly "no."

If he or she says they *are* following a standard procedure then ask the next question: "How do *you* know?"

The only way to know if the salesforce is abiding by a standard process is to follow President Reagan's maxim, "Trust but verify." There must be procedures in place that make it clearly and immediately visible as to whether the process is being followed or not. *If management focuses only on the output of the sales process (closing sales) but does not spend time monitoring faithful adherence to process steps, the ironic outcome will be the inability to manage the output.*

If you think about it for a moment, this seeming contradiction makes sense. Improving every other process in your business or personal life starts with analyzing and improving each step that leads to the result. Trying to change the effect without changing the causes is futile. It is akin to expecting a different result by doing exactly the same thing.

This is like a golf coach instructing you, "Hit the ball better!" For anyone who plays golf, or has taken a lesson, the silliness of this directive will be immediately clear. If you only focus on hitting the ball, you rarely improve, unless you happen to be an especially gifted athlete. A good coach will help you work on improving each of the steps that lead to good ball striking, such as your setup position, balance, takeaway of the club, and the sequence of initiating the swing. Hitting the ball well is the target outcome of doing all those things properly, but cannot be controlled directly.

The culturally ingrained behavior of senior management not to delve deeply into sales processes is what makes troubleshooting and improving overall sales results so difficult. The actual sales process, including the value-added (and expensive) steps that lead to a closed sale, get short shrift when it comes to management's attention as compared to the closed sales themselves. If you want to change the effect (output), you have to change the causes (inputs, or in this case, process steps).

In the following chapters, we are going to see how a Lean Selling™ approach both optimizes and enforces process, while providing the closed-loop system that lets management know that things are under control (i.e., predictable). An important step in making this happen is the use and collection of metrics, and investing time to delve more deeply into sales processes. We will cover both of these topics in the next chapter.

Key Takeaways from Chapter 9

1. There are a few minimum requirements for an organization's sales process to qualify as a process.

2. Unless sales processes are clearly documented, communicated, and enforced, they are unlikely to be adhered to by everyone.

3. Unless all participants follow the sales process, it will not be able to be improved or leveraged.

4. Managers must audit compliance with their sales process if it is important to them.

Chapter 10

Measuring the Effectiveness and Efficiency of Your Sales Process

In Chapter Ten
→ Metrics
→ Role of CRM Systems
→ Sales Process Improvement

How Often Do You Get Metrics from Your Process?

The one sales metric all sales managers and senior executives receive is revenue. They may also get other statistics, such as the number of new customers or repeat purchases for a given timeframe. If they value analytics, they may look at certain ratios, such as revenue per sale or average sale value per salesperson. Such simple analytical metrics can generally be easily captured and reported.

However, these metrics are all variations of ways to measure the *output* of the sales process. They provide no information on what is happening *during* the process. For example, **one of the most important metrics you can measure about your sales process is cycle time. That is, how long does it take, on average, for a Buyer to become a customer after first contact with a salesperson?** This is a very important metric because it has profound implications for the scalability and efficiency of your sales process. Time is money, and the longer your average sales cycle is, the more expensive it is. Conversely, the faster you sell something and get paid for it, the less expensive the process is.

If your organization produces a product or delivers a service, can you imagine doing business if you had no idea how long it would take to produce the product or deliver the service? Can you picture what would happen if your customer service department couldn't give your customers any indication of when they might be able to help them with a product or service problem? Although product development schedules are notoriously sketchy, what organization would accept open-ended schedules for the development of anything outside of the domain of space exploration or curing a previously incurable disease?

Why is it that sales organizations are not generally held to the same standard to report the elapsed time it takes for them to do what they do (close sales)? Possibly, it's because there is a commonly-held belief that the Buyer is in control and unpredictable, and that there is little or nothing a Seller can do to control that. On the other hand, maybe it is that there is scant management interest in how long sales take as long as quotas are met (or not).

A corollary metric to sales cycle time is a concept I will call Buyer Aging. This is synonymous to accounts receivable aging, which is watched closely (like a hawk) by financial executives and regularly reported because it is a key driver of an organization's cash flow performance. The longer the sales cycle, the longer the Buyer Aging will generally be. This simply implies that the Buyer is in the sales cycle longer, which wouldn't initially seem to add a lot of additional information. However, since aging is an average value, it also tells us whether "Buyer inventory" is getting "stale or obsolete" while it is in the sales process.

Previously, drawing on the model of a production process, I built a case that Buyers, at least in theory, intrinsically have more value as they proceed further along in the sales process (if for no other reason than they should be closer to buying). This is rational because the Seller and his or her organization have made investments in the Buyer at every step of the Selling process. The value invested had to go somewhere. It went into the Buyer. If Buyers stall in the Selling process for long periods of time, they cause the average Buyer Aging value to increase.

How Are You Doing?

If you are a manager or senior executive who has sales reporting to you or as part of your organization, do you know what the health of the sales production process is, all the time? If not, why not?

Sales status reporting is generally unstructured, sporadic and anything but real time. Why is that? The main cause, I think, is that sales results are the only measurement many managers use to determine how their sales process is performing. Still, if the only thing you are measuring is Closed Sales, then you will not get any visibility into the activities that are actually *creating* Closed Sales, and whether there is a problem or an improvement that could be made there.

In order to get more visibility into the upstream sales processes and to build more predictability into the sales pipeline system, it is necessary to create additional relevant metrics. These metrics can provide an instant status report on the operating condition of the entire sales system.

To return to the accounts receivable analogy, this is like an account continuing to age (not paying its overdue bills month after month), which raises (a bad thing) the value (another metric!) of the accounts receivable aging (generally measured in "days sales outstanding"). In most companies, when accounts pass a certain number of days outstanding, they are referred to the collections department. If collections are unsuccessful, after they pass a second milestone in time the amount due is often written off as bad debt, since historical statistics indicate that the longer a debt remains unpaid, the less likely it is to *ever* be repaid.

If we would apply the same logic to our sales pipeline, **the longer a Buyer remains in the sales process without progress, the less likely it becomes that he or she will ever buy anything.** Does this mean we should we remove or re-characterize Buyers who are languishing in our sales process for months and months, or do we just leave them in our CRM, hoping against hope that they come back to life?

If we don't remove stuck Buyers from our sales process, then we don't really know what our opportunity pipeline looks like, and we may fool ourselves into thinking that the chances of making the revenue forecast is rosier than it really is.

The Role of CRM Systems

Curiously, with today's CRM systems, the data needed to provide these types of information in the form of reports is often available within the system, but is rarely readily accessible in a form that management can use. There are many reasons for this, which are beyond the scope of this book to delve into, but as I implied before, **the CRM system is only as good as what is fed into it, and what is fed into it is frequently not accurate, consistent, or complete.** Further, unless every member of the sales team is using the CRM in the same way, you do not have reliable global data about your entire sales process. That is why having a CRM system by itself does not ensure that you have a functional sales process or the means to manage it properly.

Further, while a CRM system can automate and, to a certain extent, enforce process, it does not model your unique sales process out of the box. I know that most modern CRM systems come with a simple built-in sales process structure, starter templates, and ways to modify them. However, in my experience, an organization should clarify how its sales process is *actually* working and how it *will* work, and *only then* invest the time and effort to have the CRM system conform to that, rather than the other way around. Unmodified CRM templates will likely be useful only for the most simple and generic sales processes.

How Often Do You Review Your Process?

Let's assume you have a sales process as we have defined it. Is it a process that was put on auto-pilot some time ago, or do you regularly have a team review it in order to ensure that it reflects the reality of the way sales are currently being performed? If there are disconnects between the assumed process and reality, how do you reconcile this? Should the process be changed or should conformance be better enforced?

There is not one right answer to this last question. The first step is to acknowledge that there is a "disconnect." This is not necessarily a bad thing, as salespeople may have learned a better way to get results faster by eliminating wasteful steps. Perhaps they may have instinctively responded to changes in the marketplace or Buyer patterns by changing their behavior or the sequence of process steps.

☑ LEAN LEARNINGS

Root Cause Analysis

Definition

This is the discipline of looking for the underlying cause of a problem and fixing it so it doesn't happen again. This is to be differentiated from addressing symptoms, which may be causes of problems themselves, but not the root cause. The Five Whys is a technique used to promote delving deeper than the apparent cause when problem solving.

Application to Lean Selling

As with many processes, there is often great confusion when troubleshooting sales processes in determining what is a symptom and what is a cause. Often the initial usual suspects are merely symptoms of an upstream cause such as lead generation or a lack of training or communication. Lean Thinking tells us that fixing symptoms will bring temporary relief, but unless we get to the root causes of problems, the same issues will resurface, like a weed that was cut but did not have its roots pulled out.

The problem emerges when this disconnect is ignored and no concerted effort is made to bring the sales process and Selling reality back into alignment. Selling and the marketplace are dynamic. Still, if you allow your sales process to fall out of step with the way sales are actually being performed, then you will no longer have one real, living sales process. You then will likely have as many different sales "processes" as you have salespeople. The all-important strategic objectives of sales repeatability and scalability will then be lost. If you do not regularly engage in determining whether your documented process matches the actual process, you will not be able to have confidence in it or rely upon it.

How Often Do You Modify Your Process?

Selling is a dynamic area. Changes in the marketplace, your company's products and focus, and Buyers' preferences are all reasons to regularly review your Selling process. Reviewing a sales process for candidate tweaks and changes is a team effort and should include not only the sales personnel and managers, but key players who support the sales process, including those from departments outside of sales. Although getting the entire team together is an investment of everyone's precious time, it will pay for itself many times over by avoiding the costs of misunderstandings and miscommunications that can happen after a process is modified.

In a Lean Selling™ process, modifications can happen at any time. The people executing and monitoring the process must stop and convene whenever the process is not yielding the results (that is, not meeting goals based on the measurement of objective metrics discussed earlier) that everyone expected. This same group, in a Lean Selling process, is empowered by management to make changes to the process that they think will get the process closer to yielding the expected result.

These changes constitute an "experiment" in the truest sense, in that we never know in advance whether a process change will actually yield the result we are aiming for. Treating process changes as experiments also requires that there be an *a priori* hypothesis about the expected change in results after the change in process, also expressed in terms of objective metrics.

If the process change yields the hypothesized result, then the process can be stabilized and monitoring resumed. If it does not, then the team will have to reconvene, consider why their hypothesis might have been incorrect, and craft another experiment to improve the process. This is a repetitive cycle of continuous improvement and learning.

The Case for Metrics and Monitoring—
An Example

An example may help illustrate this concept. Let's say that the sales process metrics assume that 50% of the leads that are given to salespeople will be qualified within three days, thereby enabling them to move further through the Selling process. Let's also assume the process is actually yielding only 25% of leads qualified within three days and 30% within one week. The predictive cascading effect of that will be that sales will fall short of the forecast (by at least 40%), assuming all other process steps yield results as planned. The team will have to convene to consider various alternatives for the shortfall. Here are some examples of what the team might consider:

- Leads are not being properly qualified before being handed off to a salesperson based on previously agreed-upon criteria.

- The lead generation process and the salespeople are not using the same criteria to qualify a lead.

- The 50% figure is not a reasonable target (assuming it hasn't been met previously); it should be halved. (This conclusion would imply that the salespeople may require nearly twice as many leads to meet the sales forecast.)

Each one of these possible causes yields a unique action plan and experiment to improve the process (in this case, potentially for lead generation activities as well as sales). These are only a few examples of potential causes of the problem that can be considered as candidates to pursue for improvement.

If we had not previously established expectations of our process expressed as metrics and monitored these metrics continuously, we might not be aware that there is a problem until there appears a drastic, surprise reduction in the revenue forecast. Then it would probably be too late to do much about it in the near-term. Further, without such metrics and a well-defined process, we might find it difficult to know where to look for the source of the problem.

The **Lean Selling System** gives participants a set of tools for troubleshooting shortfalls in process output, delivery times, or quality. We will begin to introduce a number of these tools in the following chapters.

Key Takeaways from Chapter 10

1. *A sales process is not of much use as a management tool unless it generates a snapshot of meaningful metrics that indicates how well it is working.*

2. *CRM systems can have a role in the sales process, but it may not be what you currently think it is.*

3. *Sales processes should be reviewed regularly to ascertain whether they still reflect the way things are being done.*

4. *Management should decide, in collaboration with sales process participants, how to close gaps between process theory and reality.*

Chapter 11

Major Types and Causes of Waste in Sales Processes

In Chapter Eleven
→ Buyer-Seller Disconnects
→ Wasteful Activities
→ Wasted Time
→ Overproduction

Differing Goals Between Buyers and Sellers

The mother of all waste in sales is that Buyers and Sellers have different objectives. Sometimes this is by plan, but often it's because neither party asks the other what their objectives are for working together. If it's by plan, then that's twentieth-century-sales thinking. If it's because of a lack of training and new ideas for how to do things, Lean Selling™ can address that issue.

If we step back from the Buying and Selling processes to get a more objective perspective, it might seem strange that Buyers and Sellers would have differing goals. In this book we have already discussed at some length how a Seller can't sell without a Buyer, and a Buyer can't buy without a Seller. Therefore, it would seem that there would be a natural motivation for mutual cooperation in order to better achieve the goals of both parties. Of course, this isn't the first example in human history where people don't pursue the rational, pragmatic path for irrational, non-pragmatic reasons.

Using a Lean Thinking approach, if we want to discover potential ways to change this unproductive behavior, we first have to understand why the behavior exists in the first place. Here are a few possibilities to consider:

- **Buyers and Sellers have an imbalance of required knowledge to effect a Buying decision**, whether in business-to-business transactions or consumer purchases (from mobile phones to health plans to automobiles to financial advice). This has led some short-sighted Buyers and Sellers to decide that they should exploit any existing informational disparities rather than try to reduce them. (Chapter 1 of this book discusses how this disparity is rapidly diminishing.) This is a win-lose mindset problem.

- **Buyers and Sellers have not been shown how cooperating in the sales process could be beneficial for both parties.** This is an education problem.

- **Buyers and Sellers don't know how to cooperate.** This is a training problem.

- **Buyers and Sellers don't have the methods to cooperate.** This is a lack of tools problem.

- **Buyers and Sellers have not been expected to cooperate**. This is a Selling system problem.

A Lean Selling process effectively addresses all of the above shortcomings. Of course, the above list is very rational and, as a result, it is missing the emotional drivers that underlie these behaviors, including:

- **Buyers don't want to reveal too much information** because they feel it will weaken their negotiating position.

- **Sellers don't want to reveal too much information** because they feel it will weaken their negotiating position.

- **There is emotional vulnerability in exposing that you are dependent** on someone else for what you require.

- **There is a risk in choosing to trust someone to help you** to solve your problem.

- **It requires a commitment to agree to help someone else** solve his or her problem.

Everything described above mirrors the environment that Toyota faced when the company first pioneered the Lean Supply Chain. Toyota had to find a way to get vendors to commit to continuous improvement and to lower their prices over time. Toyota realized that if it did not

☑ *LEAN LEARNINGS*

Waste

Japanese: *Muda* 無駄

Definition

Taiichi Ohno, considered the father of the Toyota Production System (later referred to as Lean Manufacturing), identified seven types of waste in production processes. These are:

1. Transportation—Unnecessary movement of goods and materials on a factory floor
1. Inventory—Excess goods that are waiting to be processed or sold
1. Motion—Unnecessary movement
1. Waiting—Waiting for a process step, often related to in-process inventory
1. Over-processing—Performing unnecessary processing on a good or service that does not have value to the customer
1. Over-production—Creating more supply than there is demand for
1. Defects—Quality problems that require time to fix or are not found until they reach a customer

Application to Lean Selling

Although these wastes were originally identified for manufacturing production processes, a sale is a service production process and demonstrates similar wastes. For example:

1. Transportation—A salesperson traveling to a customer site when a phone call or Skype® conference would have sufficed
1. Inventory—Buyers sitting in the sales pipeline but not moving forward
1. Motion—Salespeople making non-value-added contact with a Buyer to "check in"
1. Waiting—Buyers who stall in the sales pipeline and don't complete activities as scheduled or committed
1. Over-processing—Sharing unnecessary information with a Buyer, which increases the perceived risk of a Buying decision and complicates the Buying process
1. Over-production—Providing too many options for the Buyer, which confuses the decision process
1. Defects—Unqualified Buyers get into the sales pipeline or customers do not get what they wanted from the sales process

provide an incentive to vendors to do so, the company would only be asking them to work harder and to be creative on their behalf, with the reward being reduced profits for the vendors (in the face of increased profits for Toyota). Being long-term thinkers, the leadership of Toyota realized that while "squeezing" vendors might lead to increased profitability in the short-term, it was never a viable strategy for the long-term. (Remember the Golden Goose?)

Toyota came up with a new win-win (versus win-lose) way to work with vendors that revolutionized relationships with supply chain partners, which they still employ today. First of all, rather than annually "bidding out" for the best price on a selected component, Toyota made a long-term commitment to a selected vendor and *possibly* one or two backup vendors. This made it economical for Toyota to make investments in teaching its vendors how to implement their Lean methodologies in their own factories, so that the vendors would get better and more efficient at what they do.

Additionally, at the beginning of the relationship Toyota and a new vendor agree on a mutually acceptable price, and at the same time agree on target price reductions based on assumptions about the vendor reducing its costs over time. In this way the profit margin for the vendor (the vendor's selling price minus its cost to produce) does not decline over time, even as this selling price is reduced.

But that's not all. Toyota typically shares the savings it realizes from vendor cost reductions with the vendor.[1] In this way the companies are partners in the benefits of continuous improvement. As a result of this new type of supplier relationship, Toyota acquires a vendor that is getting better and better all the time (in quality as well as efficiency), and the vendor gets a lower cost of production, which can be used to gain additional market share by reducing prices, or to increase profit margins—or some combination of the two—when selling to other customers. It is truly a creative win-win solution to an age-old supplier-customer dilemma.

Another related example of Toyota's forward Lean Thinking is illustrated by the way that it deals with the aftereffects of its own internal efficiency improvements. The improvements from applying Lean Thinking and methodologies to production processes can be very dramatic, in the early stages and beyond. This almost always leads to excess production employees not required by the improved process. While this is great for the company, what about all the people who were made redundant? Are they likely to be fans of Lean improvements, in their hearts or minds?

This problem, at its essence, is not conceptually much different from the vendor case described above. The players have changed, but not the ethical and practical dilemma. Toyota knew that it would be difficult to gain support for continuous improvement using Lean methodologies if the people implementing them thought it would lead to losing their jobs or to demotions. That would be, to exaggerate a grisly metaphor, like asking them to dig their own graves.

It is important to note that modern Japan has a deep cultural commitment to life-long employment. Nevertheless, it is not an inviolable commitment, particularly if a company meets with some dramatic, unexpected disaster, or finds itself otherwise suddenly with lots of employees with nothing to do. (In the case of massive layoffs, CEOs of Japanese companies have been known to voluntarily resign to take responsibility for breaking their promise to the workers not to lay them off.)

How did Toyota decide to handle this? They promised their workers that no one would lose their job because of increased efficiencies and other improvements that created excess workers. Fortunately, they have been able to live up to that promise. What do they do with the extra people? They put them to work figuring out the next improvements Toyota could make or the next new businesses Toyota could enter, until sales growth eventually absorbs the excess staff. Since Toyota is constantly improving its processes, this is an ongoing, relentless program.

I share these examples because they illustrate an important element of Lean Thinking, which is to provide motivation to the people making improvements by showing them how they will benefit, and by sharing the benefits of continuous improvement. Both the vendor and employee solutions cited above are examples of how to take relationships with built-in, endemic, long-term, structural distrusts and turn them around to be truly win-win, trusting relationships. Trusting relationships are reinforced through behaviors consistent with what was promised.

If Lean Thinking can demonstrate a way to do so in areas with seemingly intractable conflicts, such as with vendors and employees, it can facilitate doing so with Buyers and Sellers using a Lean Selling process. Aligning Buyers and Sellers on their goals helps to eliminate the waste of time and the inefficiencies that result from working at cross-purposes.

Do Your Salespeople Chafe at the Idea of Production Work?

Most salespeople, particularly those who work in the field, would not like to be thought of as production workers. That is, they wouldn't like being compared to the people who work on a manufacturing line, doing the same (supposedly) boring job or task over and over again. They consider themselves too creative and fancy free to be production workers.

I find this interesting. One of the most commonly used words in conjunction with "sales" is "production." Rarely do I hear words like "creative," "panache," or "artistic" combined with the word, "sales." That is not to say that selling (like many business activities) doesn't require creativity, panache, or even some artistry from time to time to solve problems and work effectively with customers. It's just not what the vast majority of salespeople are measured on. It's *production*, the same as in a factory.

Unclear Buyer Requirements

A majority of sales professionals in a recent survey listed a deeper understanding of Buyer requirements as their number-one area for improvement in their sales process.[2] Buyers can often be notoriously bad at clearly identifying what they want. A primary reason is that they often don't really know what they want until they see it. Even carefully written specifications that may accompany a Request for Proposal (RFP) fail to consider everything that's needed. (Have you heard of "change orders" after a contract is awarded?)

In software development, even with a significant and serious effort to create a complete specification for a reasonably complex software application, ultimately *as little as 45% of the final feature set came from the original specification.*[3] That means that as much as 55% of the feature set required was "discovered" after the specification was written, even if many months and considerable staff hours were expended to develop a state-of-the-art and "complete" specification.

The second reason is that Buyers don't always know how to describe what they want. It is sometimes not easy to explain to someone who is not inside your head exactly what you are thinking about. Buyers have requirements that they are aware of, and also those that they are not consciously aware of (or don't yet know about). It is unlikely Buyers will be able to clearly translate their conscious requirements into a form that a Seller can understand, let alone inform a Seller about unconscious or unknown requirements.

The third reason is that both Buyers and Sellers make assumptions about what the other is saying or asking for, without testing these assumptions. This is dangerous and can lead to a significant waste of time and money. Good listening skills are important here, being attuned to both the logical and emotional elements of what is being said. This is where face-to-face (or video conference) meetings can provide the advantage of facial expressions and body language. (There are good books that delve more deeply into this topic identified in the Resources section in the back of this book.)

These causes of miscommunication are partly due to the reality of human nature, but it is in the best interest of both Buyer and Seller to make sure the other party understands what they are thinking and asking for. Rather than trying to change the nature of the beast, it will be more fruitful to use a Lean Selling methodology that acknowledges this reality and addresses it to minimize communication errors. Simply put, this methodology views the gathering of requirements as a "discovery process" rather than a single event of interaction and information transfer (as a specification assumes). It also tests, *continuously*, that Buyer and Seller understand each other and that nothing important in the requirements has changed because of new information or external forces.

Spending time developing or providing the wrong product or

service (that is, not the one the Buyer wanted) is a tremendously wasteful use of time and resources. It is *not* a good way to become a trusted supplier.

Unnecessary Activity

Another significant contributor to waste in the sales process is unnecessary activity in many forms. It might be an unnecessary meeting, presentation, or product demonstration. Some Sellers are on auto-pilot and will be compelled to go through their selling routine ("Let me tell you a little about our company," or "Let me show you a quick demo.") regardless of whether those actions have any value for the Buyer or the Buying process. And remember, **all Selling activity that does not have value to the Buyer is waste, for both the Buyer and the Seller. In fact, it is *anti-value*** because it causes the Buyer to distance himself or herself emotionally from the Seller. (Remember: time is money, and wasted time is wasted money, for the Buyer *and* for the Seller.)

If you are a Seller, do you have meetings with Buyers just to "check in"? That may have some value for you if you actually get an update on the progress of a sale, but is it of any value to the Buyer? If not, it is waste.

I know that many salespeople have been taught to get as much face time with Buyers as possible. If you are treating the Buyer to a round of golf at an exclusive country club (assuming your Buyer plays golf), that might have value for the Buyer (although not necessarily for your sale). Other than that, unless you are a personal friend or relative (and maybe not even then), Buyers don't usually want to see you unless you have something of value to offer them. They really do have other things to do with their time.

The goal is to get Buyers to *want* to see you. How? By adding value (defined by the Buyer) in every meeting or telephone call you have with them. How can you be sure you are adding value? Ask them. Make sure you know what they value and then figure out how you can provide it. They may, in fact, look forward to seeing you.

If you are a Seller, take a look at all the activities you do in a typical sales process. If you are a sales manager, do it in aggregate (assuming you actually know what activities your salespeople are doing). Ask yourself two questions about these activities:

1. **What value did that activity add for the Buyer (not just for me or my company)?**

2. **How can I be sure?**

Waiting Time

"Chilling your heels" is a common and one the most frustrating aspects of a Selling process (possibly just behind losing a sale, but maybe even ahead of it). It seems that Selling is destined to be a waiting game. If you are a Seller, in a given week or month, have you ever stopped to calculate how much total time you spent on a given opportunity that actually moved it closer to a sale? I'll bet it's a really small percentage of your month. How do I know?

I know because Selling is one of the most inefficient processes that there is, especially when it comes to time. One of the most fundamental metrics that Lean methodologies use when analyzing processes is the percentage of time actually adding value divided by the elapsed time, or the Value Added Ratio (VAR). It is not uncommon for this percentage to be in the single digits in processes that are not Lean. My estimate is that for sales, it may be below a single digit (that is, the VAR is less than 1%).

How did I arrive at this number? There are approximately 173 working hours in the average month if you work a 40-hour week. If you spend one hour per month actually creating value for a given account, then that is 0.6% of your total available time. If you are a Seller, how many "active" accounts do you have where you struggle to figure out how to add one hour of true value per month?

Underproviding and Overproviding

These are two of my favorites, because they are so pervasive. Let's consider underproviding first. From the Seller's perspective, underproviding means simply that the Seller does not provide everything the Buyer requires at each stage of the Selling process, when he or she requires it, in order to enable the Buyer to move confidently forward to the next step in the Buying process.

However, now we know from Lean Selling that there is a corollary for the Buyer. From the perspective of the Buyer as a provider, underproviding means simply that the Buyer does not provide everything that the Seller requires at each stage of the Buying process—when he or she requires it—in order that the Seller can move confidently forward to the next step in the Selling process. Remember, a sale is a duet, not a solo performance.

Overproviding also comes in Buyer and Seller varieties. The Seller overproviding is more recognizable and includes deluging the Buyer with information about your company and products, talking about things your product can potentially do, and talking about additional services your company can offer, none of which the Buyer is interested in (at the current time).

Not only does this waste the Buyer's time by reviewing information and materials that the Buyer doesn't value, but it also creates unconscious confusion in the Buyer's mind and heightens his or her anxiety and perception of risk about making a decision. **The cure here is to focus on the objective. This means to only provide information that will help move the Selling or Buying process from where it is to the next step.** Any additional information, although it may be valuable to someone at some point in the sales process, is, at *this* point in time, waste.

When a Buyer overprovides, he or she is sharing information that is superfluous to the purchase decision currently under consideration. Buyers may sometimes do this to throw a Seller off the scent (because the Buyer is not being completely forthcoming), or he or she may simply be confused. A Seller has to be careful not to assume that everything a Buyer shares is pertinent to the Buying process. Remember, assumptions have to be tested before they are acted upon.

In Lean Thinking, anything that is provided before it is required or requested is waste. The same is true in Lean Selling.

Key Takeaways from Chapter 11

1. Sales processes exhibit many costly types of waste.

2. The root causes of waste are poor communications between Buyers and Sellers and lack of alignment on goals for the sales process.

3. Waste includes unnecessary activity, underproviding and overproviding.

4. Sales processes should be reviewed regularly to determine whether they still reflect the way things are being done.

5. Management should decide, in collaboration with sales process participants, how to close gaps between process theory and reality.

Chapter 12

A Simplified Selling Process

In Chapter Twelve
- → Steps of a Sale
- → Process Inputs and Outputs
- → Process Dependencies

Five Steps of a Sale

There are as many different ways to describe a sales process as there are sales organizations. However, I think the vast majority of these can be largely overlaid on the simplified process illustrated below.

Illustration 1: Five Key Steps of a Sale

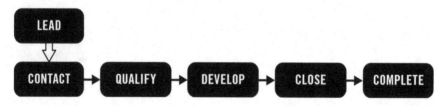

Step #1

We will set our beginning "fencepost" for delineating the scope of our sales process at the point that a salesperson receives a lead. This lead could come from a number of sources. It could be from the marketing department or a lead-generation team. It might be from a form that someone filled out on the company website, or it could be a lead the salesperson generated by himself or herself as a result of a cold call. A lead will be of varying quality (defined as its propensity to turn into a sale), often depending on how much "nurturing" was done on the lead before it was handed over to sales.

A nurturing process may have been done over a period of days, weeks, or months, by some combination of marketing and pre-sales functions, depending on how the particular organization develops leads. By the time a salesperson first contacts the lead, the potential Buyer may have been exposed to a narrow or broad range of information about the company and its products and services. A lead generated from a cold call would be considered "raw" in that it has had no nurturing, and we can assume the potential Buyer has little or no knowledge of the organization the salesperson represents or its value proposition.

At any rate, for our purposes, the sales process now begins. The very first thing a salesperson has to do is to make contact with the lead. In the past, this was almost always done by phone, but today, especially for certain types of products and services, this initial contact might be through email or other electronic means. Since the potential Buyer represented by the lead has shown some interest in what the company can do for him or her, the salesperson's first objective is to make contact and start to assess the level and nature of the interest.

Step #2

Once contact is made and there is a dialogue started (in person, by phone, or through messages sent back and forth) the next objective for the salesperson is to qualify whether this person fits the criteria required to indicate that the Buyer is likely to do business with his or her company. Basically, the salesperson wants to know if he or she should be investing time in this person and moving the lead into his or her sales "funnel" or "pipeline."

Illustration 2: Sales Pipeline vs. Sales Funnel

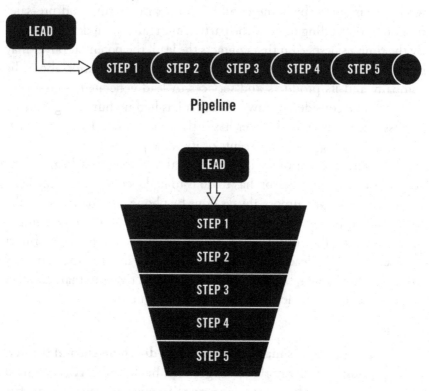

How much qualification a salesperson has to do at this stage is dependent on how selective the organization is about its potential customers and how much qualification was already done on the lead before it was handed over to the salesperson. Qualification questions might include company size by employees or revenue, location, industry the prospect participates in, capital equipment the company has installed, timeframe to purchase, and existing budget to potentially purchase the organization's products or services. These are generic criteria. The actual qualification will be specific to the organization and the type of customer the company serves.

Step #3

Once a lead is qualified, the salesperson will attempt to engage the Buyer in sales development activities, moving the lead through the pipeline or down the funnel toward closing a sale. What happens now varies widely based on what is being sold, to whom it is being sold, and the idiosyncrasies of the organization's particular industry. This stage will generally involve a deep dive into the Buyer's requirements, will often include the supplying of stock or custom literature to the Buyer, and often involves a product demo or sample. Surely the Buyer will, at some point, require either standard pricing or a custom proposal and delivery estimates prior to making a Buying decision. Just how much time the Seller will spend face to face with the Buyer will also vary considerably by organization. The Seller's objective here is to do whatever is necessary (within reason and the law) to get the Buyer to reach the point of making a Buying decision favorable to the Seller's organization.

Step #4

The magical time in every salesperson's (and sales manager's) job is when he or she hears that the Buyer has decided to purchase or commit to the company's product or service. This is typically considered the close of the sales process, commonly referred to as "closing." There may still be some details to work out like delivery scheduling, contract terms or other legal issues (hopefully and ideally not), but in general the Seller's primary goal has been achieved.

Step #5

When the product or service has been successfully delivered and, if necessary, installed, the sales process is generally considered complete. This is our other "fencepost" in this example. Many organizations do not consider the Seller to be responsible for executing this part of the process, but the Seller at a minimum has to follow up periodically to ensure satisfactory completion, if for no other reason than the person usually won't get paid unless the product or service is delivered and accepted by the Buyer.

Funnel vs. Pipeline

A sales pipeline is conceptually a horizontal flow of steps of sales development for each opportunity, like water that flows through a pipe, while a funnel is usually depicted vertically, starting wide on top, where leads drop in, and narrowing at the bottom, where closed or completed sales fall through. The funnel graphically indicates that only a fraction of leads that come in the top actually come out the bottom. The rest leak out from the sides (or get endlessly stuck inside the funnel). Either depiction is essentially capturing the same information, with the main purpose to show status of opportunities in the sales process. Ideally, a pipeline or funnel would also indicate "movement" of an opportunity and how long an opportunity has been "stuck" at its current state in the process.

With Lean Selling™, my personal graphical preference is to use a pipeline instead of a funnel, for two reasons.

1. A pipeline looks more like a process, typically depicted in Lean process diagrams as moving from left to right. This depiction can easily represent Flow, which we will cover in Part IV of this book.

2. A funnel shape assumes a certain attrition of opportunities as a given (because its shape is wider on the top where new opportunities come in than at the bottom where they close). The "ideal" shape would be closer to equal on top and bottom, like a pipeline turned 90 degrees. We will go deeper into this subject when we cover the topic of waste later in this book.

Some organizations will not consider the sales process complete until the product is paid for (one indicator of satisfactory delivery). Others will not consider it complete until the Buyer is willing to be a reference for the organization (a higher standard indeed!).

Inputs and Outputs

What are the inputs and outputs of this simplified selling process outlined here? Clearly, the primary input is a lead, meaning the name, title (if a business Buyer) and contact information of someone who has expressed interest in the products or services the salesperson sells. Without that, there is nothing to start a sales process with. The output of the process is a decision from the Buyer the lead represents to purchase from the salesperson's organization, as signified in a purchase order, online order, or signed contract. This seems simple enough.

Dependencies

However, the devil is in the details. What happens between a lead being placed in a salesperson's hands (or CRM system) and a Buying decision can be all over the map. This is because, even when there is a process like the one here that is faithfully followed, there are dependencies that prevent the process from "flowing" smoothly. Rather, most sales processes move in fits and starts. A dependency in a process is something that a process step is dependent upon completion before that step in the process can be executed. Let's take a look at a few examples.

In our simple example, the salesperson gets a lead and then attempts to make contact. Note the use of the word "attempts." It is not easy to reach people these days, and it is getting harder, as you have probably experienced yourself (unless you are one of those exceptionally fortunate people that others call back, either because they have to or because you are offering them money). Everyone seems to be extremely busy, and it is rare that someone is waiting for the phone to ring with a salesperson on the other end.

As a result, the salesperson may not be able to reach the lead right away. How long will it take: a day, a week, a month? Of course, it depends (there's that word again) on how urgent the lead thinks his or her problem is and how likely the prospect thinks it is that the salesperson's organization will be able to help. It also depends on how many other balls the lead is juggling at the moment, and where this initiative sits in the queue with other important priorities.

Of course, the salesperson does not have visibility to any of this information until he or she finally makes contact with the lead. There may be some notes that were passed on with the lead based on others' previous contact regarding the urgency of the need, but the fact remains: nothing moves forward until the salesperson can have a live or electronic discussion with the lead. In other words, a dependency of the Contact step is being able to actually get a response after first reaching out to the lead.

The next dependency has to do with the following step in our process, Qualification. In order to qualify the lead, the salesperson must be able to elicit information to make a determination of Buyer suitability. Not all Buyers are completely cooperative at this stage. They will be happy to tell you how to spell their name, letter by letter, but if you ask more challenging questions, such as, "What is your timeframe to address this issue?" (In other words, "When do you think you will *buy* something?"), the Buyer may not be so forthcoming.

It might be because he or she doesn't know, or it could be because the prospect does not want to be pinned down. It could also be that the prospect is not actually authorized to buy anything; he or she is just gathering information for themselves or for someone else. But if the prospect admits as much to the Seller, he or she may not get the snappy response and open-ended services the Seller can provide.

This creates a dilemma for the Seller. He or she might not have enough information to qualify the lead, but he or she may not have enough information to disqualify the lead either. What does a salesperson do? It depends a lot on the individual salesperson, his or her experience, and how full the sales pipeline is. **Qualification stringency by individual salespeople appears to be highly correlated with how full one's sales pipeline is**; when the pipeline is full, Sellers just don't have time to fool around with a Buyer who is not serious, doesn't exhibit urgency, or may be wasting their time.

This, of course, implies that those salespeople with more sparse pipelines don't have enough to do and are perfectly willing to let Buyers waste their time, as well as the company's resources in adding value to a "fake," or unqualified, Buyer-in-Process. The main point here is that the salesperson is dependent on the Buyer's behavior to be able to qualify the lead, in order to move his or her sales process forward.

Even when the salesperson is fortunate enough to qualify (or disqualify) the Buyer expeditiously, there now arises a new dependency to executing the Develop stage of the process. The activities that go on here can be quite diverse, depending on the complexity of the sale. This stage of the sales process requires that the Buyer focus a lot of attention and energy into being developed.

It may be necessary to bring other people from the Buyer's organization in at this stage, which complicates the process greatly. If it is a major or strategic purchase under consideration, it may require the input (or concurrence) of a team that crosses organizational boundaries. It is likely that each participant on the "buying team" will have his or her own concerns and objectives regarding the decision to purchase.

Putting the increased complexity of the Buyer-Seller interactions and content to be discussed aside for a moment, it is simply a lot more difficult to schedule a group of busy people than it is one busy person. This can lead to required meetings and discussions having delays between them that add absolutely no value (the delays, that is) and slow down the Selling and Buying process, often considerably. Again, the Seller at this stage of the process is highly dependent on the cooperation and desire of the Buyer to move things forward.

In an ideal world, when the Develop stage is complete and the Buyer (or Buying team) has made a decision to buy from the Seller, it would seem that getting through the Close stage should be a snap. However, it rarely is. Why is that? Because of all those pesky details that have to be worked out with contracts, credit, legal, and so forth. Of course, for smaller, insignificant purchases, this may not be the case. Nevertheless, for large or strategic purchases, it almost certainly will be.

One reason it is so hard to get closure after a decision has been made is that the sales cycle takes so long. The world has been changing between first contact and a decision. Participants in the process lose track of that. As a result, when they finally reach a decision point, they may find that the original budget is no longer available, requirements have changed, a reorganization is afoot, or a myriad of other things have happened—or are about to happen—that throw a monkey wrench into their Buying process. Sometimes these items can be addressed quickly and relatively easily. Sometimes they lead to putting the Buying process on the back-burner or on hold completely.

In your career, have you ever had the experience of completing a lengthy and complicated sales process where the deal was done, but when it was time to sign on the dotted line, your Buyer was unexpectedly no longer with the organization, or surprisingly transferred to other responsibilities? I have. If you or your organization is not selling in Japan or certain European countries, you can bank on it happening all the time if your sales cycle is too long.

Key Takeaways from Chapter 12

1. There are five basic steps to a simplified sales process.
2. There are inputs to and outputs from each step of the process.
3. Each step is dependent on something being completed in a previous step.
4. The longer the entire sales process takes, the greater chance there is for something to derail it.

Chapter 13

A Simplified Buying Process

In Chapter Thirteen
→ Steps of a Purchase
→ Process Inputs and Outputs
→ Process Dependencies

Five Steps of a Purchase

The simplified selling process discussed in the previous chapter will be very familiar to anyone who has participated in or closely with a sales organization. In companies, the sales "process" of an organization is mentioned frequently (regardless of whether it meets our hurdle of actually qualifying as a process, as discussed earlier). Simply put, it is understood as the "things salespeople do" to close business for the company.

You don't hear about the Buying process much. In fact, have you ever heard about it in your organization? You won't hear much about a Buying process in the vast majority of sales training programs, either. What you will hear a lot about is closing techniques and in-vogue selling methods like "story-telling." Neither of these is focused on the Buyer or the Buying process, only on closing a sale. Even if neglected, there is a Buyer and a Buying process in every sale, and from a macro view, the latter looks a lot like a Selling process. However, hardly anyone talks about it. Why is that?

Maybe it's because Sellers, their managers, and their organization's executives think that the Buying process exists in a parallel universe: vaguely present but never seen and never interacting with the other universe, the Selling process. The two processes pass each other like ships in the night, generating to each other an occasional eerie sensation that something is out there, but unable to distinguish it in the darkness. Let's develop this invisible, alternate reality idea further.

There is no company activity more important to CEOs, investors, and Boards of Directors than sales. Companies live or die on revenues. There is no process that is more important to understand to make sales than the Buying process. Your company could double its sales just by turning a fraction of Buyers' *No Decision or Status Quo* decisions into Buying decisions.

A majority of sales professionals listed sales cycles that end in *No Decision* as the most likely reason they weren't meeting their sales quotas.[1] How can organizations ignore the Buying process as if it didn't exist? Might it finally be time to acknowledge this and bring this Buying process out of the darkness and into full view?

Illustration 3: Six Key Steps of a Purchase

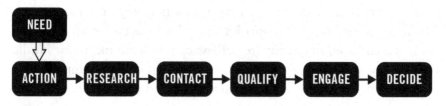

Step #1

First, the Buyer takes action based on a need that or his or her organization has. That need, in business at least, is often couched as a solution for a current or potential problem or relief from a business pain. It is important to acknowledge that not all needs are acted upon. Generally, there are a whole host of problems that organizations and individuals have, but they are unable to address them all at once. A priority of problems to be solved eventually emerges. Sometimes the priority is based on urgency; sometimes it is based on the potential value of solving the problem (or the potential cost of not solving it).

Something has to happen to get the Buyer to make a decision to take action. It might be an internal crisis or an external threat. It might be the unexpected appearance of funding that wasn't there before. It could be a new strategic direction that the organization's leadership has decided to pursue.

The Buyer may decide to take action or he or she may be directed by someone else to do so. Whatever the cause and circumstances, the Buyer is now ready to prioritize finding a potential solution for a perceived problem and invest (valuable) time in doing so.

Step #2

The next step the Buyer will take is to do research on who could potentially help him or her figure out what to do to solve the problem. It is possible that the need and solution are crystal clear, but often they are not. In some cases, the Buyer will have a trusted vendor that he or she thinks might be able to supply a solution, which he or she will reach out to initially. If not, he or she may turn to a trusted advisor to see if he or she can get him or her started on the right path to finding someone. These days, people will tap their social networks or use blog sites or Web community groups to post a question, and they may get assistance from someone they don't even know personally.

If none of these paths yields an answer, then the Buyer has a lot of work ahead to come up to speed on the various offerings that are available in the marketplace. The Buyer then needs to develop a game plan to get educated quickly on his or her options. Fortunately, for today's Buyer, the Web makes that effort much more efficient than in the past.

It is worth noting that a cold call to a Buyer while he or she is in this or the previous stage is often fruitful because the Buyer is in the early stages of his or her Buying process, has not made up his or her mind about what he or she wants to buy, and will likely be open to working with someone who can help to figure it out. In this case, fortunate timing plays an important role.

A cold call before the need is recognized or reaches a high priority level, or after the Buyer gets much deeper in the Buying process on his or her own, is not likely to yield as much. That's one of the reasons that prospecting for Buyers through cold-calling is often described as a "numbers game." (Perhaps it should be called a "timing game.")

Step #3

Once the Buyer has completed his or her research, he or she will start to reach out and contact potential suppliers of the required products or services. This is where the parallel universes of Buyer and Seller briefly coexist in a single point in space and time, before returning to their disconnected states. If you work for a company that has a strong brand, and it aligns with what the Buyer is looking for, there is a good chance he or she will contact your organization. The same is true if your company is in a specialty niche. For everyone else, it's a lottery unless they have a well-thought-out and well-executed marketing strategy. For organizations that are fortunate enough to be contacted by a potential Buyer, their sales process begins at this point.

Step #4

The Buyer will use knowledge gained from first contact together with available resources and information to determine which suppliers to "short-list." Since the Buyer by now has likely done significant research or has solid recommendations from his or her network of experts, he or she may ask the Seller to complete a questionnaire (the answers of which he or she will compare with the answers of all the other Sellers he or she has contacted or will contact). This is an uncomfortable position for a Seller. It is like being in the witness chair in a court of law. You get to answer the question and only the question that is asked, and don't get to ask any yourself. The Buyer is clearly in control in this case, and the Seller is reacting.

Step #5

The Buyer must next engage with one or more Sellers, but may attempt to carefully control the nature of the engagement to maintain an "arms-length" relationship and protect his or her own time. At some point, for most purchases, the Buyer will have to cozy up a bit more to the Seller in order to find out what he or she doesn't know, get product demos, samples, etc. Hopefully, at this point, if not before, the Seller will be able to begin to establish a more egalitarian and collaborative relationship, for the benefit of both of them.

Step #6

Once the Buyer feels he or she has all the required information from vendors, he or she is ready to make a decision (or not). It would seem at this point that the parallel universes would converge once more, but oddly, it seems they often drift farther apart. Buyers require help making decisions, particularly when fear of risk holds them back. But they often recoil instead, depriving them of a resource, the Seller, who might be able to help address their concerns.

Of course, as we know, decisions do eventually get made and sales are closed. So the picture I am painting may seem unrealistically grim. Or is it? The majority of sales opportunities that go into the sales pipeline never come out the other end. What happens to them? They end up in a state called *No Decision*[2] or *Status Quo*. It's hard to know why without understanding what's going on in the Buyer's universe.

Double Sales Without *Increasing Marketing or Sales Expenses*

According to sales experts, a salesperson's number-one competitor, figuratively and statistically, is **No Decision** or **Status Quo**. Did you know that, across the sales spectrum, more opportunities are lost to No Decision than all other competitors combined? For example, in the information technology (IT) industry, when a Buyer makes a decision, a Seller has a 50% chance of it being favorable, and a 50% chance it will be unfavorable (favorable for a competitor). These sound like pretty good odds for a Seller, don't they? They do, until you realize that *only 30% of Buyers make a decision by the end of the sales process. 70% of sales are lost to No Decision or Status Quo*.

The math is fairly straightforward in this case; every time you get a Buyer to make a decision, you win a customer half the time. These are good odds. If you increase the frequency of a Buyer making any decision by the end of the sales process from 30% to 60%, *you will double your sales, without increasing the number of leads that come into the pipeline or the costs that would accompany such an increase in leads.*

It's good that we now know who the *real* competitor is.

Inputs and Outputs

The input to our simplified Buying process is a need that rises to a priority that will be acted upon, accompanied by the financial resources to make a purchase to address the need. This need is often stated in the form of a current problem, potential problem, or opportunity. The output of the Buying process is (ideally) a solution to the Buyer's problem.

Dependencies

The Buyer is dependent on research (including available personal and social networks) to help identify a potential solution provider. If this is not fruitful and the Buyer can't figure out from Web-based research whom to call, the process might end there or be put at a lower priority than another important project that is not as challenging to address. In that case, the lucky salesperson mentioned previously may never be contacted.

The Buyer is also dependent on the Seller while in the engagement stage. The risk for the Buyer here is that he or she doesn't know what he or she doesn't know. If the Buyer demands tight control of the process and preserves an aloof approach to the relationship to the Seller, he or she may miss out on learning about potential solutions that can help.

Finally, the Buyer is dependent on finding a solution that he or she can defend the purchase of. If the Buyer is not confident that the solutions he or she has uncovered and spent time learning about will indeed solve the problem at hand, he or she may bring No Decision into the process. This is unfortunate, because while there was a will to solve a problem, the process didn't quite provide a way. The Buyer's problem will remain unsolved for another day

Key Takeaways from Chapter 13

1. *There are five basic steps to a simplified purchasing process.*

2. *There are inputs to and outputs from each step of the process.*

3. *Each step is dependent on something being completed in a previous step.*

4. *No Decision or Status Quo is the biggest competitor sales-people have.*

Chapter 14

Step By Step

Deliverables

Each process step has a "deliverable." Simply put, a deliverable is what the widget (in the case of producing a physical product) or intangible (in the case of delivering a service) is supposed to look like at the end of each process step. It includes all the characteristics that the widget would have (such as being a certain color after a painting process) or a service would provide (such as a diagnostic result after completing a medical screening test process).

All repeatable processes require inputs into their process to be within certain parameters or "specifications," in order for them to go through the process and to ensure a predictable output each time. When the inputs to a process are not within these parameters (referred to as "out-of-tolerance"), we say there is a quality problem.

In mass-production employed in high-volume manufacturing for most of the twentieth century, quality problems between process steps were often not discovered until late in the production process, if not at the very end. This has proven to be very wasteful, because significant value has been added to a widget or service that is defective and will either have to be reworked to meet post-production quality standards, or discarded as scrap. It is also wasteful because it requires specialists who are members of a "quality department" to ensure that widgets meet manufacturing standards, as well as highly skilled labor from a "rework department" to try to salvage defective products by attempting to correct production (or raw material) defects.

In Lean production systems, there is a concept called "error-proofing" that aims to ensure that the input to a process is never out of specification or contains a quality problem. In fact, in a Lean process, if a quality problem is detected at any point in the process, *the entire production process stops until the cause of the problem is identified and corrected so it won't happen again.* This prevents bad quality parts from being propagated through the production line, and it also eliminates the classic mass-manufacturing quality department as well as the required rework. Neither is needed anymore.

You might find this information interesting but might also be wondering how it relates to sales. The connection is that **once we accept the fact that sales is a process, then all the Lean improvements and best practices that have been developed to dramatically improve processes should be applicable to sales processes as well.**

To provide a simple demonstration of this point, let's imagine we have a sales prospect that has been injected into a company's standard sales process. For the sake of illustration, let's assume that this sales prospect is "defective" in some way, so that he or she will *never* be capable of becoming a customer in his or her current form. There could be a myriad of reasons, but to pick a glaring example, let's say he or she lives in or plans to use your organization's creations in a country where it is forbidden by your country's export controls. (This seemed a bit more dramatic than making the problem that he or she didn't have a sufficient budget, or couldn't afford or financially justify your organization's output.)

In any case, regardless of the cause of the misfit, if this person is inserted into the sales process with his or her "quality defect" unrecognized, your organization could spend a lot of time and money adding value to a defective input. Unfortunately, at the end of a long costly process, you will not have a new customer, regardless of how hard you worked and how brilliant your efforts were. All will be wasted.

Now, I'm sure most sales organizations ask qualifying questions up front that would eliminate many of these obvious nonconformities. Still, I know that many organizations find out only at the end of their sales process that a prospect has been a misfit from Day One and should never have gotten into the sales process.

This is the reason why the input quality is as important (if not more important) than the output quality, when it comes to processes. Every process step should "error-proof" the output of the previous step and not allow quality problems to flow through the system. To clarify: this is not just at the first step of the process. It's at *every* step.

Referring back to Illustration 1 from Chapter 12, let's say a Buyer suddenly and unexpectedly requests a detailed proposal that will require significant investment of time (and time is money) from your organization to prepare properly. For argument's sake, let's also say that delivering a proposal should be contained within the Close process of our simple illustration. If the Buyer has not completed the Develop process to our "specification," then to move the Buyer into the Close process would be to allow a quality problem to be propagated. If we believe in our process (and we do, or we wouldn't follow it) then that can't be a good thing.

We are unlikely to get the result we are looking for at the end of the process, which is a sale. In fact, our failure to stop and correct the quality problem will likely *reduce* the chance of winning the business. Further, this scenario portends "salvaging" by a "rework team," which may be successful, but which may also inevitably result in the loss of the business and the investment that went into it. I believe most organizations and individual salespeople have experienced something similar to this scenario.

Therefore, deliverables are important because they demand the formulation of very specific expectations at every point between process steps. In Lean systems, there is an inviolable organizational commitment not to continue to move quality defects (anything that does not meet the documented expectations of the deliverables) along in the process. Let's take a look at some potential examples of deliverables, starting with the key steps of a sale.

Illustration 1: Five Key Steps of a Sale

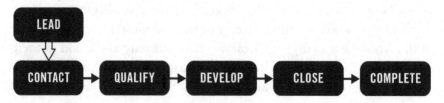

Lead → Contact

When a lead is passed to the salesforce, there should be very specific criteria it has to meet. The person delivering the lead (e.g., marketing department or lead-generation team), and the person receiving the lead (sales manager or salesperson) must have identical specifications as to what characteristics this lead must have to enter the sales process. Some examples for a business-to-business transaction might include:

- **Geographic location (country, state, province)**
- **Company revenue (greater than and/or less than $X)**
- **Number of employees (greater than and/or less than N)**
- **Industry (included / excluded)**
- **Purchase timeframe (# of months)**
- **Title or organizational level of lead (Director, VP, CEO)**

This list of qualifying criteria can be as short or long as makes sense. It shouldn't be so long that it would eliminate every customer you currently have, but it shouldn't be so short as not to eliminate those that have historically shown to be unlikely to buy from your organization.

So a specification for a lead deliverable might read something like the following: "A person at a director level or above, with headquarters in the U.S., in an organization with annual revenues between $50 and $500 million and 100 to 1000 total employees, which supplies components to the aerospace or medical products industry, and who is looking to make a purchase decision within 90 days." The supplier of the lead certifies that, to his or her knowledge, the lead meets all these criteria. The receiver of the Lead (the Seller) may have additional qualifications to complete during an initial conversation with the lead, but in this example these are the minimum criteria for a lead to get into the sales pipeline.

Incidentally, even if the lead does not meet all the criteria, it is not necessarily discarded or ignored. It can be passed on to another sales group that works with smaller (or larger) companies or to an international distributor, for instance.

Contact → Qualify

Once the lead is accepted, a salesperson will have to reach out to the lead and either establish live contact or set up an appointment to do so. If the sales process is very simple, and purchases are of insignificant amounts, it is possible that this can be done electronically. Example deliverables at the end of the Contact process are:

- **Seller has made contact with Lead.**

- **Lead is willing to schedule time for deeper discussions with the Seller about requirements.**

These would appear to be logical minimum requirements to move to the Qualify step. If the Seller is unable to make contact with or get a response from the lead, or the lead is unwilling to engage in deeper discussions, then there isn't any practical way the Seller can qualify the lead.

Qualify → Develop

Some example deliverables from the Qualify process step might be:

- **Confirmation that lead does indeed meet the minimum specifications required to be a lead.**

- **Confirmation that the lead has sufficient other characteristics of a serious candidate to make a purchase.** (These may be beyond the go / no-go criteria first used to screen the lead for entering the sales process and will be unique to each organization. This is where judgment and experience of a salesperson come into play, but this information still can be quantified, for example, by using a simple scoring system or other rubric.)

Develop → Close

The Develop stage can be the most variable in terms of its fluidity and length, which will depend on many factors. These include the complexity (technical or regulatory) of the product or service, its price, and its strategic importance to the Buyer's organization. Regardless of how involved this process is, the deliverable will be similar across many different types of sales situations. For example, the deliverables could be (Buyer here refers to either an individual or buying team):

- **The Buyer has expressed a preference for your organization's product or service.**
- **The Buyer can clearly enunciate the justification for that preference**
- **The Buyer is ready to make a decision to purchase and has the authority to make that decision**
- **The Buyer has or can get the funding to purchase**
- **There are no potential legal issues unresolved**

Close → Completed

Some of the more obvious deliverables of the Close process will be one or more of the following, depending on the type of product or service being purchased:

- **Signed contract**
- **Check or purchase order or credit card**
- **Schedule for delivery**
- **List of any preparations the Buyer's organization has to make prior to delivery, along with an action plan to complete them**
- **List of any installation, customization, or training that the Seller's organization must provide post-delivery, along with an action plan to complete them**

Completed

We now come to our final list of deliverables. Requirements organizations may have before they classify a sale as completed could include:

- **Everything the Buyer and Seller organizations committed to complete pre- and post-sale has been successfully finished.**
- **The product or service is working at the customer's locations**

and delivering the value the Buyer expected and the Seller committed to.

- **The Buyer organization pays for the product or service timely and in full.**

- **The Buyer is willing to serve as a reference for the Seller and his or her organization.**

That covers the five key steps of a simplified sale. Remember, however, that there is also a Buying process we outlined in the previous chapter and graphically described in Illustration 3. I suspect that Buyers may be less inclined to think about what they are doing as a process, but that doesn't mean that it doesn't qualify as one.

In Chapter 8 we defined a process as a series of steps or activities that someone follows in order to create something. **Is there something a Buyer wants to produce with the Buying process? Yes; it is a confident purchase *decision*.** Clearly, there are certain steps a Buyer must follow to get to that point, even if he or she is not consciously aware of them at the beginning of the Buying process. Might the Buying process have deliverables as well?

As it turns out, there are indeed deliverables in the Buying process. The Buyer—unless "buying" is his or her primary job—is unlikely to think about the output of each step as a deliverable. However, it would behoove the Seller to think about them that way, and also for the Seller to coach the Buyer on thinking that way, as we will learn in just a bit. What then might these deliverables be? Let's go through each Buying process step as we did with the sales process to see what they might look like.

Illustration 3: Six Key Steps of a Purchase

Need → Action

The very first thing that kicks off a Buying process is the awareness of a need, a belief that there is potential resolution, and a decision to do something about it. The Buyer could be delegated the responsibility to buy something by executive decision, or by his or her own decision. Also, there could be a latent need that a marketing or cold-calling activity brings to the forefront.

Buyers will not act to seek a solution unless they believe one exists. This is a typical reaction when Buyers don't have the confidence that a problem can be solved or don't know how to solve it. **Marketing and other lead-generation activities can challenge Buyers' limiting beliefs and give them hope, thereby creating a Buying process where there was none before.**

The Buyer will have to have some idea what problem he or she is aiming to solve before he or she will know what action to take. So then, examples of "deliverables" at this step might be:

- **Description of problem or need**
- **A list of who is affected by the problem**
- **Estimates of the hard (measurable) and soft (difficult to measure, but important) benefits of addressing the need**
- **A list of who will use any ultimate solution**
- **A timeframe for having something in place to address the need**

A Buyer may or may not take such a systematic approach to Buying, depending on how frequently he or she has gone through this process. Many Buyers never think to ask these basic questions. Fortunately, there are Sellers who can coach them through this process. Unfortunately, the Seller coach may not know about the Buyer requirement, and the Buyer probably doesn't know that coaching is available. The Buyer also may not realize that there is a fairly standard process to follow.

Action → Research

The Buyer must come up with an action plan for making a Buying decision within the required timeframe. Before he or she can move to the next step, the Buyer must have something resembling the following set of deliverables. These may not be documented, but should be. This is another opportunity for the Seller acting as a coach to add value to the Buying process, assuming the Seller somehow manages to get involved at this early stage.

- **Places to look for providers of the type of solution sought**
- **The amount of time that will be spent researching**
- **Potential people within the Buyer's organization or personal network who might help find a potential provider**
- **How the research will be done**
- **What information the research should provide**

How many Buyers do you think take this type of systematic approach to Buying? If they did, do you think they would be more successful Buyers? If you, as a Seller (and Buyer's Coach) taught them how to do this, do you think the Buyer would value this service? Do you think the Buyer would think of you differently than the other myriad salespeople they might come in contact with during this Buying process?

Research → Contact

At the end of the Research step, the Buyer should have a deliverable that is a list resembling the following:

- **Information on which vendors appear able to meet minimum product or service requirements**
- **A rough estimate of the cost of each vendor or at least a ranking from least to most expensive**
- **Public or personal (network or social media) reviews and testimonials about the vendors**
- **Location of vendor (if applicable)**
- **Experience of vendor working with similar companies or on similar problem areas**

This information deliverable will enable the Buyer to eliminate vendors from contention and begin to reach out to the remaining ones to complete a next level of screening, evaluation, and ranking to decide which vendors to engage more deeply with.

Unless your organization's marketing or lead-generation activities uncover a potential Buyer earlier in the Buying cycle, the first time you, as a salesperson, may know about an opportunity is when the Buyer contacts you. Of course, you could have already been eliminated as a potential supplier by now, rightly or wrongly. In that case, you might never even know that there was an opportunity. However, if you, or your organization, are fortunate enough to get that inquiry call from a Buyer, this will be your first chance to coach the Buyer. How? Simply by working with the Buyer to complete the remaining list of deliverables in the following process steps that the Buyer didn't realize was required.

Start Coaching ASAP

If you think that being a Buyer's Coach is a cool idea, then the sooner you start the better. Why wait until a Buyer contacts you? By then he or she may have done some research and come to some silly conclusions simply because you weren't there to help!

It would be much better if you could get connected with Buyers when they are first starting their Buying process. How can you do that? It's called Marketing. If you have a clear idea what your ideal Buyer looks like and where to find him or her, then the right marketing campaign can help ensure that you will be the first person he or she contacts to ask for help and ideas.

What's that? You say you don't know what your ideal Buyer looks like or where to find him or her? Then you have some work to do, quickly. Make an appointment right away to talk to the person in charge of your marketing team (hopefully it's not you) and ask them for their help in figuring it out. There's no time to waste!

Contact → Qualify

Okay. You are in touch with a Buyer and it is your first (and best) opportunity to put on your coaching hat and see how it fits. The chances are that your Buyer hasn't quite realized that he or she is in a Buying process that has defined steps, let alone thought about the importance of creating a list of deliverables for each step. These are things that the vast majority of Buyers may never think about at this early stage of the Buying process.

However, since you are a Buyer's Coach you know that the Buyer will require a deliverable at the end of the initial contact, which will be a requirement to successfully execute the next step in the Buying process, the Qualify stage. This deliverable is a predetermined plan of how they are going to determine which vendors to eliminate and which to keep after contacting them. It should contain items like the following:

- **Minimum criteria to qualify as a vendor**

- **Additional beneficial, but not required, vendor criteria, ranked in order of importance to the Buyer and his or her organization**

- **How the Buyer is going to confirm where each vendor stands on each of these criteria**

Sure, it's a lot of work to coach a Buyer on this, and you are adding tremendous, unexpected value for the Buyer in doing so. However, don't you want to know the answers to these questions anyway before you engage with the Buyer?

Qualify → Engage

If the deliverable from the last stage was done correctly, then the Buyer should now have what he or she requires for making a decision regarding the vendors he or she wants to engage with in deeper discovery. This is in the form of the deliverable which documents where each vendor stands against the list of requirements and preferences developed in the previous stage. In addition, before entering the Engage stage, the list of deliverables must be expanded to include:

- **What the Buyer hopes to gain through engagement with vendors on further discovery of products, services, and organization**

- **How the Buyer plans or would like to do this discovery**

- **How much time the Buyer is going to allocate to the process**

- **How much participation the Buyer wants from the vendor**

- **How long the Buyer wants the process to take**

At this stage, a Seller coaching a Buyer to explicitly define these items will help avoid an open-ended Engage process without a clear deliverable. Now, let's take a look at what the deliverable is at the end of the Engage process for the Buyer.

Engage → Decide

At this point, the Buyer has completed research, built relationships with one or more potential vendors, and there is only one thing left for the Buyer to do: make a decision. So, it would seem only natural that our list of deliverables at this stage would be focused on what the Buyer requires to make a confident, timely decision.

- **List of participants (if more than an individual) who will make the decision on vendor selection**

- **How that decision will be made**

- **When it will be made**

- **Whether there is anything required from the Seller organization (such as technical specifications, site visit, or a proposal)**

As with the earlier Engage stage, the Decide stage has a propensity to get bogged down frequently, with an indeterminate end. This list of deliverables can help the Seller coach the Buyer to a decision.

Decide

Hopefully, the Buyer will see your value as a Seller that goes beyond the product or service your organization provides and make a decision to purchase from you. The list of deliverables at the end of this stage will be what both the Buyer and Seller are required to prepare in order to facilitate the completion of a successful Buying process. These can include:

- **When any required paperwork (such as contracts or purchase orders) will be delivered**

- **A timeframe for when the product or service will be delivered**

- **A list of actions that the Buyer and Seller organization must take pre- and post-delivery to ensure a successful implementation**

Even in the unfortunate (and, hopefully rare) case that—despite the fine work the Seller has done as a Buyer's Coach—the Buyer decides for a valid reason to buy from someone else, you will have still successfully done your job as a Seller *as long as the Buyer makes a decision*. **Remember, your biggest competitor is always *No Decision* or *Status Quo*.**

Handoffs

If we compare the sales process in Illustration 1 to the purchase process of Illustration 3, we can see some parallels, literally and figuratively.

Illustration 4: Parallel Universes

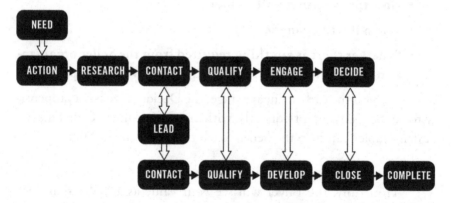

We see that Buyer and Seller universes first converge at the point of initial contact. From that time on, the Buyer and Seller are co-participants in each other's processes, as mentioned earlier. However the Buyer and Seller came to first find out about each other and make initial contact, it is clear that they will have to work together to complete the rest of the process as outlined here. This, then, raises the questions of *how* they work together, which has brought us to the current topic of handoffs.

First, what are handoffs? Think of a relay race where a baton is passed to a team member. The baton receiver must secure the baton before he or she can make his or her run. In this case, imagine the Buyer and Seller are the only runners, and they pass the baton back and forth each lap until the race is complete.

Illustration 5: A Relay Race

If we look back at Illustration 4, we see there must be handoffs wherever the process steps require interactions between the Buyer and Seller. Let's look at each of these interactions in turn.

Contact ↔ Contact

Here we have the usual pleasantries, exchange of contact information and determination of best ways to communicate. Generally, this is an appropriate time for some background about the Buyer situation and *brief* overview of the Seller's organization to be shared. However, the Seller's objective should be to get into coaching mode as quickly as possible. The Seller has to have his or her eye on the deliverable of this Contact stage, as listed earlier. The Seller should focus his or her efforts on helping the Buyer complete that deliverable in the initial call. That's about it. Once the deliverable is completed, the Seller should request and secure another time for them to discuss how his or her organization stacks up against the list they have just developed (the Buyer's Qualify stage).

If the Seller allows the Buyer to move into the Buyer's Qualify stage without completing the deliverable for the Contact stage, we have a quality problem, and the process must stop. For the Seller to participate in a Buyer's Qualify process without this deliverable will not be doing the Buyer any favor.

Remember, coaches are supposed to help people do the right things that will support their goals. How can a Buyer make a decision in the Qualify stage on which vendors to continue to work with, if he or she hasn't first clarified what he or she is looking for in a vendor, and how he or she will determine which vendor has it?

Qualify ⟷ Qualify

In the session where Buyer and Seller are going to qualify each other, the Buyer now has his or her list or agenda (that the Seller helped him or her create) and the Seller also has his or her list of what he or she is looking for in a Buyer. Of course, the Seller is now prepared to address the requirements of the Buyer in some detail and offer some proof (documentary, technical, social, or other) that his or her organization can indeed meet the minimum criteria, and possibly some preferred criteria as well.

If there is something the Buyer is looking for (either on the mandatory or "nice-to-have" list) that will be difficult or impossible for the Seller to provide, this would be a good time for the Seller to confirm how firm the requirement is, or how important the additional beneficial criteria are. There is no point in proceeding down the path of a costly sales process if you have little or no chance of meeting the minimum Buyer criteria, or several of the important optional ones. If you happen to *know* (because you did your research before the call, which wouldn't have been possible if you had allowed the Buyer to drag you into Qualify on the first call) that none of the competition can offer these capabilities either, this would be a good time to share that with the Buyer, offer some proof, and see if the Buyer is willing to modify the requirements.

Assuming the Seller has not yet graciously eliminated himself or herself from the opportunity, now is the time for the Seller to go through his or her list of requirements to complete the Seller's Qualify stage, either directly, one by one, or through a process of asking the Buyer questions that should yield the information. Which path to pursue is a question of personal style, but I recommend the latter. A Seller may or may not want to share too much information about his or her own process with the Buyer, if for no other reason than a Lean one: the Buyer may not care about or value that information, at least at this point in time.

It is possible that the Buyer and Seller may each have to go offline and confirm the answers to questions that they asked each other during this stage. Don't be discouraged by this. It is a good thing and establishes credibility that the Seller wants to provide accurate information to the Buyer (not "winging it"), and vice versa. Simply set up another time to address those issues. Remember how important it is to build a relationship that adds value for the Buyer at each step. Increasing trustworthiness is something a Buyer values.

Engage ←→ Develop

The Buyer and Seller must work very closely at this point in the process, and the Seller must make sure that everything is converging toward closure. What the Buyer and Seller do during these stages can vary widely, depending on the type of product or service under consideration. It is very common that the Buyer and Seller ask each other for information, demonstrations, or examples in these stages, each acting as a knowledge and information supplier to the other.

Nevertheless, it is critical that the Seller continues to be a coach to the Buyer, making sure that the previously discussed Buyer deliverables are completed (and shared with the Seller) at each stage of the Buying process. This is in addition to the Seller completing his or her own deliverables for each stage of the Selling process. Remember, the Seller has the responsibility to ensure that at every process step the deliverable from the previous step is of acceptable quality—in both the Selling *and* Buying processes.

Decide ←→ Close

Here we come to the idiomatic (not idiotic) place where the "rubber meets the road." Everything done so far has been to get to the point of a decision. This can be a time of great stress for both Sellers *and* Buyers. It is a time of uncertainty for the Seller that can lead to a feeling of loss of control. For the Buyer, it is mainly about risk: the risk of making a bad, or not the best, decision.

However, the Seller has coached the Buyer through the entire process and the path to a decision is clear to both of them. This can be a time for the Seller to acknowledge the Buyer's feelings of risk and offer ways to mitigate them. The Seller can point to all the fine work they have done together in approaching this decision process in a professional, thorough way.

If the Seller works closely with the Buyer as described here, there shouldn't be many surprises at this point in the process. If there is some hesitancy on the part of the Buyer to move forward, the Seller should ask specifically what that is, and review each step of the plan they previously put in place (the deliverable of the Engage step) in order to facilitate a decision.

Elapsed Time

How long, then, does this entire process take? According to every sales executive or CEO I've ever spoken to, longer than it should. Still, how long should it take? No one seems to have a good answer to that. However, Lean Thinking and Lean Selling do have an answer: no longer than it has to. Then how long does it *have* to take? The only way to answer that question is for a team within the Seller's organization to take a deep dive into these processes to figure that out.

Lean methodologies do not claim to know in advance the minimum time it can take for a process to be completed. It does, however, continuously test the boundaries of how fast things can get done, with a mindset of continuous improvement along with the application of Lean tools and methodologies. I will introduce two of these methodologies here, in wrapping up our discussion of the Buying and Selling processes.

Inventory

Inventory is the buildup of partially or fully completed outputs of a process step, waiting to be processed by the next step. Most of us are familiar with the term "inventory" in the form of finished goods (which have completed a production process and are ready for sale), stored in a warehouse waiting for an order so they can be shipped to a customer. When the buildup in inventory is between steps in the production process, it is called Work-in-Process, or WIP.

☑ *LEAN LEARNINGS*

Minimizing Inventory

Japanese: *Muda* 無駄

Definition

In a production process, it is always preferable to reduce inventory to the minimum amount that will allow a production process to keep flowing without stopping. Excess inventory is a sign of lack of flow and is a source of quality problems. Inventory costs money to create and store, and the greater the amount of inventory any process has, the more of a company's cash there is tied up in it.

There are three primary types of inventory, listed in order from the least to the most expensive type as labor and other costs are added during the production process:

1. **Raw materials**

2. **Work-in-Process (WIP)**

3. **Finished goods**

However, as mentioned above, Lean Thinking states that there are other, even more important, reasons to reduce inventory beyond considerations of cash requirements.

1. **Excess WIP inventory hinders process flow**

2. **All three types of inventory can delay the time it takes to detect quality problems in a process**

Application to Lean Selling

Every Buyer who enters the sales process represents a form of sales pipeline inventory until a sale is completed. The longer the Buyer stays in the sales pipeline, the more investment that has been made in developing the Buyer. Finished goods in this context would be analogous to a Buyer who has been through the entire process but does not move forward to make a Buying decision for whatever reasons. Also, Buyers who stay in the process too long expose it to quality problems such as changing Buyer organization requirements and budget priorities, new competition, and Buyer job change. The shorter the sales cycle, the lower the overall customer acquisition cost, and the less likely it is that external factors will derail the Buying process.

Earlier I conveniently coined the acronym BIP to represent a "Buyer-in-Process" in our simplified sales process; that is, a Buyer who has entered the Contact stage but has not yet made a Buying decision. In order to accelerate a sales cycle or Buying process, Lean Thinking would guide us to eliminate inventory, in our case, BIP, between process steps.

I will provide one example to illustrate the point. Let's say that the Seller has done a superb job of coaching the Buyer through the Buying process, and now the Buyer has successfully completed the deliverable of the Engage process. However, something goes wrong and the Buyer does not move into the Decision process (this seems to be a common occurrence in the real world of sales, by the way).

This would be an example of stagnant BIP inventory. BIP inventory that does not "move" is not a good thing because, as noted before, significant investment has already been made through value added to the Buyer to get to this stage. It is like finished goods or products sitting on a shelf that don't move (sell).

One of our key objectives in creating a Lean Selling™ process will be to keep Buyers moving, from Buying step to Buying step, without hesitation or interruption. Inventory is bad, slows down a process, and is often the cause of quality problems. We must minimize it in every way we can.

Waste

There are many types of waste identified by Lean Thinking. The waste we are the most concerned about in a sales process is wasted time. Wasted time in sales includes the time spent on any activity (by Seller or Buyer) that does not add value to the Buyer making a Buying decision. Every activity in a sales process must be evaluated to determine if it adds value to the Buyer and helps to create the required deliverable in each step in the process. If not, it is waste. If your primary job is sales, one day track the time that you spend on actual selling activities and try to determine how much is wasted and how much is value-added time.

Why Do Sales Take So Long?

Salespeople, their managers, and business executives all want to know why the sales cycle takes so long to complete. There is no one answer everyone agrees with, so the default position is that it just takes as long as it does.

Here are some of the more common theories we hear from salespeople:

- **It takes a long time for people to make a decision.**
- **There are a lot of people involved in the decision to buy and a lot of selling to do.**
- **There are a lot of competing interests for budget.**
- **There are a lot of competitors, and companies have to evaluate the competitors' offerings as well.**

All of these are probably true to some extent, but are they really the cause of a sales cycle that is longer than it has to be?

The problem with all of the above rationalizations is that they lead to an acceptance of the Current State as inevitable and unchangeable, rather than leading to some possible courses of action that could be pursued to change it. Here are some alternative theories that Lean Thinking would have us consider:

- **The sales process started too soon.**
- **The sales process started before the Buyer was ready.**
- **The Buyer didn't know what he or she actually required.**
- **The Seller didn't fully understand what the customer required.**
- **The Buyer doesn't know how to make a decision.**
- **There was a lot of time wasted waiting in the process when things were not moving forward.**

If we try to fix a problem without knowing what the underlying causes of the problem truly are, then we will not make much progress, or we could make it worse. **Ask your sales team how many of these Lean Thinking explanations they believe might be applicable.** Then you can start talking about how you might empower your salespeople to get more control over the length of the sales cycle.

Let's start with how salespeople are spending their time. According to industry experts, the average salesperson spends between 20–40% of available time actually selling. What do the salespeople do with the rest of their time? Well, from a quarter to half of their time is spent prospecting (finding new business), and a similar amount on administrative tasks.[1, 2] Is there an opportunity to **use Lean Thinking to analyze how time spent on prospecting and administrative tasks (more than 50% of available selling time) can be reduced, thereby freeing up that time for Selling? The impact could be equal to doubling the size of your salesforce!**

The other form of wasted time is related to inventory. Every time there is inventory (BIP) at the beginning of a process step, there is waiting time, which is waste. One of the main reasons sales cycles take so long is that there is so much waiting time between or within steps. One foundational Lean methodology calculates the percentage of all time spent creating value in a sales process divided by the elapsed time of the entire process.

As mentioned before, this can be a very small percentage. Why? It is, I believe, because the same problems that have plagued mass manufacturing processes and mass service delivery processes also bring sales processes to their knees. Only Lean Thinking and a Lean approach to addressing the current waste in sales processes can effectively address this problem. The end result of this transformation is called the **Lean Selling System**.

Key Takeaways from Chapter 14

1. *Every step of the sales process should have a specific output, or deliverable.*

2. *There are various handoffs between Buyers and Sellers in the sales process, analogous to a relay race.*

3. *Lean methodologies aim to reduce the length of the sales cycle by reducing waste.*

4. *Sales processes create inventory when they have wait times, and this is an indication there is waste in the process.*

Chapter 15

How to Synchronize Buyers and Sellers

In Chapter Fifteen
→ Buyer-Seller Communication
→ Sales Process Goal Setting
→ Clarifying Buyer Requirements
→ Expectations and Commitments

Communication

As with most relationships, good communication is the basis for a successful relationship between Buyers and Sellers. The different types of communication that Buyers and Sellers engage in can be quite varied and demanding. It can include the following topics:

- **Narrative of the need or problem the Buyer wants to address and why**

- **Technical description of the Buyer's product or service requirements**

- **Value proposition of the Seller's organization**

- **Features, functions, and benefits of the Seller's product or service**

Additionally, it is important for the Seller to listen carefully on many levels, not only to what the Buyer is saying, but also what he or she is feeling. In a face-to-face meeting (or video conference), the Seller can observe and interpret body language and facial expressions.

With dialogs either in person or over the phone, and even with voicemail messages, a Seller should listen carefully to voice intonation to assess the feeling behind the words, not just the words themselves. What should a Seller be listening for? Buyer emotion. Correctly reading the emotional components of Buyer communication can give the Seller insight into not only the mind, but also the heart of the Buyer in these important psychological areas:

- **Level of commitment**
- **Comfort or discomfort** (in general or with a specific topic under discussion or question)
- **Fear** (usually about making the wrong decision or not being able to make a decision, looking bad with peers, or damaging his or her career)
- **Risk perception** (usually a manifestation of underlying fears)

Every one of these dynamics can significantly affect the likelihood of a Buyer making a decision. Also, as we have already repeatedly established, the primary purpose of the Selling process is to get the Buyer to make a decision. Therefore, it is important for a Seller to be sensitized to—and watching and listening for—clues as to where the Buyer stands emotionally.

Establishing Goals

There are many opportunities in a sales process for the Buyer and Seller to better understand one another. A very effective method for accelerating that process is the mutual establishment of goals that Buyer and Seller are working toward. Typically, these will be in the form of milestones with dates attached to them, as well as a notation of the responsibilities of each of the parties for reaching the milestone. Examples of milestones can include:

- **Creating a shortlist of potential vendors by __/__/__**
- **Finalizing product requirements by __/__/__**
- **Completing legal review and signoff by __/__/__**
- **Complete product demonstration and assessment of customization required by __/__/__**

These are just a few examples. The Seller should think about all the things that have to be done before the Buyer can make a decision and write them down in the form of milestones, with a blank next to each of them for the date (similar to as shown above). Leave a space for the name of who is responsible for meeting the date.

Show the list to your Buyer. Let him or her work with you on adding additional items the Buyer believes he or she will have to complete before he or she is able to make a decision. Work together with your Buyer to fill in the dates. If this collaboration is done in a thoughtful way, without shortcuts and not in a superficial way, the Seller should be in a position to make a preliminary assessment of a target date for a Buyer decision. Write it down in big numbers and letters. This will become the overarching goal that will guide the relationship until a decision is made.

These milestone dates can serve as the foundation of creating a "Buying Plan" with your Buyer. What is a Buying Plan? It's the analog of a Seller's sales plan, but for the Buyer. It's time for the Seller to put that coaching hat on again if it is not on already. **Very few salespeople, in the early stages of the sales cycle, take the time to gain commitment from, and build a relationship with, the Buyer through working on a "Buying Plan."** A Buying Plan can document all the anticipated steps and resources that will be required for a Buyer to make a Buying decision by your mutually-agreed-to target date. Oh, and don't forget to have both the Buyer and Seller sign the plan and date it.

Clarifying Requirements

One of the greatest areas of opportunity for misunderstanding between Buyers and Sellers is in the area of the specific requirements for a product or service. One of the main causes for this is that while most Buyers *generally* know what they want, they don't really know *specifically* what they want. Also, unless your Buyer has an engineering degree (and sometimes even then) he or she may not be "wired" to clearly specify requirements in the form that your organization would like to see them in.

This is a well-recognized problem across industries, and for years, the antidote was thought to be the creation of an all-encompassing, detailed specification. First of all, unless you are in a business that involves, or resembles, government procurement, you are unlikely to see anything describing requirements that comprehensive from a Buyer. Second, it would be prohibitively expensive to do so for most purchases. Third, if the Buyer did create one, it would still have errors and omissions, and things "we didn't think about." Fourth, it would take so long to complete it that by the time it was finished, the requirements would already be obsolete for most businesses.

This is why so much purchasing is focused on buying "off-the-shelf" products and services, to avoid creating a specification for a custom solution. The customization burden then shifts to "fitting" a product or service within the Buyer's organization, and identifying any configuration that may need to be done to a standard product or service.

A Lean approach takes a different tack. First of all, an overarching goal of Lean processes is to get required steps done as efficiently as possible without sacrificing quality or variety. Efficiency includes both eliminating waste and speeding up processes. ***Shortening a sales cycle from nine months to six weeks, for example, greatly reduces the chances that the original solution the Buyer envisioned (or problem that led him or her to contact you) or the solution you proposed will become obsolete during the sales process.*** It also minimizes the chances of experiencing a disturbing pattern of sales that may be uniquely American: decision-makers changing responsibilities or companies in the middle of a sales cycle. The longer a sales process takes, the greater the chances of that happening.

What's Your Story?

Here's an idea I borrowed from Lean Software development that the Seller can use as a tool to synchronize with the Buyer. In software development, one of the major process quality challenges is software engineers not having an accurate or complete understanding of user requirements. The second challenge is an outcome of this: users rarely get what they wanted or expected when the software is delivered.

The way that Lean Software development attacked this chronic issue head-on was with a knowledge-gathering tool called a "User Story," a brief vignette of what a user wants to be able to do with the software. A User Story becomes a micro-specification, and the collection of dozens and dozens of these User Stories ultimately form the complete specification for a software release. It's a simple but powerful solution to an age-old problem of getting software developers and the ultimate users of the software on the same page (literally and figuratively).

This idea can be adapted to Lean Selling™ in order to get Buyers and Sellers on the same page as well. A Seller can steadily build a complete set of Buyer requirements from a series of brief "Buyer Stories" about what the Buyer wants to be able to do or what problem he or she wants to resolve once your product or service arrives on the scene. Not only will the Seller be adding tremendous value by helping the Buyer to clarify and refine his or her requirements, but the Seller will also ultimately likely be the only vendor that really understands what those Buyer requirements are.

Expectations and Commitments

Most salespeople don't ask for commitments from Buyers or ask them about their expectations for them. Even more rarely will a salesperson tell the Buyer what his or her expectations of the Buyer are! Why is that? Is the salesperson afraid of pushing the Buyer away?

Does he or she think he or she hasn't earned the right to ask such questions or share such thoughts?

These are limiting beliefs that a Seller should disabuse himself or herself of. Verbalizing expectations and asking for commitments puts a Seller at a peer level with the Buyer. It immediately establishes his or her role as a value-provider and potentially as a coach as well as a partner. As a Seller you have to quickly establish that you likely know more about the "process" of Buying than he or she does, since you do this for a living. That, and also because you have read this book!

Don't Buyers expect Sellers to do what they committed to do, whether it's showing up for a meeting on time, or delivering information that was promised when it was promised? Do you hold your Buyers to the same standard? Why not? Creating a Buying Plan will be a meaningless exercise unless the Buyer and Seller take the milestones, dates, and responsibilities seriously. The "Make a Decision" date is critical, but if the Seller nonchalantly accepts slippage in the milestone dates (and the excuses that accompany them), your decision date is no longer real because there is no commitment to it, on the part of the Buyer *or the Seller.*

Tools for Synchronization

We have already discussed several tools that Sellers can use to create synchronization with Buyers. These include the collaborative creation of deliverables and receipt of handoffs for each step of the process, the mutual creation of goals, milestones, and dates, and the shared creation of a Buying Plan.

Still, by definition, synchronization is not a one-time event. All of these items are part of a living plan. As new information is gathered, new requirements are uncovered and new challenges emerge. All of these commitments and plans should be collaboratively modified to establish a new working plan. This continuous interaction of Buyer and Seller on specific agreements and commitments will provide a platform for synchronization. Synchronize well and often!

Key Takeaways from Chapter 15

1. *Synchronizing the Selling process with the Buying process is a critical key to success.*

2. *Sellers should be assertive with Buyers about setting goals, clarifying requirements, and gaining commitment.*

3. *There are tools a Seller can employ to ensure synchronization with a Buyer, such as a Buying Plan.*

Chapter 16

An Integrated Buying and Selling Process

In Chapter Sixteen
→ A Shared Buying-Selling Process
→ Building Quality into the Process
→ Making Closing Predictable

One Process, Two Participants

At this point we have looked in detail at a simplified Selling process, a simplified Buying process, and where the two intersect. We have enumerated several ways that Buyers and Sellers can synchronize their efforts at every step in the process in order to keep a Buying decision on track. We especially focused on the shared stages of the processes, which are represented graphically in Illustration 6.

Illustration 6: Shared Process Stages

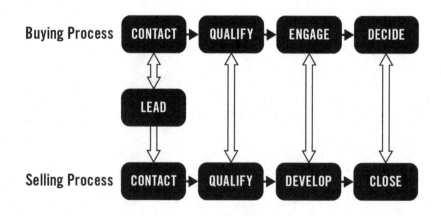

What if we were to create a graphical representation of the combination of the two? This would drive home the point that these steps are not really parts of two different processes, but rather the same process with a responsibility for execution that is shared between Buyer and Seller. We have implied this concept before, but a graphic would make it more explicit. If we then add back the unique steps that Buyer and Seller execute by themselves, we would be able to represent a single new process, called the Buying-Selling Process. This newly-minted process is shown in Illustration 7.

Illustration 7: The Buying-Selling Process

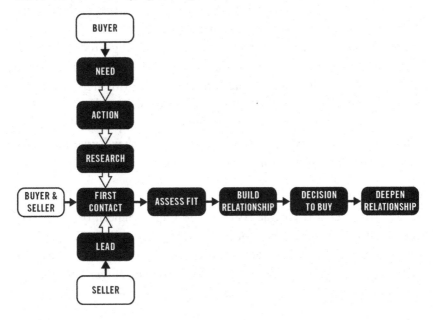

You may notice that the four steps of the process shared between Buyer and Seller have been renamed to be more generic and less specific to what a Buyer or Seller would do individually. This graphic shows that a new Buying-Selling opportunity starts with a Need (Buyer) and a Lead (Seller), which then converge at First Contact.

First Contact

Called Contact in the unmerged versions, this is the first time a Buyer and Seller have the opportunity to come together. Each is coming for a different reason, but from this point on, both will work together toward achieving their mutual goals.

Assess Fit

Previously called Qualify, this is the stage when Buyer and Seller try to determine whether they are right for each other. Each comes to this stage with a different set of criteria, but in the end they must mutually agree to work together.

Build Relationship

Formerly referred to as Engage (Buyer) and Develop (Seller), this description better encompasses what goes on during this stage. There may be many activities in this step, but they are all geared toward creating a relationship between the Buyer and Seller, their organizations, and the product or service. What happens during this step can have as much or more influence on the Buying decision than the actual product or service itself. What happens during this step should be a *true collaboration to create something new that neither Buyer nor Seller could create without the other.*

Buying Decision

Earlier termed Decide (Buyer) and Close (Seller), this new term keeps the focus on what the process is about, while reinforcing that it is a shared responsibility. The Seller has to do everything he or she can to support the making of a Buying decision, and the Buyer has to follow through on everything he or she has committed to do.

Deepen Relationship

This new process step replaces Completed for the Seller, driving home the point that this new process is not just a transaction that ends with a Buying decision, but rather a potentially long-term, rewarding affiliation that can yield benefits for both parties into the future. For the Seller, deepening this relationship starts with the delivery and successful deployment of a promised product or service, and for the Buyer, it opens the possibility of having an ongoing, trusted resource.

☑ *LEAN LEARNINGS*

Error-Proofing

Japanese: *Poke Yoka* ポカ避け

Definition

Error-proofing is building into processes appropriate types of systems and checks that prevent a defect from being propagated through the process. We sometimes colloquially call this "idiot proofing," making absolutely sure someone can't make a mistake.

Application to Lean Selling

If we think about how often salespeople reject leads that are provided by marketing or another lead-generation group as "unqualified," we can see the value of error-proofing. Salespeople are also guilty of propagating quality defects through the sales pipeline when they do not sufficiently qualify Buyers at each step of the process for "readiness" to go to the next stage. Error-proofing can address these quality problems by, for example, making sure that prospects are not entered into the sales funnel if they don't meet minimum criteria, developed with input from the sales team. Also, salespeople can be tasked to complete a qualification checklist that must be finished and provided to the sales manager before moving a Buyer to the next stage in the process.

Ideally, this relationship can lead to additional opportunities for the Seller to address additional requirements and new needs that arise in the Buyer's organization. Also, the Buyer now has a reliable resource to turn to the next time a need arises, even before beginning his or her research.

Lean Thinking and their implementations have always emphasized long-term relationships between suppliers and customers. Using Lean principles to nurture long-term relationships has been shown to yield phenomenal gains in productivity, efficiency, and quality that short-term, competitive relationships do not. Ideally, the Lean Selling™

paradigm shown in Illustration 8 can yield an ongoing source of revenue for the Seller's organization, and an ongoing source of creative solutions for the Buyer's organization.

Illustration 8: The Lean Selling Process

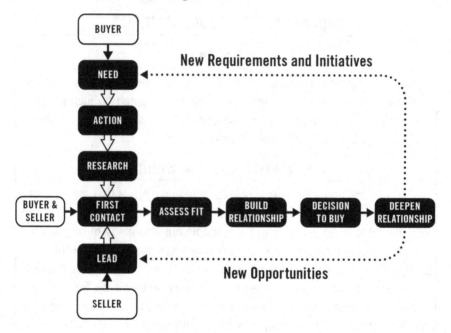

Building in Quality

We have previously discussed the Lean methodology of ensuring that defective output from one process step does not become defective input for the next process step. By using tools such as checking that each process yields the deliverables expected before moving to the next process step, we can ensure the quality of the sales process and improve predictability of the output.

With our new way of looking at the sales process as a Buying-Selling process, as depicted in Illustrations 7 and 8, we have a new opportunity to create joint deliverables at each process step, allowing Buyer and Seller to have visibility into each other's requirements. Previously I advised against a Seller sharing a "Seller's" process with a Buyer; we are beyond that now, since we have one process.

Error-Proofing Customers

Recently my wife and daughter went shopping for a student study desk for my daughter's room. They decided to go to a national retail chain store that is known for having low-cost, value-oriented, self-assembly furniture. They decided on a desk, selected among a set of options for a configuration that included a set of under-table drawers, picked the boxes required (with the brief assistance of a sales associate), and purchased and drove home with the boxes.

When my daughter was nearly finished with the table assembly, she told me she couldn't find the legs. I couldn't either. I went online to see if I could figure it out, but I couldn't. I decided to call the store but couldn't locate a phone number for the store or for support. After about 15 minutes and countless clicks, I found a telephone number to call.

I then waited on hold for 62 minutes (there was no "call me back" option) until someone picked up on the company's national support line. I lost count of how many times I had to listen to a recording telling me how important they considered my call to be. Finally when someone answered, she was pleasant, and after researching my issue for about 10 minutes, she told me that the legs had to be purchased separately. The customer service representative offered to transfer me to another department to order the legs, but I would have to pay shipping, or I could return to the store (which is 45 minutes from my house) to get them. I told her that my family picked the boxes that the sales associate directed them to (or so I was told). For that reason, I was not happy about having to pay a shipping charge (and I had *no* idea how long the wait would be to reach the next department) or doing an hour and a half of unnecessary driving. I asked to speak to a supervisor. Fortunately, I only had to wait an additional five minutes to speak to a supervisor, but she was not able to waive the shipping charge, either.

However, what I really wanted to know from the supervisor was how the company could let a customer purchase a table without legs. Her answer: "Some people already have the legs." Since struggling students comprise some of their customers, I was imagining that one poor soul couldn't afford to the buy the table **and** the legs, so last month he just bought the legs. "Okay," I said. "But why don't you at least ask the customer this question at check-out: 'Hello, ma'am. I see you are purchasing a table without legs. Was that your intention?'" She didn't have an answer to that question.

This entire experience could have been avoided by **error-proofing** the customer buying process. The company's system could be set up to ensure at check-out that a purchased configuration is rational. I have purchased from this store before, and I know it can be very confusing to pick the right components. I **wasted** approximately 90 minutes on a Sunday afternoon trying to resolve the issue because the vendor did not *error-proof* the purchase. That time was worth more to me than the cost of the desk, particularly since it couldn't be replaced. The lesson: error-proof your customers. If they make a mistake because your purchasing process is too complicated or confusing to follow, it will reflect badly on your company's quality of experience. They will blame your company for it, not themselves. And it has a real cost for the customer.

It now seems only natural that the Buyer and Seller would share the same list of deliverables at each stage of the process. This may seem a radical idea, but would you want to undergo a medical procedure if you weren't sure you and your doctor had the same objectives for the outcome?

Transparency is another underlying principle of Lean Thinking. If the people you are depending on don't know what you require or are expecting of them, they are less likely to deliver it. There are additional ways a Lean system yields consistently high quality and predictability. We will cover these in Part IV.

Predictability of Sales Closing

Predictability is a close cousin of quality, in that a high-quality process is also very predictable. Another way of saying something is predictable is that there aren't many surprises. Predictability, also expressed as "forecasting" in sales, is something everyone involved in sales is aware of, and the bane of a sales manager's existence.

It just seems so hard in the real world to wrap your arms around when business that is currently in the sales pipeline will close. The ability to accurately predict sales is very important to a business because it is the major driver of the revenue forecast. As we know, the revenue forecast is what the CEO or president runs the company by.

Still, sales cycles seem to be very unpredictable. That is another way of saying that there are a lot of surprises. Why are there so many surprises? It has to do with poor communication and deficient planning on the part of Buyers and Sellers. Good communication and appropriate, goal-oriented planning does not happen naturally. People require tools to enforce the behaviors that foster this. In the previous two chapters, I have shared a number of these. Using these tools will increase predictability of a sales process and should eliminate most, if not all, surprises. **Sales forecasting may elicit less drama as it becomes more reliable with Lean Selling, but what sales manager or CEO is going to miss the drama?**

Key Takeaways from Chapter 16

1. Buying and Selling should not be two processes, but one.

2. Error-proofing is a way to build quality and reliability into the sales process.

3. Lean Selling methodologies can greatly increase the predictability of sales, often expressed as a forecast.

Chapter 17

The Extended Sales Team

Who Cares About Sales?

Several times already I have mentioned the importance of the sales function, and risked overstating the case by comparing it to an organization's heart or bloodline. Therefore, the title of this section might seem superfluous. Everyone cares about how sales is doing, right? While that is a politically correct statement, unfortunately it's often not the case until there is a revenue crisis and nearly everyone in the organization suddenly feels at some personal risk.

It's not hard to understand how this situation of benign neglect for the sales function has developed. After all, everyone has a job to do, just like salespeople do. Engineers engineer and accountants count. Customer Service personnel provide service, and marketing people market. Production workers produce, managers manage, and executives execute. It seems that, left to its own devices, organizations will devolve into this type of thinking.

This is often referred to as the "silo" effect, where each function is performing its job the best way possible, but the organization is not functioning as one integrated system with a common purpose. In such organizations, there is little sustained cross-communication between functional silos. This leads to all manner of problems and inefficiencies, from missing product delivery dates, to quality problems, to unhappy customers.

The sales department doesn't "work for" the engineering department any more than engineering works for sales. The marketing department doesn't work for the sales department, but neither does the sales department work for marketing. As noted, everyone has a job to do, but in most organizations functional silos create enormous inefficiencies and quality problems that directly impact company profits and market share.

We have already said that nothing happens until something is sold, and that closing sales is where the rubber meets the road. Therefore, it is true that **the sales department has a very unique role in the organization in that it can confirm—or call into question—everything that the company is doing,** through its success or failure.

If a new product doesn't sell as anticipated, is the problem the product, the salespeople who don't understand how to sell it, or an unrealistic forecast (that could have come from anywhere in the organization)? There are sometimes a lot of fingers simultaneously pointing in different directions following new product launches. **The way to stop the finger-pointing is to break down the silos.**

Lean Thinking brings a fresh, revolutionary approach to this twentieth-century-organization problem. It decrees that everything and everyone in the company should focus on one thing: bringing value to the customer. This becomes the unifying mission, the rallying cry that brings people out of their silos to cooperate on a common journey of improving the lives of customers. Yes, the salesperson may be the rubber, and he or she is the closest to the road, but there's a lot sitting on top of the rubber that provides value for the customer.

Who's Supporting Sales?

Salespeople are often thought of as lone wolves, possibly because many operate in offices remote from headquarters and have to largely fend for themselves (sort of like wild beasts). It may also be because salespeople are the first to know when something is not working in the real world and have to quickly adapt if they want to survive. **Organizations rarely give sufficient thought to the tools and support that salespeople require to be effective when they are engaged in a sales process.**

Larger companies generally have a marketing department that is supposed to make the job of salespeople easier, minimally by raising brand awareness so new sales prospects don't think they are from Mars. Really fortunate salespeople work for organizations that make a sustained investment in generating leads so they don't have to spend most of their time cold-calling into accounts. Measuring the effectiveness of marketing and lead generation is an ongoing controversy. Everyone agrees it would be a good thing to do, but few seem to know quite the best way to do it.

Most organizations do not have the data infrastructure that would allow them to analyze the economic benefit of marketing, public relations (PR) and lead-generation activities. The most logical way is to review the history of new sales to ascertain which activity was likely responsible for the lead being generated.

Suppose a lead comes in from a prospect that completed a form on the company website, and the person fails to complete the drop-down box titled, "How did you hear of us?" Should that lead be credited to investments made in the website, or was it the result of one of the other activities driving the prospect to the website? We can see the challenge of getting reliable data that cleanly ties a sale to investment made in a specific lead source.

This type of thinking risks devolving into being reactive and backward-looking. The biggest problem facing most sales organizations today is that there are not enough qualified leads in their target market for them to pursue. (Note that I didn't write that there weren't enough potential prospects, just not enough qualified leads.) However, **companies rarely take the time and effort to figure out how many leads are actually *required* for their salespeople to meet their quotas.** They can't do that without having a predictive sales process (one that generates a consistent metric for the average number of sales or revenue as a percentage of leads) that allows for such a calculation.

There is much more organizations can do to support their sales team. However, without a formalized sales process, it is difficult to know exactly where and how to help change the sales equation. Also, without a focus on creating customer value that starts at the top of the organization, it will be difficult to get everyone working for—and measuring their own success by—the success of the sales team.

Mission Accomplished

Salespeople simply love it when a sales executive or CEO offers to go out and "close" a deal he or she has been working on for a while. The executive almost always returns with a "Mission Accomplished" message and directs the salesperson to "pick up the order." Of course, the salesperson is dutifully thankful. I wonder how many companies keep statistics on how long it takes after the deal is "closed" by an executive to actually get it closed.

If you are keeping any tabs on this, contact me or post on the "Lean Selling" group on LinkedIn® or page on Facebook®.

Is Everyone Playing on the Same Team?

Most people want to believe they are supporting the goals of the organization and are "team" players. The question is, which team are they playing on? The silo effect is very powerful indeed, and can only be broken down (as it needs to be) through transformational change. This is a book about sales, and it can't delve deeply into the complexity, challenges and means of changing corporate culture and reinforcing teamwork, very challenging endeavors indeed. However, **one Lean slogan often used to motivate people to overcome the paralysis caused by complexity is, "Just do it." Another I would add is, "Start somewhere, anywhere."** Lean transformations have a tendency to draw in other functional areas outside of where they originated, breaking down silos as they do so.

This is one of the things I find so exciting about introducing Lean methodologies into an organization: internal behaviors and ways of working together naturally change in order to function in a Lean way. This is not simply driving cultural change for the sake of cultural change. Rather, it is a practical, non-judgmental way of getting everyone focused on the same objective, and doing what it takes to achieve it. This objective is always about delivering more value to the customer, faster and less expensively.

Many people think that Lean transformations yield such unbelievable increases in quality because that is its focus, similar to Six Sigma, a quality initiative developed by Motorola and later adopted by GE that relies on statistical process control. However, that's not true. Lean is always more focused on eliminating waste than achieving a certain quality level. It measures quality improvement, but Six Sigma level of quality eventually comes for free. It is the same with positive cultural change in organizations that undertake a Lean transformation, in any department. Lean Thinking can be contagious and create a virtuous cycle of continuous improvement across an organization.

Lean applications originated in manufacturing, and the implementers were focused on providing more value for the customer by providing more product variety and shorter delivery times. Ironically, as discussed above, the Japanese manufacturers at this time became differentiated from Western manufacturers based on their outstanding reputation for quality, although that was not what their primary objective was. Quality was a side-effect of Lean Production, aiming to resolve the limitations imposed by mass production.

Sales Can Lead the Way

Initially, these improvements were often isolated within the production department and were not spread to other functional areas of the organization. Primarily, they were focused on making a better product.

When Lean Thinking spread to services, it opened a whole new set of possible target areas to which Lean process improvement could be applied. One of the first applications, in the automobile industry, targeted improving the delivery of repair and maintenance service on the products that had been produced in a Lean fashion. The results were at one level different than—and at another level very much the same as—they were for Lean Manufacturing. More value was provided to the customer by reducing the time wasted by customers in getting service, and the inconvenience of quality problems, such as parts required for repair being out of stock.

Once the barrier between a Lean process for tangibles (such as a product) and intangibles (such as a service) was breached, the potential applications for Lean Thinking proved to be nearly unlimited as they spread to such areas as the delivery of health care services and education, both industries in need of a major revolution in thinking.

What I find so promising about Lean Thinking now being applied to Lean Selling™ is that the sales organization is the one that has traditionally been closest to the customer, and the customer is the focus of Lean Thinking. The implications of leveraging the combination of these two facts are enormous. A Lean Selling team, representing the Voice of the Customer, can be the catalyst for a transformation where the entire organization begins to evaluate what it does in terms of the value it adds for a customer. Let the transformation begin!

Key Takeaways from Chapter 17

1. *Everyone in the organization is affected by the performance of the sales team, but not everyone is cognizant of this.*

2. *Management should look carefully at the current support systems and infrastructure to support its salespeople to determine if they are adequate for what is required for the job.*

3. *Management should look for ways to break down functional silos and create multi-functional teams, particularly as related to sales.*

Part IV

Sales as a System

Chapter 18

Teamwork

The Secret Sauce

Teamwork is the secret sauce of Lean implementations. **It is not only about getting teams as currently defined in an organization to work together better.** *It is also about redefining teams around the job that needs to be done.*

The existence of functional silos that we discussed in the previous chapter is largely responsible for the inability of companies to innovate or to improve their quality and speed to market. This is because today's products and services are sufficiently complex that they require the involvement of multi-disciplined teams in order to become excellent in the eye of a customer. In Lean systems, the customer's point of view is the one that trumps all the others.

Craftsmen to Specialists

Today's organizations are largely based on the twentieth-century paradigm of increasing specialization of workers. This was an organizational spillover from the implementation of mass-manufacturing concepts at the beginning of industrial revolution in the early twentieth century. Prior to the industrial revolution, most products were made by craftsmen, who had a variety of skills and would often take a product from raw materials to its finished form.

Craftsmen had to be proficient at all the steps required in the process of producing an item. This could require, for example, proficiency in cutting, shaping, assembling, and finishing raw materials. Sometimes craftsmen would also be skilled in working with a *variety* of raw materials. Working in this way produced elegant, one-of-a-kind items (from the best craftsmen, who built their name, reputation or "brand" on the uniqueness of their "creations").

This was the value that craftsmen brought to the marketplace. It was also the problem that the industrial revolution sought to solve. What were these problems?

- **"One-of-a-kind" meant no two items were identical, which also meant that consistency was elusive.**

- **Craftsmen were expensive to employ, and good ones were not easy to find or develop as it took many years for them to master their wide array of skills.**

- **The craft way of building things did not provide opportunity for efficiency improvements.**

A man named Henry Ford believed that there was a better way.

The Rise of Mass Production

The drivers for Ford to create the first large-scale implementation of mass-manufacturing were the limiting characteristics of craft production listed above. The first one, the inconsistency of output, which was the mark of the craftsman, was particularly vexing to him. This is despite the fact that, in the craftsman's world, the uniqueness of each item was a value unto itself. (Even today, a custom-made home is almost always considered more valuable and is more costly than one that is mass produced.)

When it came to producing something as complex as an automobile, inconsistency turned out to be very costly indeed. This is because no single craftsman had the skills to build a complete car. The engines were built by craftsmen. The leather seats were created by craftsmen. The wheels were made by craftsmen. The carriage (body) was produced by a craftsman. However, no one craftsman could create an entire car by himself.

That was done by a new type of craftsman, or a team of craftsmen (called fitters), who assembled all the above components—and more—together to make a complete automobile. The word "assembly" belies the skills of these people. All of the components used to assemble the first cars were craft-made, which means they were never alike. These components of varying specifications had to be adjusted to fit together with other varying components. The task of the assembler craftsman was to tinker with all of these parts until everything could be assembled together. It was an extremely time-consuming effort that required, in many ways, more skill than those possessed by the craftspeople that created the original components themselves.

Automobiles at the turn of the twentieth century were only for very wealthy people because they were so expensive to produce, largely due to the labor required to create both the components and the finished products. Henry Ford wanted to produce a car that the masses could afford. This would require a whole new way of thinking about how to build an automobile. Ford's approach can be simplified as having the following major objectives:

- **Find a way to build consistent components within tight tolerances (minimal variation from specification)**
- **Assemble them with low-skilled (and low-cost) labor**
- **Decrease costs by increasing efficiencies with scale (today called "economies of scale")**

This led Ford to introduce the following innovations into his or her system that became known as mass production:

- **Large batch manufacturing of components (to gain economies of scale)**
- **Moving assembly line** (to pace production and increase worker efficiency)
- **Specialization of skills** (to reduce labor cost and increase productivity)

These innovations reduced the time required to assemble an automobile *by a whopping 88%, as compared to craft production.*[1] This meant that Ford could assemble a car in nearly a tenth of the time, or could produce more than eight cars in the time it took to create one using craft methods. Ford's inventions were wildly successful in the marketplace, bringing the automobile for the first time within the economic reach of the masses. Craft production was soon relegated to small niche markets.

There was a price to pay for Ford's approach, however. The saying at the time was that you could get a Model T automobile (Ford's most famous and popular model then) in any color you wanted, as long as it was black. Ford very consciously sacrificed variety and choice for cost savings and it worked, to a point. The mass production system's intolerance to variety and rapid change would eventually become one of the shortcomings that opened the door for Lean production.

Mass Production to Functional Silos

The main aspect of mass production that we are concerned with here is its emphasis on specialization. Specialization was an important way to reduce labor costs because low-cost, unskilled workers could be quickly trained to do a single task over and over. It was also a way to increase productivity because by doing a single task over and over, a worker would become very proficient at it and over time decrease the time required to complete it.

Today's modern companies have specializations around functional areas such as accounting, marketing, engineering, research, and so forth. It is easy to understand how this evolved. Industrial age thinking about the values of specialization was carried from the production floor into the office environment. It's also easy to see why this way of thinking not only continues but also is becoming more entrenched.

Everything today is becoming increasingly complex, both because of relentless technological innovation and because of continually changing consumer preferences. Tax law and accounting procedures are so complex (at least in the U.S.) that it is not an area for a financial or legal dabbler. The innovations social media have introduced into the marketing equation make marketing people's heads spin trying to keep up with new technologies and products, as well as new cultural norms and ways of communicating to and within the market. Engineering is undergoing tremendous change as well, partly driven by new technolo-

☑ *LEAN LEARNINGS*

Consensus Decision Making

Japanese: *Nemawashi* 根回し

Definition

It is probably one of the earliest aspects of the Japanese "brand" that Westerners became aware of in addition to obsession with quality: the emphasis on making decisions by consensus. For many Western companies, this seems to be a time-consuming and inefficient way to do things, and it is. However, it is also quite effective. Japanese companies tend to spend more time than their Western counterparts on gaining consensus but much less time on implementing decisions. The Japanese culture calls for flushing out all the objections and getting everyone "on-board" before a decision is finalized. As a result, there are rarely any instances where people sabotage an implementation, intentionally or not. Western companies, by contrast, generally take much longer than the Japanese to implement once they make a decision because resistance often emerges, or new issues appear during a rollout of a new plan.

Application to Lean Selling

In general, salespeople are rarely consulted about changes in process or policy before implementation. This occurs even though it is widely acknowledged that salespeople should have a high level of motivation to be most effective. Even sales department heads are often not notified of changes that affect them and their customers. There is much room in the sales arena and the surrounding support functions to practice nemawashi.

gy and also by new, modern methodologies for building products (such as concurrent engineering and Lean-agile software development).

Illustration 9: Functional Silos

Organization

Having specialists, experts in a certain discipline, is realistically not an option today; it is a necessity. This naturally leads to an increasing depth but decreasing breadth of knowledge within any one person or department. It is easy to understand how silos develop as people mainly interact with other people who speak their language and can help them get better at the limited scope of what they do. Nevertheless, there is an insidious organizational outcome that results from this trend.

Mean to Lean

An important premise of Lean Thinking is that, when making improvements, it is critical to evaluate the effect on the entire system, not just the individual departments, components, or processes. The "system" as defined here is *everything* the organization does in a coordinated fashion to successfully deliver a complete product or service solution to a customer. One of the fallouts and eventual downfalls of mass production thinking is that it does not encourage systems thinking. That is because the focus is on making increasingly larger volumes of something at a decreasing cost through optimizing individual steps of a process. As a result, it does not consider whether the overall system, as defined above, gets more–*or less*–efficient, or delivers higher–or *lower*–quality after such "improvements" are made.

The natural organizational extension of mass production thinking is to create silos of functional departments. Every department works on getting better at what it does, but does the overall company improve? If the marketing department gets increasingly better at generating company recognition in the marketplace, but its efforts do not result in an increased quality or quantity of sales leads or revenues, does it matter to anyone but the marketing department?

Lean Thinking Eliminates Functional Silos

I don't delude myself into thinking that the pace of change, or the demand for experts and specialists, will slow. *How then can we deal with organizational silos and move to a model that optimizes the entire system of a company? Lean Thinking provides an answer, which is to create teams that cut across functional lines.* These are, in essence, cross-functional teams that collaborate on applying continuous improvement across a wide variety of organizational areas: from supply chain management to product development to marketing and sales to distribution to customer support and service. I depict this concept graphically in Illustration 10. I will expand on the implications of this and other aspects of Lean Thinking in the following chapters.

Illustration 10: Lean Teams

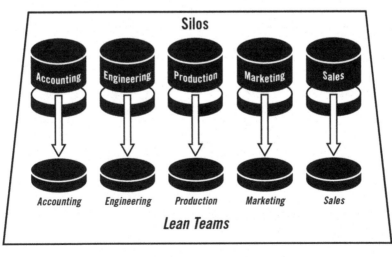

Key Takeaways from Chapter 18

1. Teamwork is the key to the success of Lean implementations.

2. Industrial age thinking has led to the creation of functional silos, which are suboptimal from the viewpoint of the entire enterprise.

3. Lean Thinking and practices naturally break down functional silos.

Specifying Value[1]

Defining Value

"Value" is a quintessential term in Lean Thinking. The primary reason organizations exist, according to Lean Thinking, is to create value for their customers, or users, of their products and services. Value can only be defined by the customer or user. Positive value is the discrete benefits, and also the aggregate benefits, an organization provides to their customers. **Negative value includes the customer cost of acquiring and using the product or service, which includes hassle and time wasted because of quality and other service problems, in addition to monetary costs.**

Clarifying Value

Clarifying the value an individual organization brings to its customers is the required first step in implementing Lean Thinking and Lean transformations. This is because all Lean Thinking and methodologies aim to increase the value that is provided to customers while reducing the cost, for both the customer and the organization, of providing that value. Reducing or eliminating waste is one of the primary methods of reducing cost in Lean systems.

It would seem that defining and clarifying the value one provides would be a straightforward task. Apparently, though, it is not. In a survey of sales professionals, the inability to effectively communicate value to the customer was one of the top three reasons listed for missing sales quotas.[2] **Why should it be so hard to communicate your organiza-tion's value to your customers? Do your salespeople know what it is? Does the rest of your organization?**

Therefore, we see that, if value is not properly defined, an orga-nization may be working to achieve the wrong goals. Practically speak-ing, is this a challenge for many organizations? I believe it is. One of the reasons is that organizations tend to look at value from the inside out, not from the outside in, which is the perspective of the customer. Another reason is that it is rare to find an organization where there is broad agreement on the value the company provides its customers across functional areas, and especially the employee population.

Increasing Value

These issues generally do not rise to the level of an apparent problem as long as an organization continues doing what it has always been doing, while holding on to the assumption that there must be inherent value provided for the customer by what it does. This is true even in the all-too-common case that there is a lack of general agree-ment across the organization on what that value actually is. However, *once a company decides it has to get better at what it does, possibly triggered by changing market conditions or fresh competition, the full cost of not clearly articulating what your organization's value is becomes clearer.*

Improvement requires change, and change entails risk. It also requires decisions be made to choose among a number of potential paths to improvement a company can pursue. However, what does an organization base these choices on? How do you make a decision about what to do in the face of so many possible alternatives? How do you know if making a specific change is going to make your company better (or worse)? Without knowing what you are trying to optimize through improvement efforts, change becomes difficult and feels very risky to pursue. Inertia is a powerful force and the mother of organizational paralysis.

☑ LEAN LEARNINGS

Five Principles of Lean Thinking

Definition

James P. Womack and Daniel T. Jones, in their book, *Lean Thinking*, posited five principles of Lean Thinking:

1. **Value—What the customer values about the product or service your organization provides**

2. **The Value Stream—The process path that a product or service goes through to create value for a customer**

3. **Flow—The continuous flow of products and services through value-adding steps without interruption or waiting time between steps**

4. **Pull—Demand created by "pulling" a product or service from the end of the process as contrasted with "pushing" it through the process**

5. **Perfection—This is the goal of Continuous Improvement, which can never be achieved, but which creates endless progress in approaching it**

Application to Lean Selling

All processes can be continuously improved using these five principles originally applied by Toyota Motor Corporation in its Lean Manufacturing operation. These principles have now been applied to a variety of service industries to dramatically improve service delivery. Sales processes can also benefit greatly from the creative application of these principles.

Value as a Decision-Making Tool

Lean Thinking provides a way out of this trap of indecision. *By positing a single, clear definition of an organization's purpose, which is increasing the value it provides from the customer's perspective, Lean Thinking supplies the necessary momentum to break out of inertia.* All decisions on what to do, and what choices to make, can be answered by asking the simple question, "Would making this proposed improvement add more value from our customers' perspectives?" There is, then, a single objective that the entire organization can aim for.

Voice of the Customer

Clearly identifying the value an organization provides is not something that should be done exclusively within company walls. It is almost always helpful to ask your customers what value they believe you offer to them. The responses can sometimes be very surprising and could lead to the company completely redefining the value they *actually* provide. Some refer to this concept of listening carefully to your customers' points of view as the Voice of the Customer (or VOC for short). Lean Thinking requires that the Voice of the Customer is a part of every decision an organization makes.

Voice of the Buyer

When it comes to sales, and Lean Selling™, the Buyer is the customer. Even if not a customer in the strict sense of the word because the prospect hasn't bought from us yet, he or she is still a customer of our Selling process. *What is the value these people want to get out of our Selling process? It is to support their Buying process.* Ultimately, it is to assist them in making a timely, well-considered, confident Buying decision.

This is what value is to a Buyer (as compared to a customer, where value is tied to the product or service delivered). **Every aspect of the Selling process should be evaluated as to whether it adds Buyer value. If it doesn't, it is waste and should be eliminated** as an activity, action, or requirement of the Selling process. The tools we will learn about in the next chapter were developed to help an organization do just that, for all of their processes. Sales processes are no exception.

Key Takeaways from Chapter 19

1. *In Lean Thinking, value is always defined from the customer's perspective.*

2. *It is critically important to gain unambiguous consensus across the organization as to specifically what value it provides to its customers.*

3. *Lean Thinking and Lean Selling work continuously to improve the value provided to the customer.*

4. *By seeking out and listening to the Voice of the Customer, organizations can get a new perspective on the value they provide, as well as discovering new ways to provide value to customers.*

Chapter 20

Identifying the Value Stream

Value Stream Mapping

Once we clearly define the value of a product or service an organization offers, the next step is to look at how that value is actually produced. **In Lean Thinking this is called the Value Stream, the set of activities an organization undertakes to produce value for its customers.**

It is common practice, when beginning a Lean transformation event, to graphically represent the "flow" of a product or service as it is being created, from the beginning to the end of the production process. There are standard conventions for doing this, and the end result is called a Value Stream Map (VSM). A VSM is a powerful visual tool that provides a birds-eye view of *how* an organization builds value into its products and services. It turns out to be an excellent tool for building organizational agreement on what is actually going on internally and externally during the process of value creation, often resulting in eye-opening revelations for the participants in such an exercise.

A separate VSM is created for each unique product or service the organization provides. If the production process is very similar for two different products or services, they may be combined into a single VSM. Value Stream Mapping is a Lean methodology to analyze processes based on customer value that results in the development of a VSM.

Creating a VSM is a team effort. The initial, high-level map is created in a session that would include participation of senior management from all functions represented on or contributing to the product or service. The goal of a VSM event is not to recommend specific changes within process steps, but rather to gain a high-level view of how the process flows and what is going on within it. As a result, it is important only that participants know enough about their functional area to provide management–not technical– information and guidance to the creation of the VSM.

When completed, a VSM should illustrate all the individual process steps involved in producing value for a customer, and graphically indicate how value flows from one step to the next. It does not delve down to the level of detail that would show what actually happens *within* a process step. A properly documented VSM would show how products and information flow, starting with a request for something (for example, an order from a customer) and ending with the delivery of it. The VSM also shows the flow of goods or services from outside vendors, as well as information flow within and between processes.

When prepared by a team, VSMs can be created on larger-than-life sheets of paper, often giant whiteboard size. There can be a lot of detail, as we will soon see. It is beyond the scope of this book to delve into the technical details of creating a VSM or to describe all the specialized symbology it employs. There are books devoted to this single topic that do an excellent job at that.[1] It is also difficult to faithfully reproduce a fully-adorned VSM that would be legible in a book of this size. However, Illustration 11 outlines the concept for a manufacturing process, where the VSM tool and methodology were first used. *(Note that a key to standard VSM symbols are included in Appendix A of this book.)*

Illustration 11: Outline of Value Stream Map

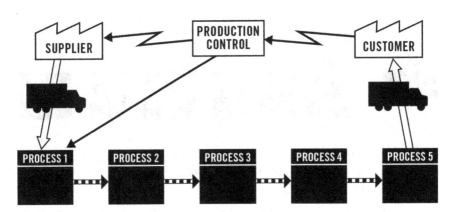

The above illustration models the production of a physical product, not a service. The first clue to this is that there are trucks in the picture, to indicate that there are raw materials or components going into the factory and that a physical product is being delivered to the customer. By convention, the external elements of the process (in this case, customers and outside suppliers) are in the top part of the diagram and information (represented by the thin bent arrows) moves from right to left. Internal processes are on the bottom, and move from left to right. This outline VSM is skeletal, showing only that there are materials or components being delivered from an outside vendor, that there are five process steps in creating the product, and that a product is delivered to the customer who requested it.

It turns out that a VSM can be used to graphically depict the creation or delivery of a service as well as a physical product. Since this discussion could get a bit technical for some readers, before anyone's eyes glaze over, let's create a VSM for a service to make it more relevant to our main area of interest. I'm not referring to just any service, though. To make it most relevant, let's reproduce the Buying-Selling process that we first introduced in Chapter 16 with Illustration 7 in the form of a VSM with Illustration 12.

Illustration 12: A Buying-Selling Process Value Stream Map

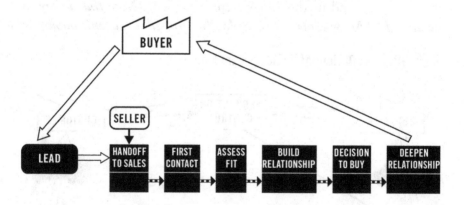

The "fence posts," or starting and ending points, of the process the VSM covers are the Lead box on the left, the starting point, and the

Deepen Relationship box on the right, where everything that was promised was delivered and the customer is happy and willing to continue a relationship with the Seller, make referrals, provide a testimonial, and do other good things.

The arrows between the boxes indicate that a product or service is moving from left to right. **In this case, the "product" that's moving from process step to process step is a Buyer and a Seller, both moving together. The "service" that has value being added to it is the increasing ability of the Buyer to make a Buying decision, according to the schedule that was agreed upon in the Buying Plan.**

Developing Metrics

A VSM is also an effective tool for capturing important metrics about a process that will be used to troubleshoot the process and consider improvement options. A properly completed VSM will yield the following metrics:

1. **The actual time for each process step**

2. **The amount of time for each process step that added value for the customer**

3. **The amount of time for each process step that didn't add value for the customer but is necessary, at least at the current time**

4. **The amount of time for each process step that didn't add value for the customer and isn't necessary**

5. **The amount of "wait" time between each process step** (the time it takes for the next process to start after the previous one is completed)

6. **The inventory between each process step** (Work-in-Process that is waiting to be processed by the next step is shown by the triangle with a capital "I" inside it—by definition, if there is wait time between steps then there is inventory between those steps)

Illustration 13: Adding Metrics to the Current State Value Stream Map

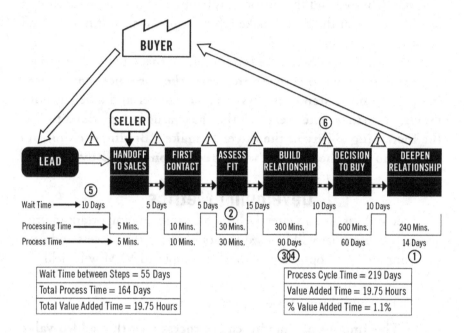

Illustration 13 marks with circled numbers the location on the VSM for each of the above numbered metrics shown in our Buying-Selling process example. Adding totals of different sets of these numbers together for the entire process yields a valuable collection of metrics.

For example, adding together the *totals* of #1 and #5 will provide the elapsed process time or *sales process cycle time* (219 days in our example). In our example, this is how long it takes for the sales process to complete once a lead is created. This number can be expressed in minutes, hours, days, whatever makes sense given the scale of the numbers.

The total amount of wasted time in the process can be found by adding the totals for #4 and #5. The totals for #5 are clear, and in our example there are 55 days of wasted time waiting between steps. As far as #4 is concerned, if you look at the three right-most boxes, you will see a big discrepancy between the actual processing time (i.e., adding value, such as a Buyer and Seller meeting to move things forward or address questions and issues) and the elapsed time of the process.

We can't immediately tell how much of this difference falls into category #4 (unnecessary waste) vs. category #3 (necessary waste). The reason this cannot be determined without further research is that much of that time is controlled by the Buyer and the Buyer organization, and we have to know better what the Buyer is doing before we can decide if it is waste that can be immediately eliminated.

For example, some of the elapsed time in the Build Relationship process step may be the Buyer waiting for information he or she has requested from someone internally or externally. This time would be waste, but currently required. On the other hand, if much of the elapsed time occurs because the Buyer just didn't prioritize the work that had to be done, that would be waste that could be eliminated with better prioritization and scheduling.

An improved working relationship between the Buyer and Seller could allow a Seller to coach the Buyer on eliminating wasted time (including waiting time), assuming the Buyer is open to this. It is fairly typical that the first pass at creating a VSM for a Buying-Selling process will raise some questions regarding whether identified waste is currently necessary, which cannot be answered without further research.

What this exercise does point out, which is very enlightening to anyone concerned about the length of sales cycles, is that about 75% of elapsed time appears to be at least partly within the Buyer's control. Now, this is probably not going surprise anyone, but it is **not** a reason to give up and say nothing can be done about speeding up the sales process. There are 55 days of waiting time between steps that the Seller's organization might be able to reduce with or without the Buyer's involvement. Reducing that time would immediately decrease the sales cycle time.

The key takeaway from this example exercise is that if you want to dramatically reduce your sales cycle time, you will have to get more directly engaged with what the Buyer is doing in this process, and coach him or her into becoming more efficient. Creating the Buying Plan is the first step in this direction. However, each Seller will have to understand the unique obstacles each Buyer has in making a decision more quickly, and creatively challenge each one.

Eventually, patterns that Buyers exhibit will repeat, and the sales organization will get better and better at coaching Buyers through the process. This is what continuous improvement is all about. The difference between the totals for #1 and #2 shows how much waste there is within process steps (as opposed to the waste of waiting time between process steps, or #5). A quick calculation shows this amount to be 162 days.

Total time for execution of all process steps = 1,312.75 hours
Total value-added time for all processes = 19.75 hours
Process time waste = 1,312.75 – 19.75 = 1,293 hours / 8 hours / day = 162 days

A very important metric that can be derived from this data is #2 (in our example, 19.75 hours) divided by the sum of #1 and #5 (219 days). This will be the percentage of value-added time over total cycle time. In our example, this calculation yields 1.1%.

219 days × 8 hours/day = 1,752 hours
19.75 value added hours / 1,752 total cycle hours × 100 = 1.1% value added ratio

It is not uncommon to see single digits for this number in "un-Leaned" production systems. For processes such as sales it is not unusual for this ratio to be less than 1%, particularly for big-ticket or otherwise complex sales. This means that 99% of sales process time spent is non-value-added.

This single metric can be a wake-up call for management teams. **"Why does it take 219 days to deliver less than 20 hours of value?" they want to know. It's a great question. This is the question Lean Thinking and Lean Selling™ continually ask.** The process of finding the answer to that question will lead an organization on a Lean journey. Fortunately, Lean Thinking and methodologies not only provide the tools to answer that question, but also to do something about it.

Current State

The metrics discussed in the previous section provide an assessment of the process under scrutiny in the form of a numeric scorecard, which is referred to as the "Current State." The VSM shown previously in Illustration 13 displayed these metrics and their connections to process steps. Documenting the Current State as an accurate representation of the shared understanding of the management team is the first step toward an organization making a Lean transformation. The Current State becomes the working ground for determining where and how to improve. Visualizing value and waste in the Current State through the means of a VSM yields several important benefits:

- **It puts the management team on the same page (literally and figuratively) regarding what is actually going on in the process of creating value for customers.**

- **It numerically depicts the magnitude of the gap between elapsed (cycle) time and value-added time.**

- **It provides a graphical agenda for management to discuss why the Current State looks like it does and to brainstorm about what might be done to improve it.**

The Current State is the "before." It becomes the baseline against which the impact of improvements that are about to be made can be measured. It is the grist of case studies about organizational transformation. At some point in the future, the leaders of the organization will describe this Current State as "the place we came from before we got to the place we are today." A requirement to get there, however, is that **the management team has to be brutally honest about the reality of the Current State.**

Identifying Waste

The VSM is a tool to uncover waste so management can decide what to do about it. Waste is often hard to see, but numbers don't lie. **That's why time—and the analytics that can be derived from measurements of it—is used as a proxy for hidden waste.** Simply put, time spent on any activity that does not add value for the customer is waste. Consequently, any activity that wastes time should be eliminated if possible. **The percentage of value-added time across the entire cycle time is the most useful metric for measuring the "leanness" of a system** and the progress in making it more Lean.

The most easily identifiable source of waste in our Current State VSM is the wait times between processes that add no value and create inventory (in this case for services, not products). The very first investigation the organization should undertake is to see how much this wait time between steps can be reduced. Some of these times are under complete control of the Seller's organization, such as the 10-day average delay in getting leads to the salespeople. Others will depend upon the Buyer as well as the Seller's organization, and each wait time will have to be looked at in depth to understand what is causing it and what might be done about it.

For example, the five-day wait time from lead "Handoff to Sales" to "First Contact" could possibly be reduced by having a lead that enters the pipeline trigger scheduling the Buyer for a First Contact call so that the Seller doesn't have to leave messages and play phone tag. There are different ways this could be accomplished, depending on how the lead enters the system.

As I noted before, our example Current State VSM shows that most wasted time is actually within the process steps, particularly the later ones, and not between them. As the organization investigates the causes of the intra-process waste, it may find that much of it is due to the Buyer's internal processes rather than the Seller's. Still, participants in Lean initiatives are constantly amazed at how much waste *can* be eliminated and how much time can be saved. It all starts with working to understand why the waste is there in the first place and what can be done to eliminate or reduce it.

Immediately eliminating other wasted time and the activities associated with it is not always possible. There are, inevitably, activities in a process that do not add value for the customer, but are necessary for the process to *work*. Required maintenance on equipment and training programs for employees are examples. In Lean terminology, this type of waste is called Type 1, or "non-value-added but *necessary*." This is to contrast it with Type 2 waste, which is "non-value-added and *unnecessary*." Eliminating Type 2 waste is an obvious first action for an organization to improve a process. It will yield the greatest return with the least effort.

The most likely reason that unnecessary waste hasn't already been eliminated is that people didn't know it was there. It was hiding, but the VSM analysis brought the waste to the surface. We may not yet know where all the waste is and what is causing it, but now we know where to look more deeply. Eliminating or reducing currently *necessary* waste we find should be tackled as a second step after first eliminating all obviously *unnecessary* waste. This is because eliminating *necessary* waste will generally require process redesign and would be better undertaken as a continual improvement initiative, not an acute surgical procedure.

☑ *LEAN LEARNINGS*

Pareto Analysis

Definition

This was named after Vilfredo Pareto, a 19th century Italian economist and engineer, and popularized by Joseph Juran in 1941 as the Pareto Principle, which is more commonly known as the "80/20" rule, that 80% of results are due to 20% of causes. This simple concept has diverse applications in many fields. In business and quality control, it implies that 80% of problems come from 20% of causes. This is a very simple but incredibly powerful tool in troubleshooting business processes, and particularly in deciding where to prioritize efforts for improvement. A Pareto chart will graphically show where the bulk of the problems or errors are, allowing a focus on attacking the problem with the biggest potential payoff. It is one of the most popular Lean tools used by Toyota in the company's improvement initiatives.

Application to Lean Selling

When looking at sales processes and trying to determine where investment of time and money in improvement should be made, Pareto Charts can be very powerful tools to help drive decision-making. This is especially true for facilitating consensus decision-making in a team environment.

Future State

When everyone is comfortable that the VSM reflects the Current State, it is time to start thinking about what a more ideal process might look like. This is where brainstorming and ideas from multiple functional areas inevitably lead to new ways to organize processes, by combining, eliminating, or re-routing steps in the process of creating value.

The VSM team will review the major places in the processes that are generating waste as well as the waiting times between processes. They will then begin to consider what could be done to improve the process by figuring out how it could be sped up. Multiple initiatives for improvement in a number of areas may be put on the table. Next, each initiative will be ranked according to its expected payoff and difficulty of implementation. Rarely do these initiatives require much, if any, capital investment. Therefore, the main considerations are the time to effect the change and how disruptive it might be to the organization until the process returns to a steady state.

When there is agreement on which initiatives will be pursued, a new Future State VSM can be drawn from scratch, and, hopefully, physically displayed within view of the Current State VSM. Target numbers should be added to the Future State to represent the goals for improvement of each step as well as the entire system, such as targeted cycle time, value-added vs. non-value-added time, value-added time as a percentage of cycle time, and so forth.

A leader is assigned to each initiative as well as members of the improvement team. The leader should be a member of the management team, or have the mandate of management to carry out the changes. The team members who will execute the plan and implement the changes should be those who best understand the process steps under improvement. They can, and eventually will, include the people actually carrying out each process step.

In our example, after completing their research, which included better understanding the cause of time delays in their own as well as the Buyer's organization, the VSM team believes a realistic target is to reduce the sales cycle time from 219 days to 62 days. *That's a target reduction in the length of the sales cycle of nearly 72%!* Illustration 14 shows how they plan to achieve this reduction. **Note that the percentage of value-added time as a ratio of sales cycle time improved by nearly four times!**

Illustration 14: Future State Value Stream Map

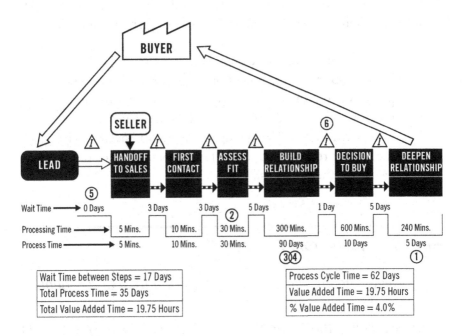

Wait Time between Steps = 17 Days
Total Process Time = 35 Days
Total Value Added Time = 19.75 Hours

Process Cycle Time = 62 Days
Value Added Time = 19.75 Hours
% Value Added Time = 4.0%

This is a highly summarized overview of the VSM process and the resulting improvement plan. A process like this could take three or more full days for a senior team to complete (not including time to do required research). As improvements are put in place, metrics are gathered to see how much progress is being made toward the Future State. Participants should not expect to achieve all the goals of the Future State after the first pass of improvements. In fact, after major changes, processes generally get worse before they get better. The improvement team continues to work diligently to minimize the size and duration of any disruptions as a priority. At the same time, the team is evaluating whether their assumptions for improvement were realistic, and also what else might be done to facilitate the transition to a new process model.

Once the goals of the Future State VSM are met and the process is stabilized, it is time to look for the next ways to speed up the process. The Future State VSM becomes the Current State VSM and a new Future State VSM is created. Teams are formed to implement the changes of the Future State VSM, and so improvement goes on, continuously.

I will close this chapter with an excerpt from the seminal book, *The Toyota Way*, where the author, Jeffrey Liker, summarizes his experience with applying Lean to non-manufacturing environments:

> My associates and I have done over one hundred kaizen [Lean improvement] events on technical and business processes and it is always eye-opening for the team how much waste is uncovered once they start mapping the value stream. Another eye-opener is the discovery that the bulk of these processes are fairly repetitive and standardizing them is possible.[2]

Key Takeaways from Chapter 20

1. Value Stream Mapping is a very powerful tool for identifying both value and waste.

2. Assessing the Current State of a process, expressed in metrics, is the first step toward a Lean transformation.

3. Envisioning a more ideal Future State for the same process, also expressed in metrics, is the second step toward a Lean transformation.

4. The third step is to form teams to make the Future State into the new Current State.

5. Repeat this process, continuously.

Chapter 21

Creating Flow

What Is Flow?

The word "flow" may conjure up the picture of a stream or babbling brook or even a river. Sometimes the flow is fast, and sometimes it is slow. The shape conforms to the geography that confines it, and it changes speed as necessary to stay connected to the water behind it and the water ahead of it. There are no pauses, hesitations, or fits and starts. There is never any "inventory" of water; it just keeps moving. (Of course, a dammed river is an exception, where the object *is* to intervene with nature to *create an inventory* of water by slowing down flow.)

Flow is a very important objective of Lean systems. Flow in Lean means that, once a process starts, the goods or materials (and for the topic of this book, even people) move through the process without pause or interruption. The second requirement for Flow in Lean systems is that *the process is capable of moving one item at a time through the entire process.*

Why Flow Is Hard

Flow in processes is devilishly difficult to accomplish. There are two main reasons for this. The first one is that that there are many external events that conspire to interfere with Flow in almost every process. Sometimes parts or people are not available when needed to complete a process step (often referred to as a "stock-out"). At other times, machines break down unexpectedly, creating a buildup of inventory preceding that process step.

The other main cause of lack of Flow is that the process was intentionally designed *not* to Flow. This is often the case when there is an expensive, high-volume piece of equipment (or an expensive, low-volume human expert, in the case of delivery of certain services) in the process. Likely, the process was optimized to maximize the expensive machinery, in order to improve the financial return on the capital investment.

In this case, inventory is not only tolerated, it is encouraged. The plan is to create large batches of finished or semi-finished product, with the objective of reducing the per-piece cost. The driving objective is optimizing the efficiency of the particular equipment. If there are multiple expensive, large machines like this, then this optimization will be repeated in multiple places in the production process.

The problem is that optimizing for a particular machine or step in a process does not optimize the *entire* process. It does not consider optimization of the entire production *system*. Further, from a Lean point of view, it prevents Flow, because it cannot allow for one item to be processed at a time, continuously, through the process.

Why Flow Is Important

Why does this matter? Because **Lean implementations have proven over and over again that, without Flow, there is waste buried in the production system.** I use the word "buried" intentionally, because the waste can't be uncovered unless you do some digging. The cost of this waste invariably exceeds the "savings" gained from optimizing for the "piece price" of the output of a single process step. Many of the problems production systems experience that necessitate constant workarounds and "expediting" are the symptoms of lack of Flow.

Lean transformations that introduce Flow into processes often require the reconfiguration or elimination of process steps, as well as some tough management decisions regarding a commitment to optimize for the entire production or service delivery system rather than a particular machine or step. In the case of product manufacturing, machines often had to be "downsized" in order to enable Flow and the optimization of the entire production system.

There are lessons from the knowledge gained in the production of tangible products that have analogs in delivery of intangible services as well, especially those that depend on expensive, rare, or expert resources. In the next chapter, we will see real-world examples of suboptimal thinking in service industries.

Flow in Sales

We have established that Flow is a very important characteristic of Lean processes. What implications does that have for the sales process? **If we wanted to pick a business process that is the antithesis of Flow, it would be the average sales process.** It is replete with unpredictability and inevitable twists, turns, stops, pauses, and restarts. Of course, we put the majority of the blame for this on the Buyer. **The common thinking is that the sales process would Flow just fine if Buyers would simply cooperate and move along in their Buying process.**

This kind of thinking empowers the Buyer, but not the Seller. It smacks of a fatalistic perspective that nothing can be done to improve the situation. Realistically speaking, though, is there anything that can be done to make the sales process Flow?

In thinking about ways to apply the most essential Lean principles to selling, I struggled with how best to accomplish Flow in a Selling process. I was all too aware of all the challenges Buyers present that prevent things from moving along. *Then I realized that it was possible for a Selling process to Flow, if only the Buying process would Flow.* I then shifted my thinking as to how we might get a Buying process to Flow.

My thinking went something like this: the goal of a Buyer is to make a decision. What do we have to do to control the time and pace of the decision process? We as Sellers can help Flow happen, by acting as coaches or by creating a Buying Plan, for example.

☑ *LEAN LEARNINGS*

Leveling

Japanese: *Heijunka* 平準化

Definition

This term originally referred to the evening-out of workload for the manufacturing process to help prevent equipment breakdown and quality problems from overworked employees. It is impossible to apply control methodologies to a process that does not have a level amount of production.

Application to Lean Selling

Many salespeople's pipelines lead to the "feast or famine" syndrome. The cause of this is lack of leveling. If a sales pipeline (individual or team) does not have leveling applied to it, then sales results will be erratic and unpredictable. Leveling in a sales pipeline means that there are the right numbers of qualified Buyers at each stage to accomplish sales targets, based on historical results and statistical probability. While most salespeople lament shortfalls in their funnel, overloaded funnels can be as much of a problem because quality will decrease if there is more demand on the Seller than can be serviced.

Compressing the Buying Process

As we have already discussed, there are certain steps a Buyer must go through to reach a Buying decision. Some of these steps take time. Like the Selling process, if the Buying process is not Lean, then there will be a small percentage of value-added time the Buyer is investing in making a decision out of the total time spent (elapsed) while in the Buying process. Although we might help the Buyer become more efficient (for example, by helping him or her to eliminate wasted activities in his or her own process), we can't eliminate many of the things a Buyer has to do in order to make a decision. Therefore, the only answer must be to compress the Buying process.

You may be thinking, "Isn't that what we are already trying to do all the time, compress the Buying process? Yet, despite our efforts to do so, it doesn't seem to speed up." This is true, but maybe we're looking at the problem from the wrong end. Maybe we have to start at the *end* of the process—not the beginning—to find a clue to the answer to our conundrum.

Well, the end of the Buying process is, as we have already defined, a *Buying decision*. This is the shared goal of both Buyer and Seller. Normally a Buying decision has a target date, or it would never get made. There are certain programs, projects, or initiatives that are, or will be, waiting on a decision. If we can fix that point in time, for example, as part of creating a Buying Plan, can this help us figure out how to compress the Buying process?

Since we have fixed the date of the endpoint of the process (the delivery date), there is only one point we can move that can compress it, or reduce the overall cycle time of the Buying process. That point is when we *start* it. I am suggesting that ***Buying processes rarely Flow because they are started too early, with the help of a co-conspirator, the Seller.***

I can feel another objection coming. Aren't people in sales relentlessly counseled to get involved as early as possible with a Buyer, so they can have some opportunity to influence the path the Buying process takes? Didn't I, in fact, allude to something along those lines earlier in this book?

I confess yes to both inquiries. However, "getting involved" doesn't necessarily mean starting a Buying process. It could mean *planning* or *getting ready for* a Buying process. How can you start a Buying process too early? The answer is when starting it early will prevent the process from accomplishing Flow.

The Buying Plan

Let's say for argument's sake that you know from experience that a Buyer, in the best case, requires two months of elapsed time to account for all the things that have to be done to reach a decision about your product or service. Let's also assume that the decision has to be made four months from now. Well, if the Seller engages in the Buying process now, he or she is dooming the process to lack Flow.

However, if we could start the Buying process in earnest two months from now, we might have a chance to start and finish it without interruption, in two months elapsed time. How could we potentially make such a thing happen without sacrificing our ability to influence and be involved in the Buying process? One way is through creating a Buying Plan.

The Seller can ask the Buyer to engage with him or her in creating a Buying Plan that will meet the Buyer's objectives for making a timely, accurate, confident decision. The first date entered on the Buying Plan is the date the decision will be made. The Seller will collaborate (and often coach) the Buyer on the individual steps he or she anticipates the Buyer will have to go through to accomplish this, and gain concurrence and commitment on each step. There may be a few steps that the Buyer requests to add that the Seller didn't consider. Each step will have a time required to complete next to it. When the list is complete, the total amount of time for all the steps becomes the planned cycle time. The Seller goes backward from the decision date by the amount of time required to complete the Buying cycle, and that becomes the start date.

Once the Seller gains concurrence from the Buyer on this continuous Flow Buying Plan, the Seller can offer to check in regularly to see if anything has changed (such as the target date for a Buying decision) that would affect the Buying Plan. They can also agree on other activities that can be done in preparing for the start of the Buying Plan. **The Buying process may not have started, but the Seller has already been hired as a coach.**

Key Takeaways from Chapter 21

1. *Flow is an ideal state of Lean processes where there is no wait time between steps.*

2. *While important, it is challenging to create Flow in a Selling process, because it depends on Buyer cooperation.*

3. *The key goal, expressed in a metric, should be to compress the time of the sales cycle from start to finish.*

4. *Creation of a Buying Plan is a way to accomplish sales cycle time reduction.*

Chapter 22

Enabling Pull

What Is Pull?

Pull is a Lean principle that turns traditional production processes on their head. A familiar Pull system is your neighborhood supermarket shelf. A wide selection of items is stacked along aisles, but only so deep, which limits the number of each item on the shelf. The store will want to have enough of each item so that at least one of each item is available at all times to prevent a stock-out, but not more. The number depth of the shelf is generally fixed, so the frequency of restocking adjusts to demand. If an item is particularly popular (that is, it moves quickly) it may be accorded two or three rows, increasing inventory available to consumers. A customer pulling an item from the shelf allows a quick glance from a stock clerk to see what has to be restocked. Today's check-out technology will generate stocking plans and even automatically generate order requirements by keeping track of sales by SKU number and comparing to orders outstanding.

Almost all classic production processes, however, are "push" systems in one form or another, in that each step of the process pushes Work-in-Process (WIP) to the next step, *whether the next step is ready to receive it or not.* This is like taking your car to the dealer for a repair without an appointment. The mechanic may get to your car some time that day, but you will have to wait. You most certainly will be without your car for a while. That's because you "pushed" it on them before they were ready to service your car, and they may have already fully booked their service capacity for the day.

Getting to Pull

Instead of making an unscheduled visit to the dealer, suppose you lived or worked a reasonably short distance from the dealer, and you happened to not be doing anything particularly urgent that day. If the dealer service department called you when a service bay was opening up, the mechanic might be able to look at your car right away if you brought it over at that time.

A more familiar application of this idea is a recent innovation in customer service phone support. None of us enjoy the time we have to wait on hold to speak to a representative. Even if we can be doing something productive (like reading or writing) while we are waiting, it is still not a pleasant experience, and one that most consumers complain about. Many customer service organizations in larger companies have implemented a system where they will call you back when a representative is available. Their promise is that you will not lose your place in the queue by opting for this service. Often they will tell you approximately when they will call back.

I personally like this option because I can refocus my attention on something else other than listening for when an agent comes on the line. Also, the music they play on hold is usually not my preference, or very good. Worse, while on hold I am often auditorily inundated with advertising messages that repeat—over and over.

The call-back option is definitely not as good as getting someone instantly when you call, but it is better than the alternative. (Incidentally, a collateral outcome of this approach achieves an important objective of Lean Production systems of "leveling" the workload for the company so it is consistent over time, leading to greater efficiencies and quality.)

This is an application of Lean Thinking to customer service. Why do I say that? First of all, by letting me off hold, they have eliminated the *waste* of my waiting time when I can't fully focus on something else. This waste is a *price*, my time, which I am paying for "free" service. Second, and germane to this chapter's topic, it is a step in the right direction of a Pull system even though it has further to go to fully qualify as Lean, as I elaborate on shortly.

Waste, Inventory, Flow, and Pull

In the traditional customer service system, you can consider all the people (tens, hundreds, thousands?) who are on hold as *inventory*, queued up and waiting for a process step. That process step is talking live to a representative who can resolve their issue. Still, that process step is not ready when you are because there is no available capacity. As a result, there is no Flow. Once again, we can see how inventory, waste, and (lack of) Flow and Pull are all related and coexist, whether we realize it or not.

In the past, **companies probably didn't think about customer hold time as waste because they were only looking at their internal process of providing customer support,** *not looking at it from the perspective of providing value to the customer.* Once the mindset changes to define value in a new way, from the viewpoint of the customer as we discussed in Chapter 19, it becomes clear that there is tremendous hidden waste in the system.

Suboptimization

The mindset that led to a process that created anti-value waste was that of suboptimization. Companies trying to hold down the cost of their customer support services try to optimize the efficiency of their service agents. Optimizing their efficiency means having them talking to customers as close to 100% of the time as possible while they are working.

Companies know that there are peak call times–they even know when they are–but they don't want to staff up for them to reduce customer wait times because it might lead to idle time for staff later. This is a service example of the same thinking that creates manufacturing processes that optimize a single machine instead of the overall system. It is a contemporary, real-world example of twentieth-century-industrial thinking.

While the company is optimizing the utilization rate (efficiency) of its customer service people (expert resources), they are optimizing for a single step in the process, not for the entire system, which starts as

☑ *LEAN LEARNINGS*

Visual Signal

Japanese: *Kanban* かんばん

Definition

Universally referred to by its Japanese name, *kanban*, this describes any of several methods that are used to support the control of production through "pull" demand rather than "push" supply that is based on a production forecast. With *kanban* in production environments, a card, an empty bin, an open slot, lights, or another visual indicator is sent from a downstream production process backwards to the preceding upstream process to request more materials, assemblies or components. In the case of a remote outside supplier, the *kanban* could be sent electronically. The upstream process is not permitted to produce anything unless the next step in the process requests it. This prevents overproduction and strictly limits the amount of inventory that accumulates between process steps to a predetermined amount.

Application to Lean Selling

There is much to be gained from making the sales pipeline visible for all to see, ideally in a physical form. Methods could then be devised for a downstream process (such as closing a sale) to signal an upstream process that a Buyer needs to be moved down the pipeline to replace the one that was removed. This approach can also be used to signal when new leads are required to be brought into the funnel so that the predicted sales closing rate can be maintained.

soon as an automated system answers the customer call. As a result, **the sums of money spent to provide quality customer service (in order to create customer loyalty and satisfaction) is diluted by the bad customer experience** of hold times. Some might call this "penny wise, pound foolish" thinking. I like to refer to it as "The Bridge over the River Kwai" syndrome, recalling the 1957 film of the same name. To me this indicates the tendency to focus on a single objective so intensely that you lose sight of the mission.

If only these companies would have had the benefit of the Value Stream Mapping process. They could have seen immediately that customer hold time was waste and should be eliminated. The call-back solution is an innovative one. As I mentioned, it is not as good as getting someone on the phone immediately, but it is much better than holding. Also, it doesn't require the company to increase staff. There is no extra expense to the company so its efficiency objective is not compromised.

Leaning Customer Service

Earlier I mentioned that the call-back method of handling customer service calls was better than holding on the line, but still not truly Lean. Although it is a step in the right (Lean) direction, there are several reasons it doesn't qualify as a truly Lean solution:

- **The vendor is doing the Pulling** (by calling you back when the rep is ready for you) instead of the customer Pulling.

- **There is waste because it requires two transactions instead of one**: I have to make a call (and possibly enter a call-back number) and also take a call.

- **I didn't get service *when I* wanted it,** but when it was convenient for the vendor.

- **There is no Flow, because the process is stopped** (resulting in wait time and inventory) when no one was available to take my call.

I could make similar comments about the car service example. Some companies have chosen to address this on-hold issue in a more Lean way. I am a customer of several credit card companies. With only one of them, when I call, a live agent answers the phone immediately. The agent seems to know who I am because he or she must use my phone's caller ID to identify me. It's interesting that I only have this experience with this company when I call about *one* of the cards I have with them. If I call this same company about the other card I have with it (which is issued and supported by the same bank, but carries a different product "brand" name), I have a different customer experience. I have to enter the last four digits of my credit card and my zip code. I also can expect to hold until an agent is available. I don't pay a fee for either card, so I'm not sure why one qualifies for the premium support service and the other doesn't, especially since I'm the same customer for both cards. I guess that's part of the "brand."

I am also a customer of an investment brokerage company that has a live support person pick up my call without wait, although this is only offered as a premium service to certain clients. Other clients have to wait on hold.

However these companies got to a more customer-friendly model for their customer service phone support process, they have definitely employed elements of Lean Thinking, if only for premium support. These examples from the service industry are worth considering because they reinforce the fact that **wherever and whenever Lean Thinking is applied, waste can be found and eliminated, while the customer experience is enhanced.** As we have seen, this applies to service processes in the same way it does to manufacturing processes. This bodes well for Lean Thinking's potential for revolutionizing sales processes in the form of Lean Selling™.

Pull and Sales

In the previous chapter I wrote that one of the biggest conceptual challenges I had in writing this book was how to take the Lean principle of creating Flow and apply it to the sales process. I proposed some ways on how that might be done. Still, while that was a thought challenge, it wasn't my biggest one. The biggest one was how to apply the principle of Pull, the subject of this chapter, to sales. It is time to address that now.

It seems so counterintuitive. There is nothing about the sales process that initially hints at being amenable to a Pull process. All the steps we talked about the Buyer going through, even with the creation of a Buying Plan, are "pushing" the Buyer from the beginning of the process to the end. I wracked my brain but couldn't immediately see how a Pull system could apply to sales without coming up with something that felt contrived.

A Radical Idea

Then it came to me. Before I share with you my insight, I have to prepare you. My next idea is quite extreme. Since you are still reading this book, you have hung in there with me while I have proposed some fairly unorthodox ideas throughout this book about how Lean Thinking could be applied to sales. I have introduced such concepts as Buyers and Sellers acting as coaches, Buying and Selling as a single process, creating and managing a Buying Plan, and *delaying* the start of a Buying process to enable Flow. ***Although you have stuck with me until now, my next idea might push you over the edge.***

We have dedicated much of this book to analyzing the Buyer perspective and how the Selling process should be supporting the Buying process. This is with a view to creating value from the perspective of the Buyer to establish a **Lean Selling System**. However, I kept asking myself how we could incorporate a Pull system into this process. I know that Pull systems were originally developed as a way to reduce inventory both in storage and between process steps, and that they are supported by such innovations as Just-in-Time (JIT) delivery of materials to the production line. Nevertheless, how could a Buyer Pull from the sales process? Well, I concluded that maybe the Buyer can't. However, Sellers can.

If we look at the extended sales process, the Buyer is a recipient of its benefit, but another "customer" of the process is the Seller. We haven't mentioned much yet about the Seller's stake in the process.

If we think about it, we know that prospecting, marketing, lead generation, and other activities that connect the outside world with our company's products and services are necessary. However, it doesn't directly add value for the customer, except that without these activities the customer might not even know our product or service existed, and therefore, couldn't benefit from it. **Well, maybe there is a different customer for prospecting, marketing, and other lead-generation activities: the *Seller.***

When we look at the Seller as the immediate customer (although not the only beneficiary) of these activities, it provides us an entirely new perspective. Now we can start thinking about the value of activities that bring prospects into the sales pipeline as determined by the value they add for salespeople. That also gives us a new, Lean Thinking way of figuring out how we might improve those activities. Once we know who the customer is, we can determine whether the value we are providing is the right value. How do we know? In this case, just ask the customer: the salesperson.

What I am suggesting, for the purpose of creating a Pull system (which is always a good thing if it can be done), is that we now shift our perspective and ***look at the value of the sales process from the viewpoint of the value it creates for the Seller***, and further investigate how we can have the Seller "Pull" from this process. How might this be done?

First, let's clarify what value is to a Seller, as a customer of the process. Virtually every salesperson I know (possibly with the exception of those who are independent agents in their own businesses) has a sales quota their organization expects them to meet or exceed. Value to a Seller is anything that supports this quota attainment, which is a steady stream of Buyers making Buying decisions, *predictably*. Most salespeople today do not have a steady, predictable flow of sales. How might we make it so?

Next, let's discuss what Pull might mean in such a system. The Seller wants to Pull Buyers from the "Decision to Buy" step of the combined Buying-Selling process first introduced in Chapter 16 and Illustration 7. How often does he or she want to do this? Let's say that the Seller's quota requires four Buyers per month to decide to do business with his or her company. That means that, on average, he or she would require one enthusiastic Buyer to close per week.

Let's also assume that the Seller has found that, for various reasons, in order to get one new customer per week, he or she must have four Buyers active in the decision process at any one time. When the Seller Pulls a Buyer from the Decision to Buy step, this action creates a "shortage" of one Buyer at that step. This shortage triggers a Pull request to the upstream process step (Build Relationship) to move a Buyer to the next stage. The movement of this latest Buyer triggers a Pull request to the upstream process step (Assess Fit) to supply another Buyer. So this continues until we get to the beginning, a Lead.

However, for a variety of reasons, Buyers frequently exit the process—sometimes called "attrition"—before completing it. These attrited Buyers have to be accounted for and replaced in the sales pipeline as well. With some amount of historical data tracking, estimates can be made of how many Buyers a Seller requires at each stage in order to account for expected attrition and still be able to meet his or her quota of one new customer per week.

Illustration 15: A Pull Selling Pipeline

Illustration 15 shows our combined Buyer-Seller process with a salesperson Pulling from the end (representing *demand*, just like a customer would pull a product off a supermarket shelf). The Lean symbol of a circular arrow indicates that each step in the process is Pulling from the stage before it, all the way back to the beginning.

These ideas of sales pipeline management are not new. What is novel is the idea of a salesperson Pulling from the sales system. What is the significance of this? First of all, it puts the goal of pipeline replenishment under the rigor and control of a process. Second, it looks at the entire sales *system,* not just the sales process. The sales system includes the inputs to the sales process, which are leads, as well as outputs from the system, which are satisfied, repeat customers. *With a Pull system approach, it will become immediately obvious from sales system metrics when and where in the sales pipeline the number of required Buyers is falling short.* This will also ultimately reveal the number of leads that must be provided on a daily or weekly basis to keep the pipeline "stocked."

Illustration 16: Keeping the Sales Pipeline Stocked

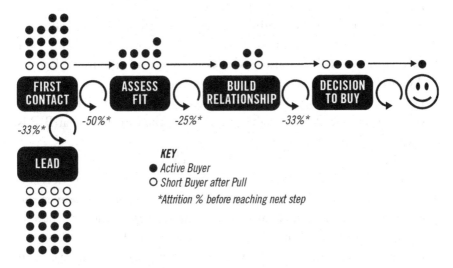

Too often, the sales process is treated as a disconnected process and not as a part of a larger system. The larger system includes the outputs of marketing and lead-generation efforts, which are inputs to the sales pipeline. The outputs and inputs of all groups involved in the support and execution of the sales pipeline must be tightly linked. Let's assume, for example, that the attrition rate from each process step to the following one is as shown in Illustration 16.

Let's see what happens when a salesperson Pulls a new customer from the pipeline. Based on the historical attrition rate, each upstream process "knows" how many new Buyers have to move in to its process step to keep the pipeline fully "stocked" at each step. A Pull system model of a sales pipeline ensures that the process is in balance, is "leveled," and allows for monitoring of metrics for early warnings of pipeline shortfall at every step.

Note that with the fictitious attrition rate we have assumed for this example, six new leads are required to replace one customer that is Pulled from the end by making a Buying decision. This is because each process step must "replenish" each Buyer-in-Process (BIP) that is Pulled to the next process step with a BIP number that takes into consideration that step's attrition rate. (You can calculate this number by taking 100 leads and multiplying them in turn by each step's attrition rate, and then dividing 100 by the resulting number.)

This "backward cascading," or ripple effect, of the attrition rate multiplies the BIP requirement as we view the process steps from right to left as shown in Illustration 16. This upstream "signaling," known in Lean terminology as *kanban*, is represented by the circular arrows between process steps, and is "transmitted" from right to left one process step at a time. The straight arrows show the direction that BIP is moving through the process.

This infers, in essence, that historically on average only about 17% of leads that come into the sales pipeline result in a Buying decision at the end of the Buying-Selling process. **Every Buyer who leaves the pipeline prematurely is a form of expensive waste.** Clearly, there is an opportunity to find out if the attrition rate can be reduced with a continuous improvement initiative (the topic of the next chapter). Such an improvement project could reduce waste (attrited leads and Buyers) in the sales pipeline while reducing the number of leads required in order to meet sales goals. Not all attrition can be eliminated; however, even a small reduction in the rate would add up to real savings in the cost of sales and marketing.

A great place to start looking for improvement would be in evaluating the quality of the leads that are provided to the salespeople. Are they sufficiently qualified? Are there clear, cross-functional guidelines on how to qualify a lead? Refer to the Case Example, "Leaning the Sales Pipeline" in Chapter 2, for a real-world illustration of the difference better lead qualification can make. Do you know what the Buyer attrition rate is in your organization?

When a Pull-initiated Lean Selling System is put in place and stabilized, sales results will become predictable because sales volume can be grown by increasing the volume or frequency of the Pull at the end of the process (by adding more salespeople or increasing quotas, or both). Doing so will Pull demand through the entire sales pipeline and create demand at each process step in the pipeline that will have to be replenished.

Any inability to fulfill demand at any process step rapidly will expose and highlight a sales process problem, and internal discussions can begin immediately about what to do to fix this. **It may turn out that** the biggest causes of sales pipeline shortfall are at the beginning stages of the process, not at the end where everyone always looks. Whatever the ultimate cause of the problem and its remedy is, the root causes of issues in the sales process can be addressed *because we have a system*, not just a process, and the system Pulls, not pushes, value through the process. This is the Lean Selling System.

Key Takeaways from Chapter 22

1. *Pull is also an important and ideal state of Lean systems, as it helps eliminate waste.*

2. *It is difficult initially to conceive, let alone implement, how Pull can work in a sales process.*

3. *Injecting Pull into the sales process will require a redefinition of one of the roles a salesperson plays to that of a consumer of the process.*

Chapter 23

Pursuing Perfection

Continuous Improvement

In the previous four chapters, we have covered four of the five core principles that form the basis of Lean Thinking: *Specifying Value, Identifying the Value Stream, Creating Flow,* and *Enabling Pull.* In this chapter we will address the fifth and final one: *Pursuing Perfection.*

As we learned in the previous chapter, Lean Thinking can improve a process and the customer experience, and further improvements can still be made. Underlying all Lean systems is an enduring principle called Continuous Improvement. Continuous Improvement encompasses both a philosophy and a practical way to implement it. This starts with the premise that all processes, including Lean ones, can be improved endlessly. This ceaseless pursuit of further improvement is what provides endless energy to a Lean system.

At first, the idea of endless improvement might sound like a motivational gimmick but not a practical one, sort of like trying to reach the horizon. However, it is actually a practical objective that yields continuing additional benefits as a result of implementing continuing improvements. Years of benchmark data from Lean production implementations around the world have demonstrated this, as the following table illustrates:[1]

Table 6 – Benchmark Data for Continuous Improvement

Improvement Area	*Immediate* % Improvement with Initial Implementation	*Additional* % Improvement after 2-3 Years
Labor Productivity	+100%	+100%
Production Times	-90%	-50%
Inventories	-90%	-50%
Quality Problems	-50%	-50%
New Product Time-to-Market	-50%	-50%

The measurable benefits from the initial implementation of a Lean production system, presented in the center column of Table 6, are almost inconceivable. I would have tremendous difficultly believing them if I had not personally seen comparable improvement results in Lean implementations I have been involved in, as I discussed in the Introduction section of this book. I don't doubt this data because I've experienced it myself (as well I trust as the researcher who reported the information).

The best way I can explain how it's possible to achieve these types of dramatic improvements is that most processes that have not yet undergone a Lean implementation are massively unproductive and inefficient, to a level that we just don't understand and can't believe. Therefore, *our level of shock and disbelief at the level of improvement is really just a reflection of the degree to which we underestimate how much waste and room there is for improvement to begin with*.

However, as inconceivable as this data may be, the data presented in the right column, representing the results of ongoing Continuous Improvement efforts in the same organizations, is even more incredible. Who could imagine that the kind of results achieved in the initial implementation could actually be improved significantly further? These are not the "outlier" results of a single very unproductive company that became radically more productive. This data comes from the "rule-of-thumb" results experienced by many companies across the globe over many years of benchmarking.

Steady State

Ironically, some readers may be wondering why an organization would continue to try to improve a system when it has already been improved so much. Possibly these same readers could see themselves pursuing improvements to get the right column, but wouldn't that be far enough? Wouldn't it be better at some point to "lock down" the system and focus efforts on maintaining this exceedingly more productive and efficient implementation to ensure that things don't go backwards? Most people are familiar with the Law of Diminishing Returns. Isn't that a factor to consider: that further improvements will be harder to make, cost more, and yield diminishing levels of improvement?

☑ *LEAN LEARNINGS*

Continuous Improvement

Japanese: *Kaizen* 改善

Definition

The pursuit of perfection may be defined by continually striving to improve processes by shortening cycle times, reducing waste (time and inventory), and increasing the ratio of value-added (as defined by the customer) time as a percentage of the total time of a process. There are several Lean tools and methodologies that support the Continuous Improvement philosophy, including the Five Whys, Value Stream Mapping, and front-line teamwork. Typically, the team executing the process will be empowered to identify improvements on its own, implement them, assess the results, and determine further actions.

Application to Lean Selling

Once you are convinced that sales is truly a process—and not merely an individual art form—then the sales process can be standardized and continually improved using the Lean tools and methodologies mentioned above. The first step is to look at all the different groups surrounding the sales team that are critical to sales success and think in terms of creating cross-functional teams based on the entire job that needs to be done. This team can then be responsible to drive Continuous Improvement in the sales process.

Actually, the answer is *no*. **There is no evidence that the Law of Diminishing Returns applies to Lean systems, any more than it applies to technological innovation.** It's quite the opposite. **There appears to be a virtuous circle that is created when the first four principles of Lean Thinking are applied. As the limits of Flow and Pull are continually tested, new waste and new ways of providing value to customers are uncovered, continuously.**

Motivation

There is another reason to never stop in the pursuit for perfection. It has to do with the creative energy that people bring to a Lean process, which is generated by the philosophy of Continuous Improvement. I actually can't envision a Lean process being kept in stasis; it just goes against the grain of what Lean Thinking is about. It reminds me of the admonition, "Grow or die."

The mentality of maintenance is not particularly exciting or motivating for employees, or their management either. This is a concern at every level of the organization and for all employees. However, **management should be especially aware of the enthusiasm levels of their customer-facing employees, especially those in sales and support roles.**

This in itself is a good reason to consider injecting Lean Thinking into sales organizations in the form of Lean Selling™. Another is that **the mindset of Continuous Improvement is a healthy one, keeps the brain sharp and creative, and is a good deterrent against job complacency. Additionally, Continuous Improvement requires continuous teamwork.** All these benefits are invaluable for people who have to deal with strangers and customers on a regular basis.

An Incremental Approach

A different debate that might be precipitated by Table 6 is one of incrementalism versus a one-time revolution. One could argue that after the initial implementation, there was still a lot of room for improvement, as proven by the data in the right column. Wouldn't it be more efficient to change the process once and get all the benefits of the middle and right column—in one fell swoop—rather than changing it over and over again?

The kind of thinking that causes this type of question to be raised must be exposed as a dangerous mental trap. It is a classic "batch" mode way of thinking: that bigger is always better. Incremental approaches to problem solving and product development (particularly in software) have been shown to yield superior results on every quality and productivity measure. This is true for several reasons:

- **When problems are complex, we can only see so far ahead in terms of crafting solutions; everything else is guesswork and decreasingly likely to be accurate.**

- **If we wait until we believe we have every possible improvement mapped out, we may never get started on improving anything.**

- **There is a high likelihood of overdesign in attempting a "complete" solution.**

- **The problems that we see after initial implementation may not even be visible today.**

- **The problems that we think we should solve today may no longer be the highest priority problems—or problems at all—after an initial improvement initiative is completed.**

Rather, an incremental (sometimes referred to as "agile") approach fits best with Lean Thinking and is consistent with the principle of Continuous Improvement.

A Self-Sustaining System

A problem with the adoption of most sales methodologies is that, over time, salespeople tend to drift back to their personal styles and comfort zones and away from the methodology unless it is rigorously enforced by management. As a result, most sales methodologies introduced into an organization may have some immediate benefit but are usually not self-sustaining. Further, organizations that strictly enforce compliance with a sales methodology are rare. This is why, in many organizations, sales methodologies come and go and come again, albeit under different names and with a slightly different focus each time.

Lean Selling is not a sales methodology in itself, but rather a system for inculcating Lean Thinking into sales processes. It is based on a set of Lean principles that have been implemented in a variety of settings and functional areas, providing a rich source of best practices and tools for implementation.

Lean Thinking always starts with defining value for the customer and then pursues the best ways to deliver that value in the shortest amount of time. There will always be obstacles that arise during that pursuit, which will be unique to each organization. Lean tools help identify and overcome these obstacles, resulting in a Lean process and system that is customized to the organization. Like all Lean implementations, a Lean Selling implementation will always be unique to the organization and the product or service it is providing.

Once such a customized Lean Selling process and system are created, an organization will naturally want it to be enduring. Philosophically, an organization would like such a system to have a life of its own—to be self-sustaining—preferably from the bottom up, not from the top down. Fortunately, our fifth and final Lean principle, *Pursuing Perfection,* **which embraces a Continuous Improvement mindset, provides the means to create a bottom-up, self-sustaining, enduring selling system that delivers additional benefits, endlessly.** In fact, an attribute of Lean systems is that they are self-sustaining and self-evolving, due to their relentless focus on Continuous Improvement.

Key Takeaways from Chapter 23

1. *A mindset of Continuous Improvement is a fundamental requirement for Lean processes, including Lean Selling.*

2. *A culture of Continuous Improvement keeps employees motivated and gives the organization a competitive edge.*

3. *Continuous Improvement, along with employee empowerment, can be the basis for a self-sustaining sales system.*

Chapter 24

Making It Visual

In Chapter Twenty-Four
→ Key Performance Indicators
→ Reporting Status
→ Creating Transparency
→ Early Warning Systems
→ Problem Solving

Establishing KPIs

In Lean implementations, making the status of processes visual is essential to monitoring progress and to being notified of problems as they occur. There are a number of very simple, creative ways that this has been done in production environments, where status reporting is essentially built into the process. For example, in a Lean production implementation, the physical movement of product or the movement of a card (thereby creating an empty slot) to request more parts from an upstream process provides a status.

Lean production encourages using lights, colors, and other physical clues to show what is going on in a factory or service process. The mechanisms that have been created to do this are startlingly low-tech. The important thing is to put a foolproof system in place so it is immediately obvious to people who have their eyes open when something is not right.

What kinds of things could go wrong in a sales process? One thing is that the sales pipeline (for an individual or sales team in aggregate) may not have the required number of Buyers at each stage of the process to meet sales targets. Another is that there may not be enough leads coming into the sales pipeline. Yet another is that a specific Buyer may be stuck on a process step for too long. Any of these can indicate that something has gone wrong with the sales process (again, individually or in aggregate), and the cause of the problem must be found and corrected to get the process on track once again.

Make the Sales Pipeline Visible

The key reason that Lean implementations have an emphasis on making things visual is that visibility highlights problems rather than hiding them. The sales pipeline is not an exception to this.

One of the reasons it is so hard to troubleshoot and fix sales process issues is that the sales pipeline is rarely visible in a way that lets everyone know exactly what is going on at any time. As a result, much of what is actually going on in the sales process remains a mystery. Possibly some people prefer it that way. Most organizations have difficulty measuring sales progress within their process; instead they opt to try to manage it from the end of the process—Closed Sales—sort of like predicting the weather by looking at a thermometer.

CRM systems can often make this problem *worse* if they are not used properly. They can become a source of obfuscation about what is going on in the sales process. The data may be in the CRM but no one is sure what it says because reports generated from the CRM rarely produce the type of management reports required to, well, manage.

Typically, sales pipeline management takes place in one-on-one meetings between managers and individual salespeople. This is time-consuming and anything but real-time. Relying on displays of charts and graphs on an individual's computer screen or printouts does not qualify as Lean visibility.

Organizations require very simple and straightforward ways of providing organizational visibility of progress (or lack of it) in the sales pipeline by individual and by team. Sometimes that means installing a low-tech solution that depends on visual cues such as colors and shapes and other clever ways to immediately convey the status of the sales pipeline.

One of the ways to monitor the sales process at a high level is by using Key Performance Indicators, or KPIs, to measure overall system performance. This can function like a dashboard in a car does, alerting to any anomalies and triggering corrective actions. Consideration must be made as to which KPIs to monitor. Some of the more obvious candidates for sales are:

- **Revenue by period (day, week, month) against target**
- **Number of closed deals by period**
- **Movement of Buyers from process step to process step**
- **Level of attrition of Buyers in the sales pipeline prematurely (lost, delayed, or on-hold)**
- **Leads that have been moved to the sales pipeline by period**
- **Inbound leads by period**
- **Number of leads being nurtured (i.e., premature for the sales pipeline)**
- **Percentage of Buyers who successfully move from one stage to the next compared to historical averages**

Status Reporting

Once sales management has decided on the specific KPIs it wants to track, the next things to determine are where the status information is coming from, how it gets into the system that is collecting the data, and how that system generates reports. A separate decision has to be made about the frequency of reporting, but the updating of information going into the system must be at least as frequent, or more so, than the reporting update cycle for the output.

In a factory production setting, the status would be as close to real-time as possible. In a large-scale telemarketing or telesales setting, that type of real-time data may also be required, especially when launching new campaigns or doing an experiment using A/B testing (testing two different offers or messages to see which one yields a better result). For lower-intensity sales situations, real-time reporting may not be required. However, it is critical that there is a fixed, repeatable time cycle for updating data and reports, whether it is hourly, daily, or weekly.

Transparency

Some thought has to be given to the physical form these reports take. They should be in the form of a shared visual that everyone who is part of the extended sales process and responsible for any of the steps within it can see at any time, from anywhere. The best way to accomplish this will depend on the physical layout of the working location. Managers may find that this objective of every process participant having visual access to the information in a public space is so important that work spaces will have to be redesigned to facilitate it. Co-location and close proximity to coworkers is critical to the success of this reporting method. Sales processes can provide some special challenges to achieving this, especially with participants traveling or in remote offices.

A key objective here is to provide transparency of all the information pertinent to the health of the process. It should be available to everyone at the same time. Ideally, it will be a shared visual such as a large whiteboard or a video screen. Physical colored magnets can also be used to visually represent status. Moving them is a bit less messy than erasing a whiteboard frequently, and they don't require any software to do the reporting. Often the lowest-tech, most visually-obvious approach is the best and most effective in monitoring Lean processes.

Early Warning

One of the key objectives of this visual system is early warning. In Lean systems, problems are detected at each process step and corrected immediately, so that quality problems are never propagated through the process. That's why KPIs or other physical or virtual markers are critical: they provide a status on every step in the process.

Let's say, for example, that suddenly the lead conversion rate drops dramatically so that very few new leads are actually making it to the next step in the sales process. This might be because an error was made upstream in one of the prospecting guidelines, such that none of the leads meet the criteria for becoming a Buyer. If this abrupt change

---

☑️ *LEAN LEARNINGS*

The Five Whys

Definition

The Five Whys is a very simple yet powerful Lean technique for problem solving. Whenever a problem appears or an objective can't be met, the question, "Why?" is asked five times. The second "Why?" is asked in response to the first answer, and so on. For example, let's say that an error is found in delivering a service. The process would go something like this:

1. *Why did the error happen?*

   A. **Because the new person didn't know**

1. *Why didn't the new person know?*

   A. **Because he hasn't been trained yet**

1. *Why hasn't he been trained?*

   A. **Because Mario is on vacation**

1. *Why didn't Mario's replacement train him?*

   A. **Because there is no replacement for Mario**

1. *Why is there no replacement for Mario?*

   A. **No one thought about it because we didn't know that a new person was starting this week.**

This technique is a key tool in the Lean methodology called Root Cause Analysis, which strives to get the root cause of problems, not just their symptoms, so they can be solved—permanently. Some managers would have stopped after the first question and commanded, "Train him right away!" But that would not have prevented the problem from reoccurring at another time with a different new employee. Asking the Five Whys uncovered a couple of deeper-rooted problems that were the real causes, not the symptoms. A root cause solution now clearly is:

1. Mario must have a backup in case he gets sick or is on vacation.

2. Someone has to let Mario's supervisor know when a new employee is starting and must be trained.

Application to Lean Selling

Whenever something unexpected or wrong happens in a sales process, stop and ask "Why?" five times. Then take corrective action to prevent the same issue from appearing again when you least expect it.

did not show as an exception, the lead-generation team or marketing group might not be aware of the error and continue to seek out and engage with the wrong prospects.

Intervention

When someone observes an obvious deviation from the expected norm, the team responsible for the process must collaborate immediately to understand what is causing the deviation and how it can be corrected. There are various Lean tools that can be used as aids in this discovery such as the "Five Whys" (see box). The Five Whys demand that, in searching for the solution to a problem, process participants go deeper than the superficial symptoms of the problem and understand the root cause. It is only by pulling out the root that a weed will not regrow.

The responsible response team must convene with a sense of urgency and make its investigation a priority. There is no higher priority in a Lean system implementation than fixing a process that is not operating within the specifications it was designed for. The solution ultimately put in place will be in the form of a scientific experiment, such as with Continuous Improvement initiatives, in that the team will have a hypothesis about what it will see change when the team implements the agreed-upon fix. Then the team will monitor the process and see if its predictions were correct before declaring victory.

Key Takeaways from Chapter 24

1. *Key Performance Indicators, or KPIs, provide an objective way to measure process health and the progress of improvement initiatives.*

2. *Lean culture requires transparency and access for everyone to critical information about performance, including KPIs.*

3. *Lean systems, including Lean Selling™, have early warning systems built in so problems can be addressed before they become crises.*

4. *The Five Whys are a technique for getting to the root cause of any problem.*

Chapter 25

Trainers, Coaches, Consultants, and Teachers

Inertia

I mentioned in an earlier part of this book that I would never recommend that an organization attempt a complete Lean transformation on its own, to Lean Selling™ or otherwise. The reason for this goes beyond the amount of Lean experience that may be contained within the management ranks of the organization. Basically, it is very important for an organization to have a resource with an outside perspective that will not be swayed by office politics or other internal considerations that employees typically have.

Another reality is that change is hard and people resist it, consciously and unconsciously. This is often referred to as organizational inertia. It takes a certain amount of energy at a different vector to change organizational inertia into momentum, and that usually requires an external force. ***In many ways Lean Thinking is counterintuitive, so it is important that the professional who leads the charge is someone who will not lose confidence in where the Lean path is heading.***

Change Agents

One name for such people is change agents. These are the people who are very good at understanding the big picture and can envision what the Future State looks like. They have excellent skills at pulling

236

☑ *LEAN LEARNINGS*

Go See for Yourself

Japanese: *Genchi Genbutsu* 現地現物
or *Gemba* 現場

Definition

Fundamental to Lean problem solving, this term means to physically go to the place where a problem originated and see for yourself what is happening. In other words, don't rely on second-hand reports or evaluations of those who have not been there. This is related to the American management phrase, "Management by Walking Around," often attributed to management practices at Hewlett-Packard and popularized by Tom Peters and Robert H. Waterman in their 1982 book, *In Search of Excellence*.

Application to Lean Selling

How often does a company CEO or senior executive physically go to the sales department or floor and listen to what is transpiring? It's quite rare. Is anyone on the phone? Is everyone on the phone? Are they mostly talking or listening? How are the conversations going? What type of problems do you see or hear? You can read all the sales reports and forecasts you want, but if you really want to know what's going on, Lean tells you to go to where the process is happening and see for yourself.

Another application of this is senior executives talking with customers (and suppliers) to hear first-hand how they view your organization and the value you deliver. Doing this one thing can make for much more productive sales discussions.

together and leading a team to collaborate on creating something new. They are also mentally tough and will face down anyone who attempts to obstruct progress. A change agent should emerge from inside of the organization, with the full support of top management in driving a transformation to a new reality.

The change agent is so critical to any major process transformation, and to a Lean one in particular, that the desired change will probably never happen without the involvement of such a person. The change agent is the one who will keep things moving in the direction of change despite the obstacles that arise internally or the setbacks that occur.

There are also a variety of outside resources that can help with knowledge transfer of Lean Thinking and principles into your organization. These resources disseminate their knowledge in different ways, and they can be roughly classified as being in one or more of four traditional categories of business and sales education and advisory services.

Trainers

Trainers normally specialize in conveying knowledge on specific methodologies or packaged programs. This modality is very common for sales, where sales trainers will typically specialize in a specific sales methodology. Delivery of a training program will normally happen over a set period of time in a group setting. The material presented will typically be prepackaged and not customized for the organization, especially with branded programs. The trainer may also be available to the organization for follow-up, fine-tuning, and troubleshooting as the organization begins implementation.

An organization can benefit from the services of a trainer for certain aspects of Lean adoption, especially when it comes to methodologies. One example of this would be the Lean methodology of Value Stream Mapping (VSM). While VSM can apply to any process, it has a very specific way it should be done. A training session for those who are going to use VSM can be of value, either as a separate session or in conjunction with an initial VSM event. Another example is training on Lean tools that support Lean principles, such as Continuous Improvement.

A Lean Selling trainer can support a Lean transition by instructing on the use of unique methodologies contained within the **Lean Selling System**. These include how to coach a Buyer, getting a Buyer to act as a coach, and creating a Buying Plan.

Coaches

A coach will generally not have a canned methodology to share, but will be good at developing certain kinds of skills in employees. Coaching is usually highly personalized, where a coach begins by assessing the current level of hard and soft skills, and the strengths and weaknesses, of an individual or team. The coaching that then takes place is adapted to best help the individual or team to reach a new level of performance in using those skills. In the case of individual coaching, the coach would work with a client to set realistic goals for improvement, providing support and accountability toward achieving a Future State.

In the case of sales, a coach could also have an individual or a team as a client, or both simultaneously. As an example, the sales team could be a client (objective: improved team performance through sales process coaching), as well as the sales manager (objective: improved team performance through sales process management coaching), as well as individual salespeople on the team (improved individual performance through focus on development of specific individual skills, role playing, addressing specific sales situations, and support in executing requirements of the sales process). With sales coaching, the goals will almost always be improvements in measurable performance, the most obvious of which is the rate of closing sales. Other goals might also include additional metrics, such as rate of movement in the sales pipeline, or the length of the sales cycle.

A **Lean Selling Coach** can address similar performance objectives, but will likely have a stronger emphasis on team compliance to the Lean Selling process, and teamwork across the extended sales team. After all, any Lean implementation is a team sport. There are specific employee "soft" skills in the areas of interpersonal communications, problem solving, and emotional intelligence that support teamwork and facilitate Lean adoption. A **Lean Selling Coach** can help develop these both individually and within the team.

Of course, a **Lean Selling Coach** will additionally focus on helping individuals and teams to internalize and develop the skills to successfully employ the unique techniques of the **Lean Selling System**. These include the use of the methodologies mentioned in the previous section, and also how to effectively execute a single Buying-Selling plan.

Consultants

Consultants are mainly generalists, although they will often specialize in a certain domain such as business strategy, operations, or sales. They may also specialize in particular industries, especially when the industries have certain unique aspects that require deep understanding of their unique business models or regulatory environment.

The main difference between consultants and the previously mentioned trainers and coaches is that consultants do not generally come into an organization with a specific improvement agenda already mapped out. While there are some consultants that use a packaged, branded methodology, most consultants will be driven by the specific challenges the organization has identified that it wants to address. Competent consultants are skilled at troubleshooting and cutting through the "noise" to understand the reality of an organization's situation and what options there are to move forward.

A Lean consultant, while armed with a background in Lean Thinking and implementation, would be more likely than a trainer or coach to begin with a high-level perspective of the organization's goals and objectives and its Current State before advising what Lean actions could be considered. Accordingly, a Lean consultant might be most appropriate for helping an organization figure out *where* Lean Thinking should initially be applied, and to develop projects to implement it in target areas.

A Lean Selling consultant can also help a company understand what outcomes it should reasonably expect from implementing the **Lean Selling System**. Such a consultant will also be in a position to estimate the time and effort to make the transition, based on experience and what he or she learns about the Current State of the company's sales process, including lead generation.

Teachers

A teacher has expert knowledge of a certain domain and generally develops his or her own methodology, or pedagogy, for conveying that information to "students." A teacher has a clear idea of the scope of knowledge that has to be conveyed, and will test frequently to be sure students are absorbing it. A good teacher will adapt his or her teaching techniques according to the knowledge absorption rates of students or the group (class).

In Japanese, the word for teacher is *sensei*. This term can be translated literally as, "one born before," or one who has previously walked the path another is taking. A *sensei* is a role with regard in Japanese society, with such a person accorded great respect and often reverence. A *sensei* is often considered to have great skill and knowledge in his or her field. The honorific term implies a person has not only advanced knowledge, but also wisdom based on accumulated knowledge.

This term is often used to address the head teacher of a martial arts *dojo*, or school. It implies that the *sensei's mission* is to share knowledge so that students can gain what he already has. In this sense, a *sensei* might also be thought of as a mentor. The main difference between a coach and a sensei is that, while both can help students or clients to learn and get better, the latter term implies a level of personal attainment. A sensei not only helps others to learn, but also personally embodies the skill, wisdom, or experience to do so.

Lean Thinking originated and was refined in Japan. In Lean, there is a term for someone who has achieved a high level in the field: a **Lean Sensei**. A *Lean Sensei* is an expert on both the philosophy and implementation of Lean Thinking, its methodologies, and its implementation. A *Lean Sensei's* classroom is the place where a Lean transformation is taking place.

A *Lean Sensei* is not a consultant, because he or she arrives at organizations with an agenda: eliminate waste and speed up processes. This goal is always the same, reducing waste and Continuous Improvement, although the actual implementation in each organization will be different. A *Lean Sensei* will lead a team through a Lean transformation and stay with the transformation until it is complete and showing positive results.

It is hard to find a true *Lean Sensei* because they are in short supply. However, if your organization is considering a Lean transformation and you can find one, by all means, hire him or her on the spot. It could be the best investment your company will ever make.

We cannot in good faith claim that a Lean Selling *Sensei* even exists today. The domain is too new. Hopefully, in the not-too-distant future, with a multiplicity of implementations of the **Lean Selling System** under their belts, there will be an ample supply of individuals who each qualify as a ***Lean Selling Sensei.***

Key Takeaways from Chapter 25

1. *Inertia is the biggest enemy of change initiatives, including a Lean Selling transformation.*

2. *Change agents are critical players in Lean transformations, as they are a force to counter inertia.*

3. *Trainers, coaches, consultants, and teachers are all available outside resources that can help ensure the success of a Lean transformation.*

4. *A Lean Selling Coach can guide your organization to successfully applying Lean Selling principles.*

When to Get Started with a Sales Transformation

- → Habit 3
- → Time Management Matrix
- → From Quadrant I to Quadrant II
- → Timing a Lean Transformation

Habit 3

In his best-selling book, *The Seven Habits of Highly Effective People*, Steven R. Covey dedicates a chapter to Habit 3, consciously prioritizing where to put your energy. Habit 3 is "Put First Things First," and it applies to organizations as well as it applies to individuals. He presents a graphical matrix which is a very useful tool for seeing how this works. I have reproduced this matrix below.[1]

Illustration 17: Time Management Matrix

	URGENT	NOT URGENT
IMPORTANT	I Crises	II Improvement Activities Problem Prevention
NOT IMPORTANT	III Interruptions	IV Surfing the Web

Adapted from *The Seven Habits of Highly Effective People* by Stephen R. Covey

As you can see, the two scales that determine the quadrant in which an activity resides are urgency and importance. Examples of the types of activities that occur in each of the quadrants are shown in Illustration 17.

Covey then shows graphical examples of what happens when our time, or an organization's time, is spent primarily in one of these quadrants. Since time is limited, you end up with a graphic that looks like Illustrations 18 or 19.

Illustration 18: Quadrant I Dominance

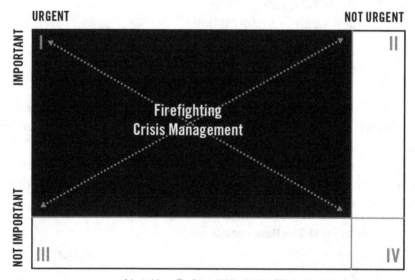

Adapted from *The Seven Habits of Highly Effective People* by Stephen R. Covey

Does Quadrant I look familiar? It is where most people spend their time in their personal and business lives. It is where organizations that are primarily made up of Quadrant I leaders spend their time as well. Since time is a limited commodity, note how spending time in Quadrant I crowds out the other three, so there is little time left to spend on them. This is especially important when there is little or no time to spend on Quadrant II, which has to do with forestalling or preventing crises.

The irony is that the more time we spend in Quadrant I deal-ing with urgent issues, business firefighting, and crisis manage-

ment, the more time we will have to spend in Quadrant I, since we will never have time to invest in averting crises. This is a vicious circle that reminds me of the saying, "I would spend time on fire prevention if I weren't so busy putting out the fires." There's a similar saying about draining a swamp and alligators.

Covey argues that the ideal goal is to maximize your energy and efforts in Quadrant II. As Illustration 19 shows, Quadrant II activities are much more forward-thinking. They are what we often call investments in people, and in the future of an organization (or personal life). As a result of spending most of our time in Quadrant II, we see that the amount of time spent in Quadrant I is greatly diminished. This is not just because Quadrant II is "crowding out" Quadrant I, but that over time there are far fewer Quadrant I (i.e., urgent) activities that demand our attention. This is because the investment made in fire prevention (Quadrant II) greatly reduced the number of fires (Quadrant I).

Illustration 19: Quadrant II Dominance

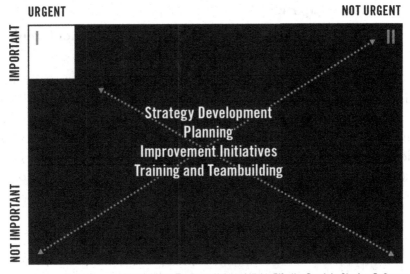

Adapted from *The Seven Habits of Highly Effective People* by Stephen R. Covey

It seems that most people I know don't like to spend most of their time on Quadrant I activities, but they do so anyhow. It seems to be a chronic problem in most organizations and people's lives today. Why is that? If it's as simple as making more investments of time in Quadrant II, why don't more people do it?

This is a question worth considering. I think most people have gotten used to being in a reactive mode, and have not taken control of their time. I see this in organizations as well, where they go from one crisis to another. Possibly people feel they have no choice because they spend most of their time at work solving (preventable) urgent problems, and then they go home and face the same thing.

I think that people and organizations don't get in front of this problem because it is hard to do. I can think of five core reasons more Quadrant II activities don't get done:

1. **Planning, reflection, and consensus-building are *hard work*.**

2. **Quadrant II activities require a *proactive attitude*.**

3. **Quadrant II activities require *creativity* and "out-of-the box" thinking.**

4. **Quadrant II activities require *discipline* to commit time to them regularly.**

5. **Quadrant II activities require *commitment* to not be pulled into seemingly urgent and important activities.**

Most people would agree that hard work, a proactive attitude, creativity, discipline, and commitment are all positive qualities. They are the types of things a truly successful person's character or an organization's winning culture can be based upon. These characteristics just don't come without effort. They require direction of our own personal values based on internal motivation, or leadership from the top of an organization.

Lean Thinking and Quadrant II

I happen to agree with Covey's assertion about the power of Quadrant II thinking. I have seen this play out in business and my personal life many times over the years. The reason I drew from Covey's ideas for this chapter is that his observations are such a great backdrop for discussing Lean Thinking. Up to this part of the book, we have spent a lot of time on the manifestations of Lean Thinking, but not as much on its underlying philosophy. Yet I believe that its underlying philosophy is the engine that gives Lean Thinking its power to transform.

Quadrant II thinking and Lean Thinking have a lot in common. First and foremost, *Lean Thinking requires the mindset of a long-term investor, not a short-term speculator. Lean Thinking is the antithesis of crisis management.* It seeks to avoid unintended crises by investing in crisis prevention. Continuous Improvement, one of the hallmark activities that results from Lean Thinking, is a Quadrant II activity that time is invested in, continuously.

The upshot is that, as attractive as the results of Lean Thinking are, it is not for organizations that prefer to manage from crisis to crisis. It would be a waste of time to pursue Lean Thinking initiatives unless an organization is ready to leave Quadrant I behind, forever.

Lean Selling and Quadrant II

As you might have already anticipated, the same argument is valid for adopting Lean Selling™. Lean Selling, as well, is something that should not be pursued by short-term thinkers or organizations that will not or cannot stay the course.

Most sales organizations and activities are filled with crises, if not at the end of each month, then certainly at the end of the quarter or year. Possibly management thinks that crises are good for salespeople, that they are motivating. I wonder if they have ever surveyed their salespeople to test that assumption.

Most salespeople I know would like to think that they have some control over their sales production. They would also like to have some confidence in the predictability of the sales results they can expect with their current efforts. Interestingly, these are the exact same things that sales managers yearn to have. People are happier and less anxious when they feel they have some control over achieving their goals.

Control, confidence, and a certain level of predictability are valued nearly universally by everyone. Crisis is the opposite of that. Are we so sure that it is really motivating for salespeople (or their managers)? Lean Thinking is a different type of thinking. It requires that we leave old beliefs and values behind (because they are not getting us where we want to go) and try something new and different. It requires that we are willing to change and to challenge ourselves and our organizations.

Timing a Lean Transformation

The answer to when is the right time to start a Lean Selling transformation is when you are ready to move on from spending the majority of your sales energies in Quadrant I, and ready to start investing in the future in Quadrant II. The right time is when you are ready to move from selling by crisis to selling by plan. It is when you are ready to move from chaos to a repeatable standard sales process that can be measured, evaluated, and continuously improved. It is when you are ready to say goodbye to Quadrant I selling and move to Quadrant II selling using the **Lean Selling System**.

In the early 2000s, American automobile manufacturers began to close the gap with Toyota on quality, at least in initial quality. I remember well the television advertisements by American automobile manufacturers touting their successes in the J.D. Power surveys on initial quality. However, as quality was measured over the life of the cars, the quality gap once again grew between Toyota and American manufacturers. *Consumer Reports* reported that after three years, American models had two or three times the problems of Toyota-built cars. Why? One expert states it is because superficial initial quality is easier to achieve cosmetically than systemic quality, which stands the test of time.[2]

For some organizations there will never be a right time to transform their sales organization using Lean Thinking. Others will start down the path, but turn back when the going gets tough, or deal with Lean Thinking superficially, as certain American automobile manufacturers did. The few companies that make it through the initial phase and stay the course of Continuous Improvement of their sales processes, however, will eventually *realize an insurmountable competitive advantage within their industries, based primarily on the way their sales organizations sell.*

This is akin to the (currently) insurmountable advantage that

Toyota has in global leadership of the automobile industry. At the time of writing this book, Toyota is dramatically more profitable and has significantly more cash in its war chest than all American automobile manufacturers combined. Only Volkswagen today is even within striking distance. Toyota, still the global leader in industry sales after recovering from five difficult years of recession, safety recalls, and extensive media coverage about runaway cars, has just reported record profits.

Of course, you are possibly considering learning more about Lean Selling because your sales function *is* in crisis. You may not think it's the ideal time to begin a Lean transformation, but it worked for Toyota after World War II, when the company couldn't remain viable without inventing Lean Thinking. Often a crisis is required to break the inertial grip of the *status quo*.

However, what if your sales organization is not in crisis, just chugging along month by month, but you believe there is much more it could do? ***If you are in a position to do so, create a crisis.*** This is a technique used by Toyota when management feels that their employees are getting too complacent.[3]

Putting more demand on the current sales process will uncover weak spots and problem areas, both opportunities for improvement that will not have been seen unless they are uncovered. A crisis can be created by simply raising revenue targets or setting goals for lead conversions or shortening the sales cycle.

When people say it can't be done, ask why, repeatedly. (Refer back to the Five Whys in Chapter 24.) When you get to the root cause, ask sales process participants what could be done to change it so it can happen. Do something. See if it improves the situation. Do something else. This will be the beginning of your Lean journey.

Key Takeaways from Chapter 26

1. The book, The Seven Habits of Highly Successful People, and Habit 3 in particular, aligns well with Lean Thinking and Lean Selling.

2. Not all organizations are ready for a Lean Selling transformation.

3. If your sales organization has gotten complacent, consider creating a crisis.

4. Use the Five Whys technique for addressing problems that appear during the crisis you create.

5. Get a team involved in brainstorming ideas to solve the problems and try something to see if these ideas work.

Chapter 27

How to Get Started with a Sales Transformation

In Chapter Twenty-Seven
→ Nibbling at Lean
→ Four Key Focus Areas
→ Senior Executive Exercises
→ Sales Executive Exercises
→ Salesperson Exercises

Are You Ready to Bite or Just Nibble?

If after reaching this part of the book you are ready to pursue a Lean Selling™ transformation, congratulations! I suspect, though, that there are many who at this point may like a lot of what they read and would like to improve their organization's sales performance but are not quite ready to take the leap. I have a suggestion for this group. It's called *point kaizen.*

Kaizen is the Japanese term for Continuous Improvement. Point *kaizen* means that you take Lean Thinking and apply improvement to a *part* of your process. In this case, it would mean applying the **Lean Selling System** to isolated parts of your sales process. Point *kaizen* can illustrate for you and your organization the power of Lean Thinking when applied to the sales process. While it won't get you the full benefits you would get from looking at the whole sales process in a systemic way, it's a start. Any start is better than doing nothing, and it's very low risk.

Four Focus Areas

For those of you who want to try point *kaizen*, or improvement, I suggest that you focus on four Lean Thinking principles as you embark upon your improvement program. A focus on these four elements alone can have a tremendous impact on productivity and performance:

1. **Value**

2. **Waste**

3. **Teamwork**

4. **Continuous Improvement**

Although we have covered each of these topics previously, let's briefly review them here. I have included a brief Lean definition of these terms and some rules for using them.

Value

Value in Lean Thinking is the benefit you deliver to your customers. This value can only be determined by your customers, not by your organization or your employees. In other words, for the purposes of this discussion, the only opinion that matters on the topic of value is the customer's. Only the customer can determine if something is of value to him or her.

Waste

Whatever your organization provides to or asks of the customer that does not add value from the customer's perspective is, for the purposes of Lean Thinking, waste. This includes any activities your organization does in the process of providing your ultimate product or service that doesn't add value from the customer's perspective. Some of this waste will be required to deliver your product or service and can't be eliminated or reduced immediately. Other waste will not be necessary and should be eliminated as soon as possible, if not immediately.

Teamwork

Teamwork is an absolutely essential ingredient for applying Lean Thinking. Lean improvements cannot be dictated; they must be developed organically by the people closest to the process. Management can set goals, and provide guidance and support, but unless it provides leadership that gets employees working collaboratively across functional boundaries—and even organizational boundaries when necessary—there will be no sustainable Lean improvements.

Continuous Improvement

Continuous Improvement is at the heart of Lean Thinking, and brings to bear many other Lean concepts in order to achieve it. A Lean transformation is not about reaching a set point and then settling comfortably into a new *status quo*. It is a mindset of continuously challenging what can be achieved. Most organizations do not have a culture of Continuous Improvement, and often employees have learned not to raise issues when they see problems. **The leaders of the organization must work to change this mindset by example so employees believe they will be *rewarded, not punished*, for identifying (and fixing) problems.**

How to Apply

Now that we've reviewed four basic principles of Lean Thinking that can have a big impact if applied, how do we begin to apply them? I suggest three different exercises that are simple and can be accomplished in a short period of time. I expect that seriously committing to these exercises and completing them in a timely fashion will open eyes in many organizations to the possibilities for improvement, and help to create a vision of an improved Future State.

CEOs, COOs, Senior Executives

If you are running the company or its operations or are a senior executive, I think you are going to like this exercise.

1. **Set aside an afternoon to meet with your direct reports.** Ask each person to write down what he or she believes is the key value that your organization provides for its customers. (You may want to prepare a simple form for this that you can hand out and collect.) If you have many different types of customers or products, you can pick one set to focus on. Either you or someone else can write the responses on a whiteboard. If there is not a consensus

on the value your organization provides, then begin a non-judg-mental discussion about what the real value is. Take as long as it requires to come to a consensus. Then, have someone capture the consensus view in a Value Statement Document. After you have circulated this document around and gained agreement from everyone on the team about your value statement, you are ready for the next step.

2. **Pick five to ten of your top customers and think about which person in each of those companies would be the best one to tell you what benefits he or she gets from your company's product or service.** If you don't know who the best person is, you may have to consult with your sales executive or the sales team member who is responsible for that account.

3. **Make an appointment to contact your customers live to dis-cuss their views of the value that your product or service adds to their companies.** Make sure they are talking about the business and strategic value you add, not just the technical value or product features. If they have trouble answering your question, ask them what bad things would happen to their com-pany if your product or service was removed from their premises tomorrow. (Make sure they know it is a *hypothetical* question, not a threat!)

4. **After completing your survey, compare the answers to the value document your team created.** Are there any surprises? Get back together with your team and go over the results. *Try to gain consensus on who was correct about the real value you provide, the customers or you and your team.* Does this change anything about the way you look at the activities you un-dertake for customers, or might it influence future decisions you make? Does it give any clues as to where you may be wasting time and energy on unnecessary or even counterproductive activities? How will you transfer what you learned from this exercise to the rest of your organization?

Sales Executives and Managers

Sales Executives and Managers are on the front lines of the sales process. In addition to providing support and training for their team, they typically spend a lot of time on administrative activities such as revenue forecasting. They usually appreciate process because they know it makes it easier for them to manage and understand what is going on. Here are a few process- and metric-oriented exercises for this group.

1. **Determine the average length of your sales cycle.** Start with closed or completed sales and calculate the number of days from when the lead was first qualified to enter into your sales pipeline. If you track the length of time a lead is at each step of your sales process, which step takes the longest to complete? Do you know why? What might be done to speed it up?

2. **Analyze the root causes of attrition of leads from your sales pipeline.** What are the top three reasons that leads come into the sales pipeline but do not complete the process? (Do not count leads that decided to do business with your competitor, only those that left the sales pipeline without making any vendor choice, that is, *No Decision or Status Quo*.) Are there common characteristics that these attrited leads have? Are these characteristics different from those of the leads that progress to the end of the sales process? Might you have less attrition if you used different qualification guidelines for deciding which leads come into the sales pipeline?

3. **Estimate the average time between a lead becoming qualified in your CRM system and the time it takes for one of your salespeople to receive it.** What can be done about reducing that time? How long on average does it take a salesperson to make initial contact with a new lead? Can anything be done to reduce that time?

4. **Identify any leads that haven't "moved" (changed state) for 30, 60, or 90 days, or more.** Can you determine why? Is the lead still viable or should it be moved out of the sales pipeline or put in a holding pattern? Do these leads have common characteristics that are different than leads that progress through the sales pipeline?

Salespeople

Lean Selling is a team sport, so we don't want the company executives and managers to have all the fun with these exercises. Here is a challenging one you as salespeople should find enjoyable, assuming your manager goes along with it. (Otherwise, you're on your own; I can't help you with that.)

1. **The next new lead you get, use the initial contact opportunity to explain your (or your organization's) philosophy about how Sellers work with Buyers.** Explain that the process is focused on adding the most value for the Buyer, *not just about making a sale.* Of course your prospects won't believe you at first, so you will have to be both persistent and consistent to convince them of your seriousness.

2. **Let the Buyers know that you would like to benefit them by sharing your extensive Buyer-support experience in helping them to reach a Buying decision that they are confident about, in the shortest elapsed time possible.** If they think this is a good idea, ask them if they would like you to act as a Buyer's Coach for them. Now, here's the kicker: tell them that, while you would, of course, prefer that they ultimately choose your company to do business with, *your main objective as a Buyer's Coach is to facilitate their making a decision that they are comfortable with in the shortest period of time, regardless of which vendor they select.* Of course, they will have trouble believing this as well, so now you must be completely transparent. You can say something like, "I know from sales statistics that when you make a Buying decision the chance of Buying from me is a least 50/50. However, industry data shows that the chances of Buyers making a decision at all are much less than that. As a result, I have a better chance of gaining new customers for my company if I increase the chances the people I coach will make a Buying decision. So, it's a win-win for both you and me."

3. **If you have them on the hook this far and they haven't wiggled off, ask them if they would take a few moments to work with you to sketch out a "Buying Plan" that lists all the steps they think might be involved in their getting to a purchase decision.** Here's your golden chance to show off your extensive experience working with Buyers and to gain credibility as a Buyer's Coach through asking seemingly innocent questions during the process about steps they may have missed. You can ask questions like, "Will you need to have . . . ?" or "Is the IT department going to have to sign off on that?" or "Will a legal review be required for the terms of our contract?" or "Are you going to require an ROI in order to get final approval?" You get the idea. **Show how knowledgeable you are about the Buyer's process and how different you are from any other salesperson they have met in recent memory, or maybe ever.**

I hope everyone has fun with these exercises, and that they become valuable learning experiences that start conversations at your organization about other ways Lean Thinking can assess and improve your sales efforts in the form of Lean Selling. Please be sure to post the results of your experiences at the LinkedIn® group or Facebook® page, "Lean Selling"; you can also direct message me on Twitter® @LeanSelling.

Key Takeaways from Chapter 27

1. *Lean Thinking and techniques can be applied to point areas in your sales process to see high impact with limited risk.*

2. *The four core principles of Lean Thinking—Value, Waste, Teamwork, and Continuous Improvement—are the ones to keep in mind as you consider how to apply Lean point improvements.*

3. There is a way for everyone affected by the sales process to get involved in personally experiencing the opportunity Lean Selling offers, from salespeople to CEOs.

4. Experiment with Lean, get out of your comfort zone, try something new and different in your sales process, and have FUN with it.

5. Let others in your organization know what you found and share your experiences with our Lean Selling online communities as well.

Chapter 28

A 90-Day Plan to Transform Sales

In Chapter Twenty-Eight
→ Ready to Go to the Next Step
→ A Pilot Approach
→ A 90-Day Plan, Week by Week

You Are Ready

The previous chapter had something for everyone, from salespeople to CEOs. This chapter, while hopefully still interesting to anyone engaged in sales or Lean Selling™, is directed primarily at the top executives of organizations. This is because this chapter provides a taste of what a full-on Lean Selling transformation might look like. Realistically, such a transformation is never going to happen without complete commitment from the very top of the organization. With that in mind, CEOs and senior executives: this chapter is for you!

Let's assume for a moment that you *are* one of those senior executives, and based on what you have read in this book so far, you want to learn more about what it would mean to embark upon a journey of sales transformation based on the principles of Lean Thinking and the application of Lean Selling. You know that point *kaizen* (improvement) described in the previous chapter is an option for you, but you want to know what other approaches you might consider that could have a bigger impact on the way you sell. That's great! Congratulations on your curiosity, forward thinking, and potential interest in becoming one of the early adopters in the Lean Selling movement!

Of course, you will want to get some idea of what would be involved. You likely will also want to know how long it will take. The answer to the latter question is actually "forever," since Continuous Improvement is, by definition, never-ending. Realistically, however, unless you have already personally experienced the dramatic improvements in speed, quality, and customer satisfaction that Lean Thinking can make when applied to your business processes, it may be a difficult leap for you to make.

This could be the first time you have been exposed to Lean Thinking. It is almost certainly the first time you have been exposed to Lean Selling, and it is definitely the first time you have been exposed to the **Lean Selling System. It is wise for you to be cautious, to see some evidence** that this can work for your organization before committing your entire company to pursue this path. In the remainder of this book I will attempt to address these questions and important concerns raised above, so that you will be able to make an informed decision about how and when you would like to move forward on improving your selling system.

The 90-Day Plan

I am going to suggest that **you consider a limited pilot program to evaluate the potential of applying the Lean Selling System in your organization.** Further, I will present this suggestion packaged in the form of a **step-by-step 90-day program** that you and your extended team can undertake to answer the question of whether Lean Selling is right for your organization. Are you ready? Here it is:

Week 1 (Days 1–7)

The first week is primarily about getting your key managers and leaders to buy into the pilot initiative and giving them an opportunity to ask questions regarding what the project is about and how they will be expected to support it. This should be accomplished by scheduling a group management meeting for this purpose. It is important for the organizational leader to clearly explain to his or her team why this pilot initiative is being undertaken, and what existing problems were the underlying motivations to consider it. In other words, what important problem are you trying to address with this pilot?

This organizational leader could be a senior executive such as the CEO, COO, president, or executive vice-president. It could also be a sales executive. It all depends on who has the authority and organizational responsibility to sponsor the pilot, largely based on which functions will be most affected by it. This introductory meeting should include all the direct reports of the sponsoring leader. All the top leaders of all the functional areas whose support is required for the pilot to be successful must attend this meeting.

When the team is gathered, the first order of business after questions and discussion is to scope the domain that this pilot initiative will be constrained to. Is it a particular group within sales (such as inside sales, outside sales, or sales support), the whole sales department, or does it also extend to include sales support functions (such as finance for the group that prepares bid proposals)? This decision will "bound," or limit, the scope of all the subsequent improvement activities for this pilot.

In addition to the organizational scope, the remaining limit on scope will be determined by the product or service that will be under study in the pilot. Different products and services can sometimes have different sales processes. If this is the case in your organization, you should limit the scope by both organization and by product or service offering.

Next, the group should agree on the membership of the Pilot Execution Team (PET) that will actually be leading the pilot. This team will include the sponsoring executive and likely some additional members of his or her team, and possibly other group participants in attendance. It may also include other key organizational leaders not present at the group meeting. Assignments should be made as soon as possible to inform appointed PET members who were not at the meeting of their appointment to this new responsibility. The group should also appoint a chair or leader for the PET.

The PET will have the responsibility of driving the pilot process forward and ensuring that senior management's intent for the pilot is preserved. A kickoff meeting for the PET should be scheduled within two weeks. The group should construct a high-level list of information that PET members should bring to this kickoff meeting.

The sponsoring leader must make sure that everyone on his or her team and anyone else who is appointed to the PET is supportive of the initiative and will not subvert it, consciously or unconsciously. Therefore, it is important to set a tone of openness for this meeting, where attendees can voice their concerns and have them heard and discussed without fear of recrimination or ridicule. It may be helpful to reinforce that this is a "90-day test," not a lifelong commitment, and that the results will be measured and evaluated, after which the team then will have a chance to weigh in on next steps with new hard data in hand. It is very important that the team members who attend this meeting understand that the primary purpose of the pilot initiative is *not* to assemble a critical assessment of the performance of their functional areas, but rather to provide a way that people across the organization can work together to help the company improve in the important area that is the focus of the pilot.

Week 2 (Days 8–14)

In the second week, those participants appointed to the Pilot Execution Team should gather information from within their area of responsibility to help support their participation in the kickoff meeting. The agenda for the kickoff meeting will be centered on determining customer value, so each participant will have to consider what research they might want to do prior to the meeting in order to be best prepared. For example, one participant may think it valuable to see which customers are generating the most revenue and profit for the product or service that is the subject of the pilot, and whether the customers who generate the most revenue are also the ones who generate the most profit.

Someone else might think it valuable to see if there are any identifying patterns that appear consistent across the very best customers, as compared to the rest. Yet another person might want to make an initial determination of whether all of the best customers get exactly the same value from the company's products and services, or different value. Each team member will have to decide what type of information he or she would like to have available in order to support his or her participation in the initial meeting.

Weeks 3-4 (Days 15–28)

In Week 3, the PET meets to tackle its first assignment, creating a Customer Value Document—which can be as brief as a statement—as succinctly and unambiguously as possible. The entire group must agree on the statement of value. If consensus cannot be reached in a reasonable amount of time, then assignments must be undertaken to do more research that will provide data to help bring the team to consensus at a follow-up meeting later that week. It is critical that everyone come to a consensus on the value that the organization provides to its customers, but that agreement should *never* be forced or otherwise coerced.

As soon as everyone is comfortable with the value statement, it should be captured in a Customer Value Document. Assignments should then be made for all PET members to interview key customers and ask them what value they believe they receive from the company's products and services. It is ideal if every PET member can do this with two or three customers.

The team will then reconvene to review its original value statement to see how it holds up after the customer interviews. If there are surprises or big disconnects, the team will have to decide how to resolve them, by either modifying the value statement, keeping it as-is, or gathering more information to determine what to do. (If the "keep as-is" course is chosen, then the team has uncovered and must acknowledge a mismatch between the organization's stated strategy and its value as perceived by customers to whom it has primarily been selling a particular product or service.)

Nailing down an *accurate* value statement that defines what value the company is aiming to provide to its customers (at least for those within the defined scope of the pilot) will be critical to the next steps in the pilot process. For example, the exercise to create a **Value Stream Map** (VSM), in which the team will participate in the following week, will be meaningless if people spend time trying to figure out how to improve delivery of the wrong value (not the one your customer really wants)!

Week 5 (Days 29–35)

This is the VSM creation week. It will take almost the entire week for the PET to create the VSM that describes the process the organization currently uses to create and deliver the product or service that falls within the pre-determined scope of the pilot, and to plot an improvement strategy. The creation of the Current State and Future State

VSMs (*see* Chapter 20 for more detail) will identify key performance metrics (KPIs) that will measure progress of the selected improvement initiatives. At the end of the process to create a VSM, one to three process improvement initiatives should be chosen that can reasonably be completed and evaluated by the end of the pilot term by the PET.

Week 6 (Days 36–42)

The PET should make and finalize member assignments for each Process Improvement Team (PIT). Each PIT will have a leader, selected by and from members of the PET, as well as additional members who are actually involved in using the process they will be improving. The team leaders must be willing to own the objective and the timetable for achieving the improvements in order to be qualified to lead the PIT responsible for the improvement.

Each PIT leader should hold a kickoff meeting as soon as possible with his or her team members to discuss the objectives of the pilot program in detail. The team members should also plot out a process transition plan from the Current State to the Future State for the process they are improving. Each PIT should plan to implement process changes as soon as possible, but no later than the start of the following week.

Weeks 7-9 (Days 43–63)

Before process change implementation begins, everyone should be clear on what KPIs will be measured to determine progress (or not) from the Current State to the Future State. Equally as important is to make sure there is a plan in place to capture these metrics. If not, then a plan must be created to capture them while the process changes are being planned and initiated.

Once everyone is satisfied that a measuring system is in place (but not before), process changes can be brought on-line or made "live," and data capture can begin. KPIs that include the original, current, and actual performance should be presented visually in an easily accessible public area where every team member can see them.

Week 10 (Days 64– 70)

New processes have been running now for two to three weeks. It is still early, but it is a good time to review the process changes made along with the disruptions they may have caused. It is also a good time to review and discuss whether there have been any surprises during implementation of the process changes. Surprises represent opportunities. New information that was unknown previously should be highlighted for everyone involved.

The best way to execute this review is in a large group setting that includes the sponsoring executive's team and all PET and PIT members. Each team should make a brief presentation of the status of their team's progress and results to-date, including new challenges and new opportunities that have been uncovered.

This will probably require a half- to a full-day meeting to get through completely. It is a big commitment of time, but this gathering should result in significant organizational learning and the collaboration and cross-fertilization of ideas across teams and with management. Each PIT may also learn valuable ideas from other teams.

Week 11 (Days 71–77)

Each Process Improvement Team should meet at the beginning of the week and decide which ideas that came from the previous week's session should be applied to modify their target process further as Phase 2 of the process transition. There may also be some additional improvement ideas that team members suggest at this time. The team should decide which ones to pursue and plan an implementation schedule.

Week 12 (Days 78–84)

This week should be dedicated to completing any remaining Phase 2 changes to the process and stabilizing it. The team will continue to collect metrics in preparation for the pilot review the following week.

Week 13 (Days 85–90)

It's now time to do a final review of the pilot. Each PIT should spend the week preparing for the group final pilot review, which should take place on Day 90. This meeting will be very similar to the previous group review, where all PIT members and pilot sponsor team management meet for in-depth reviews and commentary. The same procedure can be followed with each team's presentation, only with updated data.

The team should show how much progress, based on metrics, it has made toward the Future State goals. Identifying trends would also be important information for the group. It is essential that each team leader share new information that wasn't known before, and what he or she thinks can be done to continue to improve the modified process.

Immediately following this session, the sponsoring senior management team should meet separately to determine what it learned from the pilot, and consider what direction should be pursued next. The first decision to be made is whether the changes to processes were positive (or are trending that way) based on the goals of the pilot. In the best-case scenario, if all goals of the Future State were achieved, then the Future State VSM can now replace the original Current State VSM and become the new Current State. If not all of the Future State VSM targets were reached, then a reasonable timetable to achieve the Future State can be set by the group.

Assuming the sponsoring senior management team has seen sufficient measurable, valuable progress in one or more of the process improvement projects, the team may want to look at a longer-term commitment to Lean Thinking and Lean Selling. The team may also want to expand the scope going forward to include other processes that will take longer to change than 90 days. Additionally, the management team may want to consider including functional organizations that were not participants in the initial pilot, based on information learned during the pilot.

Week by Week Outline

Here is a weekly recap of what we've covered so far.

Week 1 Activities: Hold an introductory meeting with key staff members to discuss the purpose of starting a Lean Selling pilot initiative and key objectives. Determine the makeup of kickoff meeting participants, and schedule the kickoff within two weeks. Inform designated kickoff meeting participants of their appointment to the Pilot Execution Team.

Discuss what high-level information meeting participants should bring with them to the kickoff meeting.

Week 1 Deliverables and Milestones:

- **Roster of Pilot Execution Team (PET) members**
- **Identification of the scope of pilot (by functional and product or service area)**
- **Set date for PET kickoff meeting**
- **List of high-level information that PET members should prepare for kickoff meeting**

Week 2 Activities: PET participants gather required information about their areas of responsibility as it relates to providing value for the customer, in order to support the discussion at the kickoff meeting.

Week 2 Deliverables and Milestones:

- **Individual research to prepare for PET kickoff meeting**
- **Preparation of any documents for kickoff meeting**

Weeks 3-4 Activities: Hold the kickoff meeting with the goal of creating a candidate document describing customer value that the organization delivers. Finalize the Customer Value Document following the interview of key customers. (*Refer to* Chapter 19 *to review the way Lean Thinking defines value.*) The interview assignments should be shared among team members and executed along the lines of the Senior Executive activity outlined in the preceding chapter.

Weeks 3-4 Deliverables and Milestones:

- **A candidate Customer Value Document**
- **Research with top customers**
- **Final Customer Value Document**
- **Highlights of any "disconnects" between assumed customer value and actual customer value**

Week 5 Activities: Review Chapter 20 and hold a three- to five-day meeting to create a Current State and a Future State Value Stream Map (VSM). After identifying the areas of waste and delay in the current process, identify one to three improvement projects for Phase 1 of the transition.

Week 5 Deliverables and Milestones:

- **Current State VSM**
- **Future State VSM**
- **List of 1–3 processes targeted for improvement**

Week 6 Activities: Make and finalize assignments for Process Improvement Team leaders and members for designated improvement projects. Process Improvement Teams hold kickoff meetings and develop plans for Phase 1 implementation.

Week 6 Deliverables and Milestones:

- **Formalize Process Improvement Teams (PIT)**
- **Hold kickoff meetings for each PIT**
- **Process transition plans for moving from the Current to the Future States**

Weeks 7-9 Activities: Determine metrics that will change from initial process state to improved state, and how they will be measured. Begin implementation of Phase 1 changes to processes along with metric measurement and reporting.

Weeks 7-9 Deliverables and Milestones:

- **Ensure systems are in place to capture and report KPIs**
- **Create metric capture systems as required**
- **Implement Phase 1 process improvements**
- **Begin reporting KPIs**

Week 10 Activities: Hold a group review of the progress of each PIT, changes made, and current status. Collect group recommendations for additional changes to processes.

Week 10 Deliverables and Milestones:

- Senior management group review of progress of each PIT
- Documented KPIs provided by each PIT
- List of recommendations for Phase 2 improvements for each PIT to consider

Week 11 Activities: Each PIT determines which recommendations to pursue as Phase 2 improvements. Implement Phase 2 changes and continue metrics capture and reporting.

Week 11 Deliverables and Milestones:

- Each Process Improvement Team decides which Phase 2 changes to implement
- Phase 2 process change implementation started

Week 12 Activities: Stabilize process with new changes and continue to collect metrics.

Week 12 Deliverables and Milestones:

- Phase 2 process changes completed
- Metrics continue to be captured and reported

Week 13 Activities: Hold a group review of each team's progress and progress toward achieving the target metrics of the Future State. Discuss new information learned and identify assumptions that proved not to be true. Discuss what can be done to move closer to achieving the Future State. Collect recommendations from each group on next steps to move forward. Senior management determines next steps based on results to date and expectations of continued investment in improvement.

Week 13 Deliverables and Milestones:

- Complete pilot final review
- Identify achievements and gaps to reach Future State
- Capture ideas to further improve processes to close gap with Future State
- Senior management assessment of pilot progress, results, and trends
- Senior management determination of next steps and readiness to commit to a longer-term plan for Lean Selling

Summary and Next Steps

Engaging in a program like the one described above requires a significant commitment of time and leadership currency. **Without a doubt, such commitment will lead to an organization-wide focus on improving sales, which was the overriding objective to begin with.** While each organization is unique in both the challenges it faces and how it chooses to address them, **it is nearly assured that faithfully executing the 90-Day Pilot Program will yield new information about the sales process that was not understood before.**

Additionally, this process will almost certainly uncover new ways to improve the sales process as well. What specific areas the targets of initial improvements are in will depend upon the organization. However, **at the end of this exercise there will be a benchmark for current performance and a way to measure improvement in an objective way, using metrics.**

In addition to these "hard" benefits, there are a number of "soft" but no less important benefits that this exercise will yield:

- **The real-world practice of cross-functional teamwork**
- **Exercising delegation for problem solving and the empowerment of front-line workers**
- **A healthy, organization-wide discussion about the value you provide to your customers**

- Validation from customers of the value you *do* provide
- A step for the organization toward a mindset of Continuous Improvement
- A vision for people to see what can be accomplished with collaboration as the basis of their working relationship
- Stimulation and exercise of each individual's creativity and problem-solving skills
- An organization-wide reemphasis on the importance of sales and supporting its success

I hope that you believe that achieving even some of the benefits listed above make the commitment to the 90-Day Pilot Program worth making the investment. I realize it may seem like a lot to take on. **The good news is that there are resources available to help.** If, at any time when you are planning or after you begin your Lean Selling journey, you would like to have outside coaching help, you can refer to the information in the Appendix of this book for how to find an independent **Lean Selling Coach who can help you through the 90-Day Program.** You can also visit our website at **www.LeanSellingSystem.com/FindACoach**, or you can send an inquiry email to **FindACoach@LeanSellingSystem.com**.

Key Takeaways from Chapter 28

1. *There is a 90-day plan you can follow to see what Lean Selling can do for you.*

2. *Following the 90-Day Pilot Program to a sales transformation can provide surprising insights into your sales process.*

3. *Following the 90-Day Pilot Program can highlight opportunities that exist today to dramatically improve sales productivity—with little or no additional financial investment in sales and marketing.*

4. *The 90-Day Pilot Program is a great teambuilding exercise and a proven way to get the entire group aligned on company value and how to best provide it to your customers.*

5. *There are knowledgeable outside coaches available to help facilitate this 90-day plan, and information on finding one is contained in the Appendix.*

Appendix A

Value Stream Mapping Symbols

**PROCESS
STEP**

**OUTSIDE
SOURCES**

DATA BOX

INVENTORY

**DOWNSTREAM
PUSH**

**FINISHED GOODS
TO CUSTOMER**

**TRUCK
SHIPMENT**

**UPSTREAM
PULL**

**MANUAL
INFORMATION FLOW**

**ELECTRONIC
INFORMATION FLOW**

Appendix B

List of Lean Learnings

Appendix C

List of Sidebars

Appendix D

Lean Selling System Coaching Resources

We will be developing a **Lean Selling™ System Coach** network based on the ideas presented in this book. These coaches will be independent contractors who have access to advanced materials and instruction, which will be provided by our company, about the techniques and best practices for implementing the **Lean Selling System**. We will be compiling a list of members of the **Lean Selling Coach** network on our website at www.LeanSellingSystem.com/FindACoach to assist you in finding outside help on your organization's Lean Selling journey. You can also send an email to FindACoach@LeanSellingSystem.com if you have questions or special requirements.

If you are interested in learning how *you* can become a **Lean Selling System Coach**, go to www.LeanSellingSystem.com/Become ACoach. You can also send an email to BecomeACoach@LeanSelling System.com if you have questions that are not answered on the website.

There are public social media communities on both LinkedIn® and Facebook® you can join to network, ask questions, or share experiences about Lean Selling. On LinkedIn, search for the "Lean Selling" group and join, or just look around. On Facebook, search for "Lean Selling" and Like or Follow the page; you can also direct message me on Twitter® @LeanSelling.

In addition to developing a **Lean Selling System Coach** network, a major focus of our company will be to gather field case examples of successes and best practices gained from implementing the **Lean Selling System**. If you are interested in having your company participate in a case study or are considering a pilot implementation that you would like to discuss with me personally, you can reach me directly at Robert@LeanSellingSystem.com or at www.LinkedIn.com/in/Robert JPryor and Connect or send me an InMail.

Resources

Books

Bowden, Mark, *Winning Body Language for Sales Professionals: Control the Conversation and Connect with Your Customer—Without Saying a Word*, n.p.: McGraw-Hill, 2012

Ferrari, Bernard T., *Power Listening: Mastering the Most Critical Business Skill of All*, New York: Penguin Group, 2012

Liker, Jeffrey K., *The Toyota Way: 14 Principles from the World's Greatest Manufacturer*, New York: McGraw-Hill, 2004

Martin, Karen and Mike Osterling, *Value Stream Mapping: How to Visualize Work and Align Leadership for Organizational Transformation*, New York: McGraw-Hill, 2014

Ohno, Taiichi and Norman Bodek, *Toyota Production System: Beyond Large-Scale Production*, n.p.: Productivity Press, 2008

Patterson, Kerry, Joseph Grenny, Ron McMillan, and Al Switzler, *Crucial Conversations Tools for Talking When Stakes Are High*, New York: McGraw-Hill, 2012

Pease, Allan and Barbara, *The Definitive Book of Body Language*, New York: Bantam Dell, 2004

Ries, Eric, *The Lean Startup: How Today's Entrepreneurs Use Continuous Innovation to Create Radically Successful Businesses*, New York: Crown Business, 2011

Rother, Mike, and John Shook, *Learning to See: Value Stream Mapping to Add Value and Eliminate MUDA*, Brookline, MA: The Lean Enterprise Institute, 2003

Womack, James P., Daniel T. Jones, and Daniel Roos, *The Machine That Changed the World*, New York: Scribner, 1990

Womack, James P. and Daniel T. Jones, *Lean Thinking: Banish Waste and Create Wealth in Your Corporation*, New York: Free Press (Revised ed.), 2003

Womack, James P. and Daniel T. Jones, *Lean Solutions: How Companies and Customers Can Create Value and Wealth Together*, New York: Free Press, 2005

Software and Services Mentioned in This Book

Facebook® – Social Networking site for personal and business use: http://www.facebook.com

LinkedIn® – Social Networking site for business professionals: http://www.linkedin.com

Microsoft Dynamics® CRM – Cloud- or premise-based Customer Relationship Management (CRM) software: http://www.microsoft.com/dynamics

salesforce.com® – Cloud-based Customer Relationship Management (CRM) software: http://www.salesforce.com

TimeTrade® – Cloud-based calendar appointment scheduler: http://www.timetrade.com

Twitter® – Social Networking site for personal and business use: http://www.twitter.com

References

Introduction

1 Jeffrey K. Liker, The Toyota Way: 14 Principles from the World's Greatest Manufacturer, New York: McGraw-Hill, 2004, 269

Chapter 1

1 InternetRetailer.com, accessed August 28, 2014, http://www.internetretailer.com/2013/03/13/us-e-commerce-grow-13-2013
2 CEB Marketing Leadership Council, "The Digital Evolution in B2B Marketing," 2012, 2
3 Qvidian, "Sales Execution Trends 2014," December 11, 2013
4 Qvidian, "Sales Execution Trends 2014"
5 Michael T. Bosworth, John R. Holland, and Frank Visgatis, CustomerCentric Selling, New York: McGraw-Hill (2nd ed.), 2010, 64
6 CEB, "Why Your Sales Training Is Falling Short," March 3, 2014
7 James P. Womack, Daniel T. Jones and Daniel Roos, The Machine That Changed the World, New York: Scribner, 1990.
8 David Bailey, "Automotive News calls Toyota world No 1 car maker," (January 24, 2008), Reuters.com, accessed August 28, 2014, http://www.reuters.com/article/2008/01/24/us-autos-sales-idUSN2424076820080124
9 Womack, Machine, 92. Average performance of Japanese automakers compared to average performance of U.S. and European automakers, 1989.
10 James P. Womack and Daniel T. Jones, Lean Thinking: Banish Waste and Create Wealth in Your Corporation, New York: Free Press (Revised ed.), 2003, 74-82.
11 Womack, Lean Thinking, 86.
12 See http://www.lean.org/WhatsLean/CommonLeanQuestions.cfm#non_manufacturing and http://www.lean.org/search/?mf=2097152&mfall=22 for case studies in these and other areas.
13 Mary and Tom Poppendieck, Implementing Lean Software Development: From Concept to Cash, Boston: Pearson Education, 2007.
14 Eric Ries, The Lean Startup: How Today's Entrepreneurs Use Contin-

uous Innovation to Create Radically Successful Businesses, New York: Crown Business, 2011.

[15] Scott Douglas Stratton, "The Application of Lean Thinking to Pharmaceutical Quality Systems, Defining the FDA as the Consumer," 2004, http://www.jclauson.com/msqa/sample_thesis_fall_04.pdf

[16] Kent Beck with Cynthia Andres (1999). *Extreme Programming Explained: Embrace Change*. Stoughton, MA: Pearson Education (2nd ed. 7th printing.), 2008.

[17] Mary and Tom Poppendieck, *Lean Software Development: An Agile Toolkit*, Boston: Addison-Wesley. 2003

[18] An example is the lack of a requirement for comprehensive specifications before starting development.

[19] Emarketer.com, "Two in Five Salespeople Not Hitting Their Quotas," Mar 24, 2014, accessed August 28, 2014, http://www.emarketer.com/Article/Two-Five-Salespeople-Not-Hitting-Their-Quotas/1010700

[20] The idea that the Seller has to take responsibility to help manage the Buyer's process is quite different thinking about the role of a salesperson. The extension of such thinking is that the Buyer's and Seller's processes, which have different steps and objectives, should ideally be viewed as one process.

[21] This refers to the Lean term "value stream" that will be explained later.

Chapter 3

[1] Wikipedia.org, accessed August 28, 2014, http://en.wikipedia.org/wiki/Mosaic_%28web_browser%29

[2] CBSnews.com, accessed August 28, 2014, http://www.cbsnews.com/news/a-dying-breed-the-american-shopping-mall/

[3] InternetRetailer.com, accessed August 28, 2014, http://www.internetretailer.com/2013/03/13/us-e-commerce-grow-13-2013

[4] Multipl.com, accessed August 28, 2014, http://www.multpl.com/us-retail-sales-growth

[5] Jones Lang LaSalle, a property services firm

6   MarketWatch.com, accessed August 28, 2014, http://blogs.market-watch.com/behindthestorefront/2014/04/04/wal-marts-in-store-shoppers-prefer-amazon-com-not-walmart-com/ http://online.wsj.com/news/articles/SB10001424127887323566804578553301017702818

7   Qvidian, "Sales Execution Trends 2014"

8   CEB, "The Digital Evolution," 2

9   For some examples of these upscale services see http://www.forbes.com/sites/larryolmsted/2012/01/20/why-you-need-a-travel-agent-part-1/

10 InsideBiz.com, accessed August 28, 2014, http://insidebiz.com/news/despite-online-competition-travel-agencies-see-return-customers

Chapter 4

1   BarryPopik.com, accessed August 28, 2014, http://www.barrypopik.com/index.php/new_york_city/entry/nothing_happens_until_somebody_sells_something

2   In Lean Thinking this is referred to as the "5 Whys," a Lean problem-solving methodology.

Chapter 6

1   WSJ.com, accessed August 28, 2014, http://online.wsj.com/news/articles/SB10001424052748704080104575287153987995176?mg=reno64-wsj&url=http%3A%2F%2Fonline.wsj.com%2Farticle%2FSB10001424052748704080104575287153987995176.html

2   American Express website, accessed August 28, 2014, http://about.americanexpress.com/news/docs/2012x/AXP_2012GCSB_US.pdf

Chapter 7

1   Stephen R. Covey, *The Seven Habits of Highly Effective People*, New York: Free Press,, 2004

Chapter 8

[1] Womack, *Lean Thinking*, Chapter 3
[2] The Economist, *A Hard Act to Follow*, June 28, 2014
[3] Womack, *Lean Thinking*, pp 176-178

Chapter 9

[1] Gartner, Inc. press release, May 6, 2014, http://www.gartner.com/newsroom/id/2730317

Chapter 11

[1] Womack, *The Machine*, 150
[2] Qvidian, "Sales Execution Trends 2014"
[3] Software Productivity Institute

Chapter 13

[1] Qvidian, "Sales Execution Trends 2014"
[2] Bosworth, CustomerCentric Selling, 64

Chapter 14

[1] SellingPower.com, accessed August 28, 2014, http://blog.sellingpower.com/gg/2011/02/how-much-time-do-your-salespeople-spend-selling.html
[2] Paul Vinogradov, "Are Your People Getting Enough Quality Sales Time," May 7, 2013, accessed August 28, 2014, http://www.alexandergroup.com/blog/sales-analytics/are-your-sales-people-getting-enough-quality-sales-time/

Chapter 18

[1] Womack, *The Machine*, 29

Chapter 19

[1] This and the following four chapter titles model the organization of the five Lean Principles listed in the introduction to the book, *Lean Thinking*, by James P. Womack and Daniel T. Jones.

[2] Qvidian, "Sales Execution Trends 2014"

Chapter 20

[1] Sources for an in-depth explanation of Value Stream Mapping include Mike Rother and John Shook, *Learning to See: Value Stream Mapping to Add Value and Eliminate MUDA*, Brookline, MA: The Lean Enterprise Institute 2003 and Karen Martin and Mike Osterling, *Value Stream Mapping: How to Visualize Work and Align Leadership for Organizational Transformation*, New York: McGraw-Hill, 2014

[2] Liker, *Toyota Way*, 271

Chapter 23

[1] Womack, *Lean Thinking*, 27

Chapter 26

[1] Covey, *Seven Habits*, 151

[2] Jeffrey K. Liker, *The Toyota Way: 14 Principles from the World's Greatest* Manufacturer, McGraw-Hill, New York, NY, 2004

[3] Liker, *Toyota Way*, 51

About the Author

Robert Pryor received his B.A. degree in psychology from the State University of New York at Stony Brook and his M.B.A. from Northeastern University, where he graduated at the top of his class with a concentration in strategy and finance. Robert has been a sales, marketing, and general management executive in the computer and information technology industries for over 30 years. He was one of the early entrants into the commercial Internet industry, advising CEOs of software companies on the potential impact the emerging Internet could have on their product plans and business models. This narrow focus led to opportunities to become a multi-time CEO in the Internet space, and to be personally involved in the development, management, successful launch, and market adoption of the world's first Web video product, and one of the world's first large Web applications, named TeamCenter®, that enabled collaboration among members of geographically distributed project teams.

Ten years ago, Robert conceived and oversaw the development and launch of a Web-based soft-skills coaching service, the first of its kind. For the last four years, through his business consulting company, CEO Cubed LLC, he has helped CEOs in a variety of industries benefit from his business experiences through close collaboration with them on how best to move their companies forward.

For many years, Robert has been a student of the most popular selling methodologies and has occasionally had opportunities to train or coach organizations on these, in addition to implementing them in companies that he ran. He honed his public speaking skills in the process of being certified as an Advanced Toastmaster®. His community service contributions include more than ten years of pro bono mentoring of CEOs in early-stage companies on business development strategy and tactics. Robert's close working relationships with CEOs over many years has sensitized him to seek out three things when assessing the potential to create successful, sustainable businesses: opportunities for collaboration, proven repeatable processes, and scalable business models. His attraction to, and passion for, Lean Thinking and methodologies is due in large part to the fact that Lean environments exhibit all three of these elements.

Robert was born and raised in the South Bronx in New York City. He lived on Long Island, New York, for seven years after marrying Hiroko, his wife of 38 years, as well as living in the Boston area for 10 years before moving to Southern California in 1993. He now lives with his wife and younger daughter, Veronica, in Encinitas, California, known for its flowers, surfing, and spiritual ambiance. As this book is being written, his older daughter, Crystal, a political science Ph.D. candidate at the University of Washington, is travelling the world in the process of completing her doctoral dissertation on nonproliferation and multinational export controls for sensitive and dual use (military and commercial) technologies. Robert is a competitive singles tennis player, a certified bareboat sailing skipper, and, after 10 years, still learning how to play golf.

Index

tables are denoted with a '*t*' and figures with an "*f*"